ADVANCE PRAISE FOR *BOOKMARKED: HOW THE GREAT WORKS OF WESTERN LITERATURE F*CKED UP MY LIFE*

"Mark Scarbrough summons a host of greats—Chaucer to Henry James—to show the danger of accepting the stories we are told by our parents, our partners, and even the very authors whose books we treasure. In a brave, singular memoir that is equal parts charm, wit, and withering self-reflection, he recounts his journey through literature and life to find a self that is truly his."
—*Will Schwalbe, New York Times bestselling author of* THE END OF YOUR LIFE BOOK CLUB

Scarbrough's memoir is a riveting read, a story of his quest for love and home told in galloping prose that takes us through decades, identities, new beginnings, and second chances. It's a brave delving into his personal history peopled with characters as indelible as those in the literature he reveres until discovering that real life can't be read or performed. Luminous with grace and compassion, reflection and wit, it's about who we are once we stop falling for the stories others tell us and those we tell ourselves.
—*Helen Klein Ross, bestselling author of* WHAT WAS MINE *and* THE LATECOMERS

BOOKMARKED

*HOW THE GREAT WORKS OF WESTERN LITERATURE F*CKED UP MY LIFE*

Mark Scarbrough

PROPERTIUS PRESS

Copyright 2021 by Mark Scarbrough. All rights reserved.
Graphics and book design copyright Propertius Press. Cover image by Sebastián Bronley. Back cover photograph by Elisa Calvet. Edited by Sean Dennis. Published by Propertius Press, Lynchburg, VA. All rights reserved. No portion of this book may be reproduced, except short passages that may be quoted within a review, without express written permission from the copyright holders.

All quotations are from the public domain; all translations of non-English works are the author's, except for those taken directly from the King James Bible. Portions of this work appeared in radically different forms in *Publishers Weekly* ("The Vanity of Bonfires," 6/24/2014) and *American Letters and Commentary* ("Till Sex Do Us Part," 11/2011).

ISBN: 978-1-00535-048-2 (ebook)
ISBN: 978-1-105-40087-2 (paperback)

Propertius Press
Lynchburg, VA 24501

For her

Contents

Caution: A Preface	8
1. Pulp Fiction in Dallas	10
2. Charles Dickens in Public School	23
3. God in East Texas	35
4. William Blake in Waco	45
5. My Songs of Innocence	56
6. In the Resurrection, They Neither Marry nor are Given in Marriage	70
7. How to Get into a Fundamentalist Seminary When You're Not Sure What You Believe	84
8. Hebrew in My Underwear	89
9. The Prophecies of Love	105
10. The Parson's Tale	116
11. Geoffrey Chaucer in Kalamazoo	125
12. The Last of the Mohicans	139
13. By All This I Mean Love	156
14. How to Turn Your Life into More than One Plot	172
15. Henry James in Venice	180
16. What Literary Genre is "Good-Bye"?	195
17. How to Shove a Monk in a GM Saturn	207
18. The Vanity of Bonfires	212
19. The Book of Life	226
20. How to Make Rabbit Stew	238
21. Hiding in Plain Sight	241
22. Dante Alighieri in a Nursing Home	254
23. This Now Connected to Enough of the Others	262
Acknowledgments	267
About the Author	268

Caution: A Preface

Stop me if you've heard this one before: "I found myself in *Middlemarch*!" Or "Shakespeare saved my life!"

I call bullshit. Shakespeare never saved anyone. Least of all, me. Although I sure wanted him to. Ached for him to, somewhere in the marrow middle of my bones. And not only him but all the other literary lions, like William Blake, Charlotte Brontë, and Henry James, now dead and mounted on the wall of Western culture.

I got sucked in by their promises, the best things. A *once upon a time* that leads logically to *the end*. Characters who remain true to themselves, despite what the plot throws at them. And desires that can be—ta-da!—fulfilled. Or at least understood.

And something more tangible, too. Down in my soul's basement, where the lights are dim and my hopes are laid away in boxes, I dreamed up a mad quest through the great books to find a home. To hear the crackle in a fireplace. To feel the weight of the covers at night. To breathe in and out all that's human and loved.

Maybe I should have lowered my sights. Maybe only the main character gets home. Problem is, I've always felt like a minor one: the sidekick in a baggy sweater, the wiseacre two desks down. The guy who steps into a story, pushes it along in some vague way, and gets a one-liner as his reward: *Years later, I heard he died in a car crash.*

Or maybe I asked so much from the great books because of my upbringing. When I was ten, my parents left the Southern Baptist church. "It is too liberal," they said, seemingly in unison, a plainsong truth-telling that led us to the upland pastures of American fundamentalism. Letters were sent. Ministers were challenged. Friends were lost.

Don't get me wrong. I didn't latch onto the great books because they were forbidden. I never once read under the sheets with a flashlight. Oh, sure, I had to skip the sex scenes and turn a blind eye to the notion that a liberal could be the good guy. Authors! What can you do?

But nothing could befoul us. We were the true believers. We interpreted the Vietnam War, Nixon, and everything else as a story, a plot, rushing toward the apocalypse. The world sinned, it burned up, and we got out alive. Time was a straight line.

Once I started reading, I discovered that novels, stories, plays, and even poems were alternate timelines, descending and ascending like a grid. They even got to the same places we believed in: *just deserts* or *happily ever after.* For a long time, I wanted to homestead on that scaffolding, even though it kept coming apart and slamming to the ground. I just wasn't myself without a book in my hand.

Then I wasn't myself with one. Over time, books stopped being words outside my skin and became shadowy bits inside my brain, alternate versions of me, telling their own stories. I morphed into a bizarre body of shredded volumes, stalking the far country of my imagination. That's how I saw a long-dead poet manifest in front of me one night. How I got a job fishing monks out of gay bars. And ultimately why I tossed the person I loved over the cliff of insanity in a *hail Mary!* attempt to save my own brain from dissolving like a cheap paperback in a deluge.

All of which is to say, be careful what you read. It can fuck you up, too.

But don't worry. There's a truth beyond the great works of Western literature. Life may seem linear, forceps to tombstone. Instead, the cosmos is round and elastic, spiraled and helixed. Atoms, galaxies, your DNA—they spin and come back around. I got out from under literature's curse. You can, too.

So this story is a comedy, like Dante's, if not so divine. But there's no good news without the bad, which is part and parcel of it. In books, in life, even in the old poet's journey across the universe, the way up starts with the way down.

Pulp Fiction in Dallas

I wish I could have read my own preface back in 1973. It was the last day of seventh grade, the end of May, and a Texas blast furnace outside. The heat leaked through the cinder block of my junior high.

Dallas public schools weren't air-conditioned, so the teachers doused the lights and cranked up free-standing, industrial fans. The weaklings passed out. My music teacher called them "Yankees," although she was a grim German with a hound's underbite who pronounced it *yahng-kiss*. She gave me vocal coaching because she prized my clear tone. "Like Zjeessus," she said. "Not on tseh cross. Ehrlier."

Way earlier. Still a soprano, I was a year younger than my classmates, not yet a teenager but even more of a misfit. I was tract-home gawky, with stringy bangs and sharp elbows, a knock-off Davy Jones in J. C. Penney knits. I could have been the nerd who wound up head first in the locker room trash can. Instead, I was the smarty-pants who used his protractor to map the best arc for a football punt.

I had a few things to do before summer break. First, my buddies and I hijacked social studies to take nominations for a mock awards ceremony. We'd worked up a list of *most likelies* to be handed out by popular acclaim. A guy who'd wallpapered his locker with posters of Karen Carpenter got *most likely to be a bachelor at thirty*. A girl who'd barfed tetrazzini on her blouse captured *most likely to replace Jan on The Brady Bunch*. And by a unanimous vote, I won *most likely to trip across a flat floor*. I laughed and laughed, then blew off the next period, English, for my last vocal lesson.

I took my position next to the upright piano and gave Brahms something-or-other my best. I didn't care what I sang. I just wanted to get it right.

I'd gone whole hog for music after a field trip to hear the Dallas symphony in fourth grade. Velvet seats, a stage of tuxes—I'd never seen anything like it. Then came the Brandenburg concertos. Within a few bars, my eyes focused on a middle distance between me and the stage. I could see spiraling filaments: playful, dazzling, like arcs of electricity. I also felt an unspeakable sadness well up in me. I knocked at my cheeks to get rid of the tears, then sat back and closed my eyes to shut out the show.

Since I never wanted to feel that way again, I took up music to cure it. I focused on the notes. In the right order, they made sense, like math. In vocal competitions, I was praised for my strict tempos. As a pianist, I was hailed for my rigid fingerings.

That day, as I came to the end of a long, Romantic, Brahmsian phrase, my vocal teacher shook her head and grimaced, like at a nasty smell. "No, my Junge. Tsink of tseh Christkindl in tseh manger."

I had no idea what some of that foreign mumbo jumbo meant, except it wasn't Spanish. In Dallas, that meant it had to be classy. I heard *manger*. I tried to picture a nativity scene. There was a nice one at the mall: plastic figures in jewel tones. I finished on a long, clear note.

"Ausgezeichnet," she said, all teeth and bite. "You must have a vunderful summer."

I started to go, safe in my competence.

"Und, Schatzi, never change."

She was so bogus! Were all Germans like this? I'd accepted Jesus as my personal savior. I was done changing. Except for one more hurdle: a family conference with my counselor, a peroxide-dipped functionary who'd given me a bunch of weird tests. *Which of the following triangles matches this one? Which word is misspelled in this sentence?*

I made it down the linoleum hall without tripping. I was a preteen colossus. I stationed myself at the school's front doors.

My parents drove up in a limousine-long Chevy Impala. Dad put the whitewalls parallel to the curb. Despite the heat, Mother got out in a canvas dress and thick hose.

She was never *Mom*. She sniffed at chumminess and spoke in complete sentences. Except in extreme situations, she avoided contractions. "Decent people do not use slang," she explained. And we believed we were the textbook definition of decency: white, Protestant, Texan, middle-class.

Mother walked up, assessed the state of my clothes, found them unsullied, and touched my shoulder. A kiss would have been unthinkable in public.

Dad shimmied his wide tie against his throat. "Let's do this," he said, another thing on the long schedule his secretary typed for him every day.

I led them to my counselor's desk, stashed in a wing of the auditorium. The first of the budget cuts that would eviscerate American education had just taken effect. Harried, she explained why I, an honors student, tested so poorly in language arts.

"Dyslexic," she said, a diagnosis before it was an industry. "Fortunately, mild. But there are ways to deal with his illiteracy." She bit her lower lip to underline the severity of her solution. "He should read more."

"Read?" we three squawked.

My brain worked better in theorems and equations. I got an *A* in English by memorizing every detail.

She passed a sheaf of results across her desk and stood up to dismiss us. "Here's my parting shot," she said.

"Parthian," I corrected. "Parthian shot."

She zeroed in on me. "Get busy."

I flushed. I *was* busy. I was president of science this and vice-president of math that. I had a part in the school play, played the trumpet in this sextet, the oboe in that octet, and the piano for Sunday-night services. I kept a stressed-out overachiever's schedule long before helicopter parents.

Sensing my outrage, Dad preempted it. "We'll do our best," he said. It was hardly a promise, more like our lifestyle.

Even so, my counselor wasn't impressed. "Oh, don't worry," she said, already distracted with someone else's file. "But good books, preferably. Although anything will do."

That was a relief. We Dallasites didn't cotton to the canon in the '70s, although Lee Harvey Oswald and a certain book depository had put us on the map. Still, my parents had assembled a collection of *Reader's Digest Condensed Books*, mass-market bestsellers cut down to a hundred pages or so and collected in faux-leather volumes. They filled the wall-mount bookshelves in our den, hanging over our heads as we watched TV.

So whenever the June sun irradiated our street and made it too hot for a pick-up football game, I took my counselor's advice and carried a volume to my room. I pulled a folding chair to my desk, clicked on a gooseneck lamp, and adhered to a strict schedule. Read twenty minutes today. Read twenty-five minutes tomorrow. Read forty minutes each day next week. Wind up the alarm clock. Brrrrrrring. Done, even mid-sentence.

Because illiteracy, like everything else, could be solved with dogged determination. I had to be godlier today than yesterday and master antebellum-style manners and memorize chunks of the Bible and prepare myself to be the perfect husband and go to church umpteen times a week and maintain a 4.0., all so I could smelt the dross out of my life and ensure I didn't make any mistakes, secular or sacred. The road to hell may have been paved with good intentions, but the one to heaven was prone to hairline fractures.

I also excelled at a Christian version of '70s self-help, *Dear Abby* fused with Jesus. Once, when members of my class got to choose a book for keeps off a rack outside the auditorium, I picked *I'm OK, You're OK*. I kept it stashed in my tote next to a pocket-sized New Testament, reading a paragraph here or a verse there whenever I needed them. Like when I got a *B+* on a test. Or when I tripped and fumbled the football because the street's cracked concrete was more dangerous than a flat floor. Or when I penciled *Want to go steady?* on a Certs and my girlfriend took the thing from me and sucked it so slowly that I had to run cold water over my head in the bathroom to keep from passing out.

One afternoon, after I'd worked up to a full hour of reading, I finished one condensed novel, turned the page, and started the next in the same volume with time to spare. Who cares what I read? These stories were all alike, sanitized for families like ours. And this one, *The Stepford Wives*, was probably just another boy-meets-girl fable.

Except as I sank into this novel about housewives replaced by "yes, dear" automatons, I suddenly felt a deep-in terror, like teeth chattering between my ribs.

Good grief, these women were like me. Not that I was a robot, although I was quick to clear the table and clean my room. And not that I was a girl or "you know . . . that way," like Mother's hairdresser, Mr. Bee, who sang show tunes and cackled like a fat, old hen. But the story of these Stepford wives jarred me into the realization of something I'd long known but worked to forget. I, too, was a replacement, a simulation. I was an adopted kid.

My arrival at five days old had been a family-wide event, documented by 8mm movies shot under handheld kliegs. It featured aunts in bouffants and uncles in trilbies. My legally appointed kin have gathered for a "big surprise." Unbeknownst to them, the paperwork for the *Deaconess Home for Unwanted Children* had been filed and fulfilled in forty-eight hours.

Mother brings me out. I'm face forward, perched in her arms, my back to her chest. I bounce and kick. She smiles tightly, a little too much teeth and squint. Her thought bubble should read, *What's this?*

The camera pans the room to record the silent smiles that expressed joy back then. When the movie frame returns to me, Mother and I are already gone. She's probably putting me to bed. No one seems to notice. The film flickers on for another ten minutes, showing off a white sheet cake and bottles of 7-Up.

My adoption had always seemed happy and irrelevant, like a Disney cartoon. But as I read *The Stepford Wives*, the story I'd seen and heard seemed more like a dam. It separated all that could have been from all that was. Worse yet, time reversed course and flowed back over it.

The alarm clock rang. I turned it off and kept reading, trying to ignore the chatter between my ribs. And now something else, too, lower down in my stomach, harder to understand: a sharp drop, like what I felt on the big hill of the Runaway Mine Train at Six Flags. I used to love that thrill, hands in the air, all harmless fun, except now I felt it at my desk without a safety bar across my lap.

Time wasn't the only thing going back over the dam. I was. Back to the moment I'd been booted off my original timeline and dropped onto this one. Not the wrong one, mind you. Just *now*, a story that included me even if—this was the part I was working so hard to ignore—it didn't.

I felt a cold, clammy sweat under my shirt. I stripped it off and looked at my ribs, narrow slats under my skin. There was nothing between them. When I sat down, the chair was warm and welcoming against my spine.

Behave and be home. That was my life. And a good story. A logical progression. Except I was the character who could fit into *any* story. I was a model child, a new model of child, fully interchangeable in any family: a learning disability fixed with hard work, the periodic chart of the elements memorized, all twelve of the Old Testament's minor prophets outlined in a black binder on my shelf, everybody's answer to "what's the matter with kids these days?"

I dutifully ate food I didn't like because it was the sort of thing people in our house ate, even if I occasionally threw out the olive loaf sandwich in my lunch when no one was looking. I told my parents I didn't watch *Laugh-In,* even though I snuck over to a buddy's every so often to catch the latest. My rebellions were small, petty, almost invisible so everyone would know I was the beloved son of a mother who made a hot breakfast every morning and a dad who took us on a yearly vacation to a national park. Even on a hiking trail, our shirts were starched; our jeans, ironed. Schedules were kept; rules, obeyed; infractions, punished, often with a belt.

Fine by me. I wanted to be told how to be who I was.

I evened my chair to my desk and turned back to the first chapter of *The Stepford Wives*. I wanted to figure out those twinned sensations in me, the buzz and the drop. Maybe reading was dividing my body without splitting it, like the two lobes of the human brain in that formaldehyde jar at school.

Right at the start of the novel, the Welcome Wagon Lady arrives at the home of a couple who've moved to the neighborhood. She smiles. She hands out coupons for the grocery store.

Right there! Not what happened but *how*: the beginning of everything, the start of time itself, an alternate timeline. Reading, I was on it even if I didn't belong on it. It was like my life without being my life. Which was exactly how I felt every day of my life. In other words, I was stuck in an existential dilemma before I could spell the word. What in the Sam Hill was going on?

This: time apparently wasn't just my *when*. It was my *where*. And there were lots of *wheres*, a bookcase full of them. One of them might be a place where I could be me without trying so hard.

Was that the point of reading? To try on an alternate version of me? Could I read enough to catch a glimpse of who I might have been on another timeline, as if that 8mm home movie had never happened? Was there a me in a book somewhere who was more like the original me, before I got plunked down in this story?

I stopped setting the alarm and started reading as many condensed novels as I could. The buzzing in my ribs continued apace. But the drop in my stomach—the glimpse of emptiness at the top of a roller-coaster hill—came to feel like nothing more than the fear of falling when I'd learned to ride a bike. *That* was easy to fix. "Hold on, son," Dad had said. "Hold on."

I did. I wanted to feel the flow of events in a new plot. I wanted to wade into time, be baptized in it, and find a new life on the other side. Such thoughts might seem heady for a kid who wasn't even thirteen, but we fundamentalists worried about time all the time. *The hour is late. The end is nigh.*

What's more, reading felt like being adopted. I got lost in a plot, looked up an hour later, and said out loud, "Wait, where am I?" Then I went back to the story just because I wanted to see how it turned out, even if it wasn't really happening to me.

Other things were. One Sunday, I stood up to sing a solo in church and my voice cracked down an octave and a half. I finished in some weird, high-low mishmash, a creaky pitch over a bad vocal break. By mid-week, my voice had settled into a tenor quaver, not the basso profundo I'd hoped for.

Around the same time, I noticed the first wiry hairs on my chest. I locked myself in the bathroom and plucked them out with tweezers.

Then one night, I had a dream about my future in a Stepford Wives world. My air-brushed wife kissed me as she sawed off my scrawny limbs to sew on Rock Hudson's. I woke up to find myself playing with my. . . .

Good grief, what was the name for it? Terms from biology class seemed wrong for this dangle between my legs. And my family never used words for anatomical parts like this one. Or I used the wrong words. In sex ed, the P.E. coach's mumbly Southern accent had made me mistake *vagina* for *pajama*. "Nev-uh put yawr hand on a guhrl's vuh-jah-mah."

Duly noted! Besides, ours was an open-door house. No one ever asked, "What's going on in there?" We all knew.

Now I didn't. Late one afternoon, I was shocked to realize I'd finished a whole volume of condensed novels but skipped lunch, missed a football game out front, and lost the day.

I palmed the book in front of me. Its spine felt cool and supple. The end papers were as frilly as the wallpaper in our living room. A new volume came every month. We could have sent it back. We never did. We gave it the feather-duster treatment. But in other homes, it might have had a rougher life. It might have been stashed under a couch or thrown in a corner, the pages bent, torn. The United States was a vast country, falling apart. Parts of it were on fire: Watts, The Bronx, the Cuyahoga River. This same book might be in the hands of hippies, yippies, women's libbers, Black Panthers, communists, Jews, homosexuals, the full range of forces arrayed against something called "us." Maybe when I'd cracked open that first volume, I'd pried the lid off some kind of Pandora's box that wasn't changing the nature of time, just me.

I was a science geek. I could noodle this out.

Step 1: Create a sterile environment.

I cleaned off my desk, lined up a clunky cassette recorder, and put its big mic on a stand.

Step 2: Control the variables.

I went back to my besetting sin, *The Stepford Wives*. I pressed the record button and recited the first chapter. When I played the tape later on, I hoped I'd hear my voice on that other timeline, a me living out another story while I sat at my desk. Then I'd be able to prove how fake that me sounded. I'd be able to say something like *That's just "might be," not "is."*

But I lost clinical distance with the first words. I loved the expanse in any novel's opening. It felt hopeful and unspoiled, like the Texas prairie. Plus, the end of the story was already in sight, the moment when everything made sense, when the journey was over, even in a creepy book like *The Stepford Wives*.

I quickly forgot the point of my experiment and started recording the opening chapters of all the other condensed novels, just so I could hear the hope of each plot's ruts in the dirt, a new might-have-been where I might have been. It wasn't that I yearned to be there. It was stranger than that. I could have been there, maybe was there, but also wasn't, because I was here, at my desk, in my room. One timeline was as arbitrary *and* as real as another. I'd never heard of Stephen Hawking, but reading had landed me in the multiverse.

And one more strange reaction, too. The more I recorded those opening chapters, the less I wanted to play football. The guys were *de facto* older than I was. They had less and less patience for my protractor shenanigans. And I didn't like the way I smelled after a game—sort of like the hamper before Mother did the laundry, when she opened it and said, "We must put a stop to that."

I stacked the increasing number of cassette tapes in columns.

At first, my parents let me be. They were used to my oddball obsessions. Bach. A set of microscopes. A collection of igneous rocks. I was forever a surprise. *What's this?*

But once the tape stacks got messy, they had to step in. Dad pulled me aside one evening after supper.

"I know what you're doing," he said.

I wasn't sure *I* knew what I was doing. So why did I feel guilty?

"You do?" I asked.

"Don't get smart." He was quick to pull me in bounds. "Shouldn't you fix your reading problem in a more productive way?" He thumbed back to the Bibles at the end of a shelf of condensed novels.

We had several translations, although the collection's prize was the Scofield Reference Bible. Its footnotes lined up history to predict the end of the world. It was the approved tome at our new church, which was independent, unaffiliated, and Rapture-ready. It sat just beyond the city line in Farmers' Branch, a strip-mall suburb despite its name.

Our church wasn't a mega church. There were no mega churches back then. Our sanctuary boasted industrial carpeting and Plexiglas windows. No one shouted "amen!" No one spoke in tongues. Once a month, we sat quietly in the fellowship hall for a "pot providence" luncheon. (No one believed in luck either.) Pastor Daniel offered one prayer to bless the fried chicken and another to hasten the end of the world.

I was his star pupil. My weekdays were crammed with science clubs and music rehearsals, and my weekends were packed with county fairs and rodeos where I preached the gospel in front of our church's tent. I knew I belonged when I said what I said around other people who said the same thing. "It's better to be right than happy," Pastor Daniel counseled, although he volunteered a tight-lipped grin as if he were both.

Before all this folderol with condensed novels, the only book I'd read straight through was Hal Lindsey's *The Late Great Planet Earth*. (The Bible wasn't a book to be read, more like a how-to manual that we flipped open for random guidance.) The signs of the end were in place. Israel was gathered in its homeland. Europe was a ten-nation confederacy. During the last election, I'd calculated on the end paper of my Bible how long Senator George McGovern would reign as the Antichrist.

Although Pastor Daniel wouldn't have approved of novels, they, too, seemed like timelines—Adam to apocalypse, as well as a strange, new way to belong. But I needed to appease him. And Dad. And God, who stood right behind them. So to answer all their concerns, I connived an acceptable rebellion. I sat in the den, leafing through the Bible in a public show of piety, then recorded more first chapters on the QT in my room when Dad was at work and Mother was busy with her never-ending chores.

By August, I'd gotten through the entire collection, over two hundred first chapters. I took to listening to those tapes over and over. I felt the sheer joy of my changed voice in the words, that strange bit of a new, tenor me who still wasn't me, starting a tale that wasn't mine but could have been. Maybe I'd never find myself on another timeline. Maybe I could belong on lots of them at once. I closed my eyes and yearned to disappear, a minor rapture before the big one with Jesus.

"Mark!"

In novels, nothing was final, a fatal blasphemy for a fundamentalist.

"Mark!"

How could I know I was flirting with disaster? I liked my school, my friends, my family. This life was comfortable. Familiar. Maybe it wasn't mine, but I was living it. Or reading about one that could have been it.

"Mark!"

"What?"

"Set the table. Your father will be home in twenty minutes."

I clicked off the machine and walked down the hall, past serried family portraits. In the kitchen, Mother was rolling canned chicken and cream cheese into crescent rolls from a tube.

"You can start right here," she said, pointing to her cheek.

I kissed it once, a smack. We were safe at home.

She smiled the way she had in those home movies, all tooth and squint. "You are not fooling around with those tapes, are you?"

I bobbled my head, between a shake and a nod. I could tell she was worried because she diverted into the rules.

"Pull up your jeans. Are you fastened?"

She only let me wear hip huggers if I used safety pins to latch my shirt to my underwear.

"Yes, ma'am," I said, nodding but strangely unsure.

"Oh, sweetie, you do not need your public manners here."

She was fiercely loyal to me, the child she couldn't have, the outsider in her insular world.

Unlike many adopted kids, I'd never tried to manipulate the distance between us, although reading had helped me see it as no more than the whim of one timeline over another. Maybe that was why I suddenly wanted to jump the gap and land in her story. To have her hold me here, even if I was going into eighth grade, even if my life was no more than one plot among many, even if I was playing with myself at night. I had a sneaking suspicion that a new story might lurch into motion at any moment, driving me away from everything I knew.

Maybe she knew. Maybe to prove she could, she glanced at my shoes. "You are wearing those in the house? How are they holding up?"

They were top-shelf disco shoes. She assumed they were run-of-the-mill slip-ons, perfect for church. She hadn't noticed the white stitching in the black leather. Or the four-inch platform heels.

I'd seen them on *Soul Train*, another of my minor rebellions. I wanted to move like those dancers. Impossible. I wanted to buy those albums. Impossible. I wanted to dress like all those people. Okay, maybe.

I convinced Mother I needed a pair at Kinney's Shoes, an up-with-people chain that calmed suburban anxieties by offering mass-market riffs off inner-city styles. I distracted her from the Barry White poster behind the display, then jammed my foot in a floor-level X-ray machine to get the right fit. The clerk flipped some toggles, metal plates squashed my toes in line, and radiation flowed under my instep. "Hold still! Two more minutes! Size 10½!"

To my surprise, the shoes became more ballast than style. This keep-on-truckin' world was full of tripping hazards. Bell-bottoms. Shag carpeting. And it didn't help that Gabriel was about to blow his horn. I swore I sometimes heard that sharp intake of breath before a brass player lays into a line. My feet were always about to come unstuck from the ground.

Mother wiped her hands and bent down to press the leather at my toes. "We spent thirty dollars and you already need a new pair," she said, shaking my ankles. "You are growing so fast, our gift from heaven, and soon you will be ready to leave."

To go where? I wanted to ask. I grabbed the counter. The times were awful. Riots in Chicago. Liberals out for Spiro T. Agnew. I heard the Welcome Wagon Lady from *The Stepford Wives* say, "I know you're going to love it here."

Mother didn't notice the trickle of sweat down my forehead. "Next week," she said, "we will buy you a new pair."

No, I thought, the clarion call of fundamentalists and junior-highers alike. I'd stuck these disco shoes onto this timeline. They didn't belong here, but I did. Or should have. I tried to fend her off with the bottom line. "We don't need to spend the money."

She nodded. "You let us worry about that."

Us = me + them. The equation used to be so easy.

One time, I was rummaging in a hall closet for a missing jigsaw puzzle piece when I found a snapshot of Dad at twenty playing poker. He was bone thin, '50s cool, in a white T-shirt with a pack of cigarettes rolled up in one sleeve. When I showed the photo to Mother, she tightened her lips and offered a rare sentence fragment, a one-word plot: "Then."

They adopted me and everything stopped: the smoking, the beer, the fast cars on country roads. Such was their bargain. And I'd kept up my end. I'd melted my soul into their amalgam.

Mother pointed to the plates.

I took her wish as advice, set the table without a word, and headed back to my room.

"Mark, the boys are playing ball out front," she said. She was working on a salad of canned pears, Cool Whip, and pecans. "Do not stay cooped up."

I detoured into the living room, a furniture showroom where the vacuum tracks ran in parallel lines. We only used it for formal events: Thanksgiving, Christmas, proselytizing the neighbors. I could hear touchdown shouts outside. I fingered the sheers apart.

The guys were smiling, laughing. When they tossed the football in the air, I felt that same buzz between my ribs—for the first time in my world, on my timeline, not just in a book. As if I saw the world and read it at the same time. As if life was as fake and irresistible as a novel.

That buzz transformed into the menace of the maw. And it gained a voice. You ought to be somewhere else, it seemed to say.

I shuddered and walked back to my desk. I *was* where I belonged, even if reading felt comfy, too, like those Christmas mornings when we put on the air conditioning so we could wear our wool sweaters.

And listening to myself read was like being in the dressing room at J. C. Penney with mirrors on every side. I could see images of me in other plots. I could probably still judge which me was wrong, was fake, although I now wasn't sure what that meant, what I was faking and what I wasn't. When I tried to work out the problem, I found myself in that same spot I'd gotten to with Mother in the kitchen: wordless, silent, alone.

Without any other answers, I chose another tape, a tale of displaced people who make a home in this world. I pressed the button to play the first chapter of Richard Hough's *Captain Bligh and Mister Christian*.

It's early morning. The midshipman makes his way to the lower decks where the lights are low and dull. Just ahead, he spots Fletcher Christian's hammock. He also hears the Bounty creaking and cracking in every joint. The ship is as weary as old bones.

Right there, I could already hear the end, the mutiny, the waves against Pitcairn Island where the old Bounty was burned in the bay and the crew began a new life hundreds of nautical miles from everything they knew. I closed my eyes and sank into the story. That's when the hollows between my ribs fell silent. No more chatter, no more maw.

Aha! I'd been straddling the timelines. Or trying to stand in the empty place from which the lines of this-is and this-might-be zipped away in multiplying vectors. I just needed to slide along one at a time. When a book got to be too much, I could put it down and go see Mother in the kitchen. When the kitchen didn't make sense, I could go back to the book. The trick to reading was not to let the timelines cross. And never to fall between them.

How naïve could I be?

Charles Dickens in Public School

How naïve? For one thing, I couldn't commit to one timeline at a time. As August melted into the golden glass of September, my brain split once, then again and again. The more I read, the more I fractured into possibilities, the start of some weird, bookish bipolarity. Or maybe a multipolarity, far different from the *either/or* I'd been taught was the basis of everything. Heaven and hell. God and Satan. Me and . . . what? All the other me's?

I also couldn't have predicted the rage that came oozing out of those fractures. Sure, it had been bred in me by fundamentalism and nurtured in our Windex-ed neighborhood. I didn't know that it could also be found on the flip side of novels, hidden behind a crusty librarian's glare or an English prof's messy house. I got livid when I had to come back to my life, which was nothing much to read about.

One blazing afternoon a week before school started, I was holed up in my room, encased in a circle of light, listening to a series of recorded first chapters. I no longer cared if Mother heard. She was one story among many, part of the plot of this me, the story without a real in-the-beginning other than a home movie.

I wanted to disappear into whatever novel was on that tape. But my disease was adapting to its cure. I didn't glide along the plots as I used to. The stories seemed to push through me, as if I was the fixed point and they, the moving lines.

I glanced down and under my huk-a-poo saw the entry point of each story into my body—as if I were a blank sheet of paper and the novels were hole-punching me. Perforations of flesh were scattered on the floor around my chair: perfect circles, too many to number, too alike to put back in place.

I didn't panic at the first peek of a psychotic break that would be years in the making. For one thing, visions were *de rigueur* in my religion. I'd been primed for reality to crack and reveal the truth inside.

But for another, perforated, I felt airier, less gawky, even less anxious about my place on this timeline, probably because I was vacating it bit by bit.

Yet if I wasn't here, where was I? Who was I? And whose was I?

With quantum speed, I started flipping back and forth between the lighter me in the recorded plots and an angrier me outside them. I'd been afraid I'd slip into the empty silence between the stories. But my fate was weirder. While reading—or listening to me read—I was somehow here *and* there, in my life *and* in another, in two realities at once. Or more, many more, legions, especially since so many plots were now lodged in my brain.

I was called back onto this timeline by the sound of a football game out front. I'd started playing again with a craze for the crack of the tackle. My body was changing, too, sprouting and burbling, attaching me to the dinner table and the ground.

Problem was, these physical revisions were more nightmarish than my hole-punched visions. I found life understandable as a mental performance first, with an emotional response as an afterthought. A physical reality? I still couldn't imagine it. Without understanding the danger, I shut off the cassette player and headed outside.

The guys high-fived me. "Where's the protractor?" one of them asked.

"Shut up," I said, determined to be an asset in this testosterone brawl, an all-heart-and-no-brawn wannabe. I slashed my way toward the quarterback and dove head first into pile-ons.

One kid had gotten relegated to the other team's kicker because he had to wear his orthodontic headgear 24/7. On a fourth-down punt, I smashed through the line, grabbed the wire around his face, swung him off his feet, and ripped the metal bracket off a molar. I wanted to maim him, hurt him, annihilate him. *Thou shalt not kill* screamed in my head. *I want to be anywhere else!* I screamed back.

The guys pulled me away as the kicker coughed blood onto the street. I swore I heard the voice of that stupid Welcome Wagon Lady in my head. *I know you're going to like it here.*

"Hey, man," someone said. "What gives?"

I didn't know. I felt awful, a rank-and-file sinner. I also felt solid, strong, a barbarous body on the lam from its brain. Faking it felt good, even if my life was nothing but faking it.

The kicker hobbled home holding his jaw. But no one high-fived me. The guys tossed the football around, then gave up and scattered, almost as if they were embarrassed.

I didn't care. I was a mystic by birth and training. I searched the gutter for the molar bracket and pocketed it, a talisman of the person I was *and* the one I could be.

Mother must have seen my performance through the sheers. She seemed worried when I got in the house. *What's this?* But like any good Dallasite, she tried to make the best of it: "Boys will be...."

She couldn't finish the cliché. She looked away. "Get ready for acne," she said as she headed off to the kitchen.

Back in my room, I calmed down under the spell of another novel on tape. Music to tame a savage beast, I told myself, although I was just a science nerd doing his best to make sense of a world falling into piecemeal plots.

Back then, no Southern teenage boy had a decent way to stanch the flow of rage that seeped out of the fractures in his life. Some drag-raced down city streets; some hopped trains to New Orleans. I couldn't pull off those stunts. Fundamentalists rarely rise to opera. Our holiness is stark, a black-and-white documentary. Having acted out in anger, I retreated to passivity. That evening, after a call from the kicker's parents and a mumbled apology to them (but not him), I did something equally unthinkable. I asked for dinner in my room. I wanted to be alone, even though my family ate punctually at 5:45, a cloth-napkin affair.

My parents balked. Damnation is a slip, not a fall.

Dad started to blurt out something grandiose, this moment as a tell for the future: "I'm watching you and every day you're getting a little worse because you...."

Mother handed me a plate to cut him off. His silence marked their final answer to what was wrong with me.

I shut my door and picked at the food. I didn't want to hear what they said at the table. Mostly, I hoped they wouldn't notice how perforated I was. I went back to the first chapter of *The Stepford Wives*. I listened to that tape five, six, God knows how many times, until I was beyond a blank page, just an empty space, ready for whatever story I needed to live.

My parents didn't knock on my door, even as the tape recorder played well beyond the regulation 10:15 bedtime. That night, I slept naked for the first time: flat on my back, outside the covers. I dared anyone to walk in and see what was happening to my body, the supple down at my crotch.

No one did. Which somehow felt worse than the schizophrenic dislocation of novels.

The next morning, I tried to be less primal, a good boy. I brought my plate back to the kitchen. "Sorry," I said, head down. "Won't happen again."

Dad mussed my hair. He said we didn't need to get so "excited." Mother encouraged me to pray more.

I knew she was right, but I didn't stop listening to those tapes, as if *they* should have been able to reverse what they did to me. As if my physical footprint could shrink as my mind grew—although I started working on my body, too. I held my new craving for food in check by going on longer and longer runs, until I was nauseated. But even that exhaustion didn't work. I felt more and more like a body, less and less like a soul, even when I tried to get disembodied by a good story.

On Labor Day weekend, I went out for a run in the hundred-degree heat and began to wonder if my problem didn't have to do with those condensed plots. We treasured the Bible in its entirety, even the *begats*, although we never sat down and just read it through. Maybe I'd outgrown *Reader's Digest* novels. Maybe I needed to experience a whole story from start to finish. The way I never had my own.

I didn't listen to a tape that night. I watched *The Waltons* with my parents, the condensed novels still on shelves over our heads. "Good night, John Boy," Mother repeated at the end. How come she could mouth a plot without being overrun by it?

My answer came fast. On the first day of school, I heard about something big from the ninth graders.

"Y'all see it yet?"

"What?"

"You know."

"What?"

They rocked back on their platform heels. "You'll croak when you see it, read it."

Were they talking about a book? The unabridged version of something I already knew? "Which one?" I asked.

They rolled their collective eyes. "Dickens," they said.

I'd never heard the name before. It sounded like a cuss. Maybe that was why they said the copies were kept under lock and key.

I skipped lunch and ran laps. This Dickens thing might be my narrow escape between fury and silence, between the naked me and the gawky me, between who I was and whoever I was pretending to be. All the answers we knew were in one unabridged book, the Bible. Why not one more?

In fifth period, I met my guide: Mrs. Marsh, a middle-aged, shelf-bosomed, Southern matron who drank hot tea in class from a china cup and saucer. Later in the semester, she'd brag about being able to pencil the Lord's Prayer on a postage stamp. But she must have led a more adventurous life, too. I once saw her zip out of the teacher's lot in a Tippi Hedren-style two-seater Mercedes.

She wasted most of the first class calling the roll and writing our names phonetically on the board. I got so antsy for Dickens that I could almost taste it, a metallic wash on my teeth.

With ten minutes to go, she took off her rhinestone glasses and fixed us with her watery eyes. "This term I am pleased to begin your introduction to the wonders of litter-ah-toor," she said. "To *Great Expectations.*"

I'd never heard of it. But my expectations *were* great. Given the way the cool kids talked about it, litter-ah-toor was probably less cleaned up than a condensed novel. Given the ringing tones Mrs. Marsh used, it was also probably more Christian.

Man, books were confusing. But *Great Expectations* had to be deep and true, as anything with attributed authority was. It might allow me to believe the holes in me were filled in as I slid along its timeline—which would be complete, with no condensed bits or forgotten parts. I could sink into that glorious, sense-making world that novels promised.

Instead, Mrs. Marsh passed out a stack of mimeographs. "You cannot read the classics without understanding their foundation," she said. "We will begin with grammar."

Fair enough. Somebody at church was always nattering on about some Bible verse in Greek or Hebrew, the original languages. Maybe my problem had been a lack of preparation. And I did still have the illiteracy thing. I could always use more work.

Apparently, a lot more. For weeks on end, Mrs. Marsh drilled and diagrammed sentences she'd developed from the manner code. *A lace napkin is left on the table, but a cloth napkin is put in your lap. A gentleman pulls out a lady's chair and stands behind it while she goes to the powder room.*

Here was a problem I didn't foresee. What if one timeline was so mindlessly boring that there was no escape?

No worries. I was an expert at playing along, like when I gave answers about evolution on a biology exam to get an *A*. Or when I learned there were magnitudes of infinity. The total number of prime numbers $= \infty$. The total number of composite numbers $= \infty$. The total number of prime numbers + the total number of composite numbers $=$ a greater ∞. Impossible! God is infinite. And he is one. There are no magnitudes of infinity, nor of God, which means that. . . .

Stop! Diagram the sentence. Wait for the novel.

In the middle of a lesson on dangling modifiers, I got so irritated that I harrumphed and rolled my eyes, a rebellion close to felonious in those days. Mrs. Marsh made me stay after class.

"I'll allow it this time," she said, "because you're not an impatient boy."

She had me there. I'd been trained to wait for the Second Coming. For Democrats to get it in the neck. For the world to break open like an egg and fry in the fires of hell. Sure, I wanted to start Dickens before any of that happened. I just had to hold on. I went for longer runs.

One day, after an interminable session on possessive pronouns before gerunds, Mrs. Marsh seemed particularly pleased. "You all have become proficient in the English language and are ready for one of the great books of all time."

I held my breath.

"You will notice," she went on, "that I have not used the idiocy of a superlative with a qualifying prepositional phrase. No book is 'one of the greatest.' It is either 'the greatest' or 'one of the greats.' I will not make illogical claims even for fiction of this caliber."

I jotted down her advice—*don't go overboard*—as she unlocked the closet and assigned two girls to pass out the volumes.

If I had to guess, *Great Expectations* was probably like a PBS nature show. We didn't talk through it. Even its lies ("billions and billions of years") never tarnished its importance. Literature might be so grand, so time-altering, that there'd be no need for another book, a sort of apocalypse of reading. I'd then go back to my family and not worry about the might-have-beens, not worry about fitting in, not worry about my hole-punched body and pubic hair.

I grabbed my copy, opened it, and saw the type, smaller than a condensed book's, more like the Bible's. A good sign.

But there was something that couldn't escape a Christian trained to spot all amiss. Near the three-quarters mark, two pages were glued together. I looked around. All the copies were the same. One jock behind me whispered, "Shit, what do you think it's about?"

Cretin, I thought, using a word I'd memorized from a diagrammed sentence. I thumbed my copy again. I wanted to focus on the opening chapter, but I kept coming back to those mysterious pages. Someone had tried to pry them apart. The paper was ragged at the edges. It had been patched with tape over the glue.

The bell rang. I shoved the novel in my bag and headed off to the cooler logic of geometry. For the rest of the day, I fingered *Great Expectations*, buried in my tote near the New Testament and *I'm Okay, You're Okay*.

That evening, I sat at our dinette and held the glued pages to the fluorescents, trying to parse the words. Was there something filthy in Dickens? Was that why novels had to be condensed? Was I being protected, the way Mother put her hand over my eyes when the actors started to kiss on TV? I sniffed the print.

"Will you put that down?" Mother said from the stove.

I was afraid she'd take the book away. But I wanted to examine the pages in front of her, to get her approval for finding what's bad in everything.

She could tell I wasn't giving up. "Supper is almost ready," she said. Pork chops gurgled in canned tomato soup. "You are not going to do that silly thing of eating in your room again, are you?"

I shook my head. One rebellion at a time.

"This book's from England," I said.

29

Would she disapprove? When she didn't say anything, I added, "Dickens." Then "Charles."

She nodded. "That is the sort of book you *should* read."

She could surprise me witless, although we often seemed to have conversations she'd mapped out years before.

"I thought you didn't want me to read so much," I said.

"I was concerned"—she didn't look up from slicing maraschino cherries for the salad— "about the tape recorder."

That was the problem? Listening, rather than reading? I glanced at the book's cover. A man in a high-collared shirt gazed at a woman with a waterfall of brown curls. What could be so wrong with the two of them?

I took Mother's advice and left *Great Expectations* on the sideboard. *In the fullness of time*, I told myself, quoting St. Paul to forestall curiosity, the same thing I told myself about the dangle between my legs.

I slept soundly in my pajamas with the door open. But the next morning, when I put the book in my tote and Dad drove me to school, I could already feel the buzz between my ribs. I flipped the radio from Top Forty to Country Western stations.

"Cool it," he said, switching off the dial. After a stint as a hot-shot Air Force pilot, he'd landed a spot as a clarinetist in a professional orchestra. Within a year, he'd given up that gig for actuarial tables at an insurance company. He wanted to make sure I made the same choices.

I wanted to, too. "You ever read Dickens?" I asked.

"Of course, son. *Bleak House*. College."

He must have been confused. I had no idea authors wrote more than one book. God just wrote the Bible, after all. But I couldn't challenge Dad. He was braced for another day at the office, his forehead creased above his brows. As well it should be. The world stood on a precarious lip. Just that weekend, Billy Jean King had trounced Bobby Riggs in *The Battle of The Sexes*, 6 – 4, 6 – 4, 6 – 3.

I made it through my morning classes without a hitch, then ran for an hour at lunch in the eighty-degree, early-November humidity.

"Maybe you should slow down," one of the coaches said as I changed out of my T-shirt and shorts. But another me was already budding inside me: the literary snob. This guy taught American history by reciting the answers from the teacher's edition. What did he know?

In fifth period, Mrs. Marsh swigged her tea, rose from her desk, and opened her dog-eared copy of the novel, the pages as supple as cotton cloth. The whole thing felt like church, if Billy Jean King really had turned on the world on its head and women could be preachers.

"What is the first sentence?" Mrs. Marsh asked.

Hands went up in silence. We Dallasites held firm in the chaos.

"Mark," Mrs. Marsh said, "please stand and read it."

I did. "The first sentence?" I asked, slowing the moment to savor it.

"It cannot be in doubt."

I thought of the sheer joy of a book's beginning, an alternate universe, all that possibility and promise. The drop in my stomach was unbelievably sharp. Thank God for disco shoes. I was stable on my feet.

I took a deep breath and set to: "My father's family name being Pir . . . uh . . . uh. . . ."

Mrs. Marsh came in for the assist: "Pirrip." Except she burred it in her drawl, "PEE-rrrrruhp," with the stress on the first syllable and a rolled "r" to indicate its British provenance.

"PEE-rrrrruhp," I continued. I could feel the silence descend between my ribs, like a cold drink running down my gullet. "And my Christian name. . . ." I paused. See? Christian. "And my Christian name Philip, my infant tongue could make of both names nothing longer or more explicit than Pip."

"Precisely," she said. "What is the direct object in this sentence?"

I looked down at the page.

"Well?" she asked.

I looked up. "Nothing," I said. "The direct object of the verb *make* is *nothing*."

"Correct."

I held her liquid stare. "That's it?" I asked.

"Not an impatient boy," she said. "Please be seated."

Like Icarus, I could smell the wax melt. Dickens' words didn't feel like a thrill. They were rational and cold, like math, chemistry, or the Bible. Literature was nothing but grammar! I thought of the time, several years ago, when the old barn on my grandparents' farm had caved in. The next morning, we stared at a heap of boards.

"So goes this world," Mother said.

So goes a novel, I thought. My hopes gave way, but I didn't fall out of the sky. Glued-together pages? Probably some dumb grammar mistake, some crap about subject-verb agreement. I mean, who was this Dickens guy? Books just wanted to be like the Bible. Literature, more so, trying to be full of the right answers, if less consequential ones, prepositions and subjunctives. *Great Expectations* wasn't about time. It was a waste of it.

Mrs. Marsh went on to the next sentence: "So I called myself Pip and came to be called Pip. What is the function of the reflexive pronoun 'myself'?"

And the next sentence, and the next, catching out my peers who didn't know an auxiliary verb from a modal.

I slumped in my chair. Clearly, I'd been shanghaied by summer boredom. And by the need for self-improvement, always dicey for a fundamentalist depraved by Adam's DNA. This world, every world, the *is* and all the *might-have-beens*—the whole thing was just like noun adjuncts and adverbial clauses: a bunch of itty-bitty parts, easily aped. Maybe there was nothing wrong with pretending to be who I was. Maybe home was the best timeline in a world filled with fake ones. *Great Expectations* was indeed the book to end all the others.

The bell rang, the classroom emptied, but I didn't stand to go. Mrs. Marsh cleared her throat. "Shall you miss the glories of geometry?"

I shall never miss them again, I thought. "Thanks," I said instead.

"You," she corrected. "Thank you. And for what shall I be thanked?"

"For reminding me to pay attention to what matters," I said—then amended it: "For *your* reminding me to pay attention."

She smiled a Cheshire grin. "What an excellent student."

The tardy bell rang. Doors closed down the hall. On the spur of the moment, I decided to dodge the truant officer, skip school, and walk the three miles home. I wanted to be alone with the blessed silence in my head. I could fake a note from Mother tomorrow. No teacher ever checked the source, especially with honors students.

As Jesus said, "The truth shall set you free." I had permission to forget this whole ordeal, to be a good boy again. Or pretend to be one. It didn't matter which. Because stories were just words. Because words had to fit a grammar, an acceptable pattern. Because life was what I'd always thought it was: a set of rules.

By December, my class got up to the snarl of participles that made up Miss Havisham's drawing room. Eventually, we must have passed the offending, glued-together pages. But I'd checked out, mentally prepping for my upcoming chance to preach at the nation's largest flea market. I was to be the front man at our tent, the guy with all the answers from the Bible, the book that didn't collapse in a heap.

Once, I even forgot to bring my copy of *Great Expectations* to school. I came home to find Mother reading it. The house was decorated for Christmas with plastic snowmen in cottony, fake snow. A glass of iced tea sat on a coaster near her.

"You see why I was so interested in that book?" I asked, never thinking she'd miss the glued-together pages. I hoped she'd model my weariness at the world's ways.

"I sure do," she said.

"And?"

She smiled gently, no squint. "Pip is adopted, too."

"Too?" I asked. Or sort of yelled.

"He was an orphan," she explained.

"I'm not!"

"Come here, my sweet boy." She kissed the top of my head. "*That* is the point."

I'd say so! Adopted, I didn't need saving. Saved, I didn't need fixing. There was only one plot: the one I was living. Okay, and the one in the Bible. If I worked hard enough, they'd fuse without any illegible bits.

Mother was still smiling.

"I have to turn in the book tomorrow," I lied.

She handed it to me. "It is pretty wordy."

I never finished *Great Expectations*, although I got an *A* for diagramming Dickens' longer, original ending. I was the first kid to toss the novel back into the closet. I shivered as Mrs. Marsh slipped the key into the lock. There were no alternate beginnings. The plot of my life was tidy and obvious.

Years later, a classmate told me the problem with *Great Expectations*. Long before my year, some boy—surely, a boy—had broken into that closet and scribbled a dick on the same page in every copy. Mrs. Marsh had taken a gritty eraser to the blue ink. Then she'd applied glue. And even tape when curiosity got the better of students before me. Mrs. Marsh couldn't cut out pages from a canonical book, so she saved them by rendering them illegible. But by the time I found all that out, I was too busy ruining my adult life to take in the lesson that the great works of Western literature could not only reveal my secrets but also hold them, even the ones about dicks.

God in East Texas

Early on a February morning about six weeks later, I was wrapped in flannel pajamas and tucked under the covers. No light edged the bedroom curtains. I could hear the hollow thump of rain on the roof.

Since the small hours, I'd been quietly rehearsing my gospel pitch. Although I'd been the front man at county rodeos and smaller swap-meets, today was my debut at First Monday, the nation's largest flea market in Canton, Texas, and a three-day event despite its name.

"Dress warm," Mother warned when she came in to wake me up. "Fifty-nine degrees. Winter's sticking around!"

She padded off to start breakfast. I stretched under the covers and slowed my breathing. I could make all the timelines obey me. "Come learn about history," I murmured, "the only story God wrote."

After *Great Expectations*, I wasn't back where I started. I was immersed in the only plot that mattered. It filled the emptiness in me, fended it off around me, and made sense of the world. Didn't all that sum the definition of *home*?

When I was a kid, the Bible had seemed like a good storybook, about right for bedtime. But the snippets I heard didn't fire my imagination because they were over so quickly: Jonah down in the whale, Zacchaeus up in the tree.

As I grew up, God's Word became a good mental exercise. There was so much to memorize. And like everyone else in my church, I saw the Bible as a self-help manual with dating rules and career advice. But now that I'd started reading holy writ as a whole, I loved its scope, the past and future balled up on my spot in time.

Even so, I couldn't take any chances. As the Good Book says, "Faith without works is dead." So I'd taken a hammer to my tape recorder, bashing its dock and spindles until I couldn't use the thing again. I slipped it back into its leather case so no one would ever be the wiser, put it on my closet shelf, and stacked the tapes beside it. They were like the graves of my Civil War kin, useless memorials to a failure no one wanted to admit.

Bacon was frying. I showered, got dressed in a baggy three-piece suit, and tried to put on my disco shoes. I was then yanked out of my dreams of holiness. My toes were squashed on top of each other. It was probably my fault. My feet had likely flattened from all the running I'd done.

"No," I said to still the pain. I walked to the breakfast table without a hitch.

Mother and I prayed, then dug in.

"Dad's not getting up?" I asked.

"He needs the weekend," she said, a sentiment I couldn't understand. Life was effort. All the time.

Which Mother understood. She narrated her day ahead: loads and loads of washing. She never allowed us to use a bath towel more than once. She'd stitched a red thread in a corner of each so we'd know which end was for the face and which for the other parts.

"You are not very talkative," she finally said.

With the words of only one book in my head, I was more often silent these days—which meant that as a guy in my culture, I was godlier, too.

Outside, Pastor Daniel's green Galaxy 500 idled on the rain-slicked street. He was in the front seat, staring forward. I flashed the porch light to tell him I was ready. He waved without turning his head.

For sixty miles, the windshield wipers ticked the rhythm of time. Pastor Daniel's thin hair was combed back in a wave that showed his skull. His hands were at ten and two on the wheel.

When we got into the rolling hills of east Texas, he started fiddling with the AM dial, looking for the morning preachers.

"You mind?" he asked. "Professional obligation."

Pastor Daniel had gotten his start on an AM show, *Radio Revival*. It involved very little singing or preaching and a whole lot of praying, because the revival was always in the offing. The show had lately migrated to a local TV station but kept its original name.

After several tries, he settled on a preacher.

Is England's Queen Elizabeth the Whore of Babylon foretold in the book of Revelation?

Pastor Daniel had just finished a Sunday night series on whether the medieval divines like St. Augustine were saved. (No. In hell.)

Princess Margaret may well be the catalyst to bring about the Antichrist.

I barely paid attention. I knew all this stuff. We saw history up to current events as an architect-designed pile of symbols that unlocked the mysteries of existence. Everything meant something else.

Outside the window, the boggy fields were studded with billboards for churches. *If you don't like how you were born, try being born again.*

"You sure you're ready?" Pastor Daniel asked as we neared First Monday's gate.

"Yes, sir," I said, trying my best to be who I was.

I'd been to Canton before, but always as the kid who got lunch and kept the water glasses filled. Maybe that's why I hadn't noticed how huge the fair was. It spread across acres under a fairy-tale forest of pines that rose straight and branchless for forty feet. They'd dropped a thick carpet of needles that hushed our tires' crunch and suffocated most other plants.

We parked next to a vendor I recognized from smaller events. The man had a vipers' nest of measuring tapes around his neck. He specialized in macramé end tables, braided strands supporting sheets of glass. They dangled from meat hooks off metal bars. Under a gray tarp, he'd even staged them with examples of homey bric-a-brac: a ceramic cat wearing an Easter bonnet, a framed picture of sailors with their backs to a nuclear blast.

He waved and called out, "Hope that kid's gonna preach today. His kind make for the best sales."

Down the lanes beyond us were chipped wall sconces, yellowed wedding dresses, and loads of tittle tattle, although one time a woman—from New York, wouldn't you know?—found a Renoir among the velvet Elvises. Another guy made off with a set of Waterford for the price of gas-station drinking glasses. And then there were the celebrities, always under hat and cape: Sally Field, Sandy Duncan, even Truman Capote. "You see him on *The Mike Douglas Show*? We don't care for his kind."

Today, I recognize this scene as a stage set for Vietnam-era angst in its purest form, as well as the squinty-eyed South of resentment and regret. Back then, I felt a wide-eyed hope. The government was dealing with the hippies. The army was ready in the wings if things got worse. But we couldn't be too careful. Agnew had resigned, even if Nixon was holding strong. And the Supreme Court was in league with the devil, having just handed down *Roe v. Wade*. We had faith that we could save the United States by prayer and fasting. We hadn't thought of running our own candidates yet.

I started to ease out of the car, looking for ground that wasn't deep in muck. Under the pine needles lay dissolved clay, as sticky as quicksand. It could hold anyone in place. I'd once called it "the original cure for the Rapture." No one from our church's delegation had laughed.

"I think I need an umbrella." I said.

Pastor Daniel glanced at the cascade on the windshield. "Tough it out," he said. "Noah did."

The Old Testament was a treasure trove of verses for goosing teenagers into doing stuff they didn't want to do. But holiness was also a game, all counter moves. I tried honesty.

"Noah didn't have my shoes. They'll get ruined."

"Vanity of vanities," Pastor Daniel said.

"That's Ecclesiastes 12:8," I lobbed back. "And the next verse says, *Moreover, because the preacher was wise, he taught the people knowledge.*"

Pastor Daniel gave me his thin-lipped smile. "Okay, I could help."

The macramé man offered a hand, too. Once they had the tent stretched overhead, I dragged an easel and a card table out of the back seat. Soon, the sour-faced men from church arrived. They brought folding chairs and arranged them in a row at the back of the tent. The men then spread out newspapers and bowed their heads over the events that could trigger the apocalypse. Last year, Jane Fonda had almost singlehandedly brought Jesus back. But Pastor Daniel counseled that we shouldn't quit our day jobs. Those Kent State kids had gotten what they deserved.

Pastor Daniel motioned for me to start, so I positioned myself at the edge of the overhang, my shoes at the drip line. Ours was no raucous revival. We offered suburban Calvinism mixed with a science-fiction apocalypse. And I was the bait, a familiar sight: an eighth-grade boy with a Bible. I needed to alto-ize my voice to its pre-adolescent squeak and make the sinners come quick.

On the easel beside me was a giant chart: *God's Plan for the Ages*. It was our version of history, a map of time, and the only plot that mattered, the one those condensed novels and Dickens had tried to ape. On each end of the map, a yellow sun, warm and ripe as a fresh egg yolk, anchored the taut line of time shot through human endeavor. Off it rose "The Seven Ages of Man." First, Innocence (Adam and the Garden of Eden), then Conscience (Noah and the flood), followed by Human Government (Nimrod and the Tower of Babel), Promise (Abraham and the Promised Land), Law (Moses and the Jews), Grace (us, followed by the Rapture), and finally the Millennium (us *and* 144,000 Jews, followed by the end of everything).

I was no Puritan proctor. I refereed a multiple-choice quiz. I was a game show host who hinted, prompted, and cajoled. "Guess which age we live in!"

The chart itself offered clues. A giant cross rose off the timeline right before the Age of Grace, which was helpfully subtitled "The Church Age." But rarely did I see anyone get the right answer. The *Left Behind* lingo was brand new. Most people weren't expecting to be swept off their feet. Besides, no matter what you said, you got ushered into the gloom at the back of the tent where those sour-faced men waited in their folding chairs.

I clutched my Bible, the one with the McGovern/Antichrist math on the end paper. There was no chattering in my ribs, no drop in my stomach, even though I was about to be seen and heard by thousands in the strolling crowds. Why be nervous? Every moment was part of something cosmic, which included me, even if, like my adoption, it wasn't exactly about me.

Over among the macramé, I spotted my first mark, a mountainous woman in a dime-store housecoat. She huffed with each step, toting a bag of junk and pitching a lime green umbrella overhead. Under it huddled a teenage boy, fifteen, maybe sixteen, a couple of years older than I was. He sported a dirty football jersey and last night's blacking under his eyes. His hair was home-cut, the bangs in a straight line. But even in the rain, it showed a bit of blow-dryer feathering. He wasn't a bulked lineman, more like a lithe quarterback—which was about as close to Jesus as he could be in Texas. And I could still show him the grace of God.

The woman ran her hand down a ropy strand, put her fingers to her nose, and scrunched up her face. That's when I caught her eye.

"Y'all want to win a free Bible map?" I asked. Cheerful. Hopeful. The right tone. A performance in the service of the truth.

She squinted. "Whut?"

"God's Plan For The Ages." I made sure to speak with capital letters.

The boy looked hard at me. "Let's get outta here."

"We already go to church," she called out. "Baptist."

Bingo, I thought. Southern, I assumed. Thus, damned.

"Missionary Baptist," she clarified.

Oh, they were more conservative than we were. We allowed acoustic guitars and a few translations other than the King James. But they didn't believe in the Rapture. Inside fundamentalism's walls were endless subdivisions. That sprawl actually made it easy to know who was saved. You had to believe every single thing we did.

"You'd be a cinch to win," I told her. "And you'll get a Bible map." I pointed to the easel beside me. "Like this, only smaller. Just guess which age we live in."

I was so irresistible, a lanky kid in a big suit, that the woman lurched over to our tent. The boy came along with the umbrella, if only to avoid a soaking.

"We're game," she said.

He jammed his hands in his pockets. "I told you, let's go." His look was malevolent: lowered brow, tightened eyes.

"Y'all have a church around here?" she asked.

I was determined to act like the son she probably wished she'd had. "In Dallas, ma'am."

She wrinkled her nose, the same way she had at the macramé smell.

"Well," I said, "Farmer's Branch."

She liked the sound of that. "You country people?"

"Sure. Just figure out where we are on this chart."

She prodded her son in the ribs. "You're good at school."

"We ain't got to this part," he said.

I swallowed a sneer. The coach probably fed him the answers.

She hitched up a hip. "Aw, Jared, jest guess. Them's church people. They won't think anything bad about choo."

He curled his lip. "Fine," he said. "Law. Cuz Pop says we got too many."

"Nice try," I chirped. In my disco heels, we were almost the same height. But I slumped to give him the advantage. "Law's when God gave Moses the Ten Commandments. You know, Charlton Heston, the movie."

His mother drew in a sharp breath. "What are you watching that devil stuff for?"

I'd made a misstep. Backwoods Baptists didn't darken the doors of movie theaters.

"No, no, it's been on TV," I explained. "You could see it at home."

"Wouldn't," she sniffed. "I'm surprised you're allowed to. . . ."

I tried to get us back on track. "You get to see the plagues. And Yvonne DeCarlo."

Her son looked me up and down. "I still say it's Law. Cain't be anything else."

I could smell Irish Spring on him, a new must-have for teenage boys. And I felt something like a shudder under the walls of Jericho. It shot out of the ground and ran to my nape. I took it for the fury of the prophets. The revealed word of God was staring this jerk in the face and he wasn't paying attention!

"Look!" I stabbed a finger at the chart, the rage oozing out of every fracture on every timeline. "Right there. The cross. You know who died on the cross, right?" My voice was getting louder and lower, a growl. "And this. That's the Rapture. Have you seen people flying up to heaven? No, you have not. That hasn't happened, yet we know the cross *has* happened. So by sheer logic, if you even know what logic is. . . ."

"Gubbmint made too many laws," he smirked.

"Listen, you asshole retard. . . ."

He stepped forward so our chests touched. "Whut you callin' me?"

On cue, I heard his mother start a cornbread mewl. "Jared. You, boy. You, Jared."

"Try, try again," I taunted, leveling our heights. I followed the rules, and this moron swaggered around, acting as if he ruled the world, trying to cover the acrid stench of his stupidity with drug-store soap. The one, true story was mine. The voice of history. And of the future, too. If he'd been wearing a headgear, I'd have ripped it off his face and welcomed the beating.

Before any of that could happen, I felt a hand on my shoulder.

Pastor Daniel looked sallow in the misty light. "What's going on out here?" he asked.

Because I've never known if I'm supposed to be where I am at any moment, I've always been shocked speechless when people want to take care of me. Words evaporated in my mouth. "I . . . was trying to help. . . ."

What was the direct object of *help*? Him? Myself? My ears were red.

Jared held his ground. "He called me sumthin' bad. I can't stand that outta another guy."

The world was spinning fast. I could have gotten walloped. Then he stepped back. He probably knew his muscles were no match for my holiness.

"Who the fuck do you think you are?" he laughed.

"Jared! Language!" his mother cried.

"Coming out here to act so high and mighty? A pissant like you." He'd already backed off. It was fake, but no less threatening. "You think you got so many pretty words. Step behind this here tent and I'll beat the shit out of you. Then you can go on back to whatever farmer place you're from and tell 'em that you don't know nothin' about history." He looked down at my disco shoes and staged a sour grin. "And you probably got them at a Negro store. You don't even got the words for whut the hell you are."

I wanted to scream "no!" Maybe so many times, I could stamp out its rhythm, even if my feet seemed fused to the ground. Ours wasn't *that* story, the one about the South, about blacks and whites, about this kid's predictable and deadly racism. It was about us, about me, about who was right, or had the right timeline. I knew the end of everything. Any words I needed were clutched in my hand, the ones from Jesus in red, the ones from the prophets in my brain. Yet this kid had casually switched the plots and gone for the Dixie nightmare. And where was that story on the chart beside me?

I could hear the emptiness around me, in me, between my ribs. I felt the open chasm of history. My own, yes. Jared's, too, the

Southern hellscape of white rage. Maybe everyone's, the void that stories spun up over, that the words in the Bible should have filled. Yet not a single sentence in God's word could have explained the rabid racism in my world. Or the silence in that place inside me that was supposed to feel like home.

Jared's could. *You don't even got the words for whut the hell you are.* Hardly an answer, his sentence seemed . . . like a promise? The future? Certainly, a reverse polarity of its intent. It wriggled under my skin and stretched from my heart to my head. It was my new carotid, fizzing with hope as my rage drained away—and as Pastor Daniel took over.

"Just a misunderstanding between boys," he said. "How about a Bible Map?"

Pastor Daniel pushed me into the tent, yellowed by kerosene lanterns. I don't know what happened next. Maybe Jared got saved. Maybe he got raptured into the clouds. Hands pulled me into a folding chair. I sat down, shivering. Around me, the sour-faced men mumbled prayers. Maybe they said one for me. I wasn't listening. My shoes hurt like hell but my brain effervesced with too much oxygen. I rocked back and forth to the rhythm of the prophets and some hick kid stomping out a line dance on the floorboards of my soul, as I silently repeated my hope over and over again: *You don't even got the words for the what the hell you are.*

A while later, Pastor Daniel took a break from preaching and found me still in the folding chair. He prodded the tent's roof so the water cascaded outside.

"You want to get us some hot dogs?" he asked. He dug for some change in his pocket. "Mustard, please."

I looked down at my shoes. They'd get caked, ruined.

"Sure," I said.

I stepped into the slop without an umbrella. I could feel the mud seep over the vamps and into my socks. The white stitching turned brown.

I wandered around, ducking into booths, looking at pastel prints and knitted sit-upons. I thought about how hard I'd worked to fit in: Christian, male, polite, prophetic, right.

No one tried to fit in with me. Or meet me halfway. Everyone else was the given, the rule. They were all like the Bible. They offered solutions to turn me into me. Which I accepted *gratis* because I was a lump of still-forming flesh that could be molded, compressed, or stretched to fit any story. Such was life for an adopted kid. It might be the best I could hope for.

The next month, the men nominated a new boy to do the hawking at Canton. He was still in elementary school. He didn't need to re-pitch his voice. He parted his hair down the center, a greasy shank on either side of his forehead. He was mealy-mouthed and coldly righteous.

I went along, wore new sneakers, and sat in a folding chair. I prayed with the winners and the losers. The men now congratulated me on my holiness. If I missed the more public performance of who I was, I meekly told myself I didn't need to rehearse the future. I knew it: the Rapture, the Antichrist, the lake of fire. All I had to do was hold on. With a death grip. Forever. Even with Jared's words burbling inside me. Even though I felt like an extra in the crowd scene at the apocalypse. I was saved and lost, sanctified and irate, somebody and nobody.

The end was indeed nigh. So nigh, I didn't see it coming.

William Blake in Waco

I narrowed my high school years onto a science-lab-tent-revival axis. I made it through *Macbeth* with Cliff's Notes. *The Scarlet Letter?* No fundamentalist had to read it to know it. I did write a paper on whether the poet Henry Wadsworth Longfellow was a Christian. (No. *A-*.)

I took to sitting in the back pew at church and sneering at the guest preachers, all of whom missed the point, although I still wasn't sure what the point was. I taught myself rudimentary Greek, not so I could understand the New Testament, but so I could call into question anyone's interpretation and offer a better one. I became an even greater contradiction: a swaggering prophet in teenage-tight clothes, decades before Joel Osteen and the Jesus tech bros.

Occasionally, I glanced at the cassettes in my closet. They were a warning, not a memorial. Those condensed novels had done nothing more than splotch color on my life. I told myself that the chomping between my ribs hadn't been about books. It had been my irritation at the garish hue on things. Nothing deserved that paint.

I'd once felt the same way about *The Wizard of Oz*. My family had an old black-and-white television until I was almost in high school. I didn't know the world changed into color when Dorothy stepped out of her wrecked house. I thought the *oohs* and *aahs* were about the oversized flowers and the Munchkins. When we finally got a new TV, I saw the saturated world, the golds and reds. I hated it. "Better before," I said and stalked off to my room. I never watched the movie again.

The godlier I got, the less I fit into my family's pious but happy take on the world. I saw a holy tragedy, everything headed downhill. My parents saw a divine comedy where everything worked out. They'd also had another child, my brother—and not by adoption. Dad called us "store-bought" and "home-made."

I got in trouble more often. Nothing big, of course. I forgot to mow the lawn once in a while. I missed my curfew when I drove some girls home from a Bible study. I made my bed but forgot to tuck in the corners. I was becoming a real teenager, not a bad one, but not a model one either—and so somehow less acceptable, since we defined polar opposites as the norms.

Mother tsked. Dad sputtered. "Every day," he said, "things are getting worse."

How could that be? I could outline Isaiah's prophecy at will. I could recite about a third of the hundred and fifty psalms by heart. I could explain the differences among all the words for *love* in the Bible. I thought the Greek ones in the New Testament were more incisive, colder, and better articulated than the Hebrew ones in the Old Testament.

Because I embodied a stark faith goosed with hormones, my unspoken contradictions felt more painful when I was in the very place I *should* belong. I told myself I was holier than my fundamentalist family. They did what they could to protect themselves from my crusade. When I launched into a diatribe about the faithless world, Mother whisked my brother out of the room. When I ratcheted up the rhetoric over campus unrest on the evening news and said that a loaded gun could set the world right, Dad took my brother out to play in the yard. When I refused to tithe off my allowance because Pastor Daniel wasn't "right with the Lord," my parents made my brother sit through our oddly formal grounding ceremony, a warning for his future.

I started driving into the countryside around Dallas after school, parking near the brand-new lakes in my VW Beetle. I blared Christian pop at the sunsets in a furious attempt to silence the hope fizzing along the verbal carotid that Jared's words had implanted under my skin. When *would* I have the words to explain what the hell I was?

Truth be told, I was that bit of fuzzy penicillin mold that could save the world but ruin the meal. So my parents did what good Protestants do: they got rid of me. Not in some out-the-door scene. Holiness is not disposable. Instead, they told me to quit high school and go to college.

When I was in eleventh grade, Dad came home one afternoon and asked me to step into their bedroom, the inner sanctum of family matters, where I got spanked as a kid or my report card got a line-by-line review.

He wore a brown windowpane suit with a gold tie. He was Frank Sinatra in shopping-mall amber. "You're the odds-on favorite for salutatorian, right?" he asked.

I nodded and looked down. My Top Siders felt cool and comfortable. I'd swapped huk-a-poo for Oxford cloth.

"And being second really excites you?" Dad asked.

I couldn't meet his eyes. But I tried to explain about the C in a mandatory drafting class, the boys' answer to home ec. About not being able to draw a straight line. But I couldn't tell him that I liked second place for the same reason I now played the French horn. There were fewer solos, mostly accompaniment parts. It was easier when I was overlooked. I couldn't make a fool of myself in front of a Bible tent or with a valedictorian's speech. I could explain the hollow emptiness in me as a series of small disappointments.

And there was another reason I preferred second string: inchoate, illogical, only articulated late at night when I was at my desk, alone with the Bible's prophets. By now, my birth mother had probably forgotten me, too.

"Haven't you had enough of high school?" Dad asked.

I thought he was joking, so I time-lined the future. "What about marching in the Cotton Bowl Parade? AP Physics? Prom?"

I started to say something about applying to Wheaton College, the Yale of fundamentalists, but he stopped me short. "Don't you want a serious girlfriend?"

He had me there, even if his question was an atypical misdirection into sex when I was talking about God's plan for my life. My current girlfriend claimed she liked it when I played Bach's piano inventions because they helped her "zone out."

Dad said something about an early admission program. "I think you're done with high school." Then he clarified it: "We're sending you to Baylor. In May. For the summer term."

I wasn't enraged. More like surprised. And even amused at the absurdity of my life. I was always supposed to be somewhere else.

Admittedly, we'd had an awful week. I was appalled the nation had chosen that reprobate Jimmy Carter for president. I also knew Dad was trying to hold onto some notion of the perfect family, an

O.K. Corral of their linked DNA that locked the gate against me and my wild notions of the truth. I could see the gleam in his eye.

So partly because I was quick to blame myself, partly because I didn't want to infect my family with whatever disease was in my head, but mostly because I wanted to be the son I thought Dad wanted me to be, I nailed my SAT in math, slouched by with a barely acceptable verbal score, and bolted out of Dallas public education system at sixteen without a degree, ready to start my life in Waco, Texas, as a real guy, the kind who dates a better class and gets where he's going without thinking about it too much.

I didn't tell anyone I was leaving high school until a couple of days before the end of the term. I didn't even say "good-bye" to most of my friends. I gave my girlfriend a righteous peck and mumbled something about "being faithful." A year later, in what would have been my graduation yearbook, I got listed on the page with the kids who'd died in car wrecks.

I justified it all by telling myself that I was following God's call to be a chemistry major at a university that didn't believe in evolution. Besides, I was just passing through this redbrick campus on a boggy bit of the Brazos River floodplain. Like every other guy I knew, I was on my way to medical school—although I was a more natural fit than most. Calvinism is built into modern medicine. He who can be fixed shall be. If not, it wasn't meant to be. Besides, what's wrong with you is mostly your own fault anyway.

My academic advisor had a throwback beehive and wore big, plastic beads. Her desk was littered with photos of her holding a .22 rifle and straddling dead animals. She was part of the administration's brass, assigned because my admissions file had been stamped *permanent suspense*. It was to remain unfinished business for my years at Baylor.

When I asked her about passing as a normal freshman, she shocked me by telling me to lie. "Let's load you up with labs and keep you busy." she said. "You don't want to be a freak."

I looked out her window to the leafy quad, deserted at three in the Memorial Day heat. The grass grew right up to the sidewalk intersections. No one cut the corners. Baptists, I thought. So close to the truth. Yet so far.

"What would happen if I told people who I was?" I asked.

"I hate drama. Mint?" She rattled a little box of Tic Tacs at me.

"No, thanks."
"Hamburger?"
"What?"
"For lunch?"
"Oh, a hot dog."
She shook the box again. "Trust me."
I got the message and took one with the rest of her advice.

I marked that summer and my freshman year with the standard rituals. Our first mixer took place on a historic suspension bridge over the Brazos. Twinkle lights lined the arches. Hall and Oates pulsed in the speakers. Grizzled profs crept among us. One toted a yardstick, stuck it knee-level between dancing couples, and yanked it up, scraping any hard-ons into submission.

Some guys in the dorm had set me up with Melody: five-one, all spunk and spring. I wore cowboy boots, pinned her with a mum, and kept an eye out for the yardstick. I didn't even ask her if she was a Christian. I chalked it up to not being a freak. What's one date?

The boards of the bridge made a hollow echo of our dance steps, although I mostly kicked my feet around, trying to look as if I wasn't about to trip and fall on my face. During the third encore of "She's Gone," I asked Melody if she was enjoying her classes that term.

She smiled broadly. "You're a real stand-up guy." She pulled a small flask out of her hip pocket. "How about a nip to celebrate your status?"

I'd never tasted wine or beer, much less liquor. But since my advisor had told me to pretend to be normal, I nodded toward the flask as if I knew what I was doing. "My parents didn't raise a fool." I said.

"Well, no shit," Melody said, "but you can never be too sure. Texas, I mean."

She turned away from the crowd, took a hit, and passed me the flask. I sucked in the night air, closed my eyes, and swallowed the smallest amount possible.

"You okay?" she asked.

"A little cold," I said between clenched teeth.

"Yeah," she laughed, "and it's ninety degrees at midnight."

"Just studying too much," I explained.

She smiled, less broadly, more relaxed. "Very sweet, no matter what."

Later, on the steps of the girl's dorm, she tongued my ear, something no fundamentalist girl had ever done.

"Call me," she said.

I did. She was a slightly more daring version of everyone I knew. She listened to Fleetwood Mac, not The Captain and Tennille. She drove twenty miles over the speed limit but never missed a dorm curfew. Plus, she was a Methodist—which was sort of like being a Christian, but with booze.

We became an item, and I made it through a year and a half without cracking open a novel or reading a poem. But like Jesus, the great books can come back in the blink of an eye. I needed to finish up my required courses and waited too long to register. A seat opened in an eleven o'clock lit survey.

"Surprise!" my advisor said. There was a new picture of a dead buck on her desk. "Caddie Anderson. You're in luck."

I still didn't believe in luck. "Who?"

"One of our most popular profs. You got in as a fluke. Or an act of God. Take your pick."

I also didn't know you could pick.

Baylor's baccalaureate requirements were a tad quirky. Every Arts and Sciences undergrad had to take a course called *British Literature Before Robert Burns*. The Scottish poet divided the canon. After that, you could take a course in American lit or dig into the unthinkable buffet of world lit. The less imaginative among us finished what we'd started: *British Literature After Robert Burns*, William Blake through the Victorians and on to Ted Hughes.

"So patient with that wife of his, that Sylvia Plath," I heard one professor say.

Right at the get-go, I knew Caddie Anderson's type. She was illicit in a Waco way, like Annette Funicello as Mrs. Robinson in a remake of *The Graduate*. Anderson rarely sat down, looping the classroom to whisper poetry in our ears, her breath sickly sweet with the scent of clove gum. She also taught creative writing. She was said to "lack the *pee-aitch-dee*."

One warm Wednesday a few weeks in, she was doing circuits, her hair a studied mess, her reading glasses down her nose.

I'd long since outgrown literature. I was an eighteen-year-old sophomore who'd placed out of all the science and math requirements in his freshman year and now had enough credits to call himself a junior. I'd managed to get good grades without standing out. I was pretending to be me on all counts and getting away with it. And I wasn't disassembling another family. Altogether, in some mirror-lined dressing room of self-consciousness, it felt like what my life was supposed to feel like.

"When I was one-and-twenty," Anderson read, a thick anthology balanced on one palm, "I heard a wise man say. . . ." She paused for dramatic effect, as if A. E. Housman's poetry needed any. "Give crowns and pounds and guineas, but not your heart away."

I'd never seen a crown or a pound. I'd never been to England. The words were just soapy drivel, maybe all lies, although I was no longer quite so adamant about stamping them out, maybe because I had to pretend to be older than I was. And because Melody had started taking the pill, although we still hadn't slept together.

"I'm doing it for us," she'd said.

I hadn't known how to respond. I didn't believe in premarital sex. I also didn't believe in condoms. I'd just said "thank you," the polite way out of any difficulty.

Except Caddie Anderson, who was still on a Housman mission:

> *Give pearls away and rubies*
> *But keep your fancy free.*
> *But I was one and twenty*
> *No use to talk to me.*

To pass the time, I decided to mentally rehearse organic chemistry. *Hydroxyl radicals are produced by a decomposition of hydroperoxides and. . . .*

The sciences were still an old-school, Puritan endeavor at Baylor. The quantum mess hadn't made it to the hinterlands. Everything ended in decay, usually by heat, rarely by ice.

Anderson passed by me. Her skirt ruffled against my shoulder. Had she no dignity?

> *When I was one-and-twenty*
> *I heard him say again,*
> *"The heart out of the bosom*
> *Was never given in vain;*

She made her way to the dais that held her desk.

> *'Tis paid with sighs aplenty*
> *And sold for endless rue."*
> *And now I'm two-and-twenty,*
> *And oh, 'tis true, 'tis true.*

Rue? Who was Housman kidding?

"Are y'all listening?" Anderson asked, sighing out her Texas despair. "Did y'all feel that?"

Who was *she* kidding?

Not herself. "Can nothing reach you people?" she muttered, fluttering her hand at us, a fuck-off common among Southern women of a certain age.

She leafed through her book, accidentally tearing out a page and jamming it in somewhere else. Careless, profligate, she was fashioning an Eden no one wanted. And I was Adam on a sunny day.

She landed on another poem. "Ah, William Blake," she said. "Crazy bast. . . . Genius, really. A prophet."

Pfft, I thought, I know prophets. I stared into space, worrying about the valency of chemical radicals.

She started to recite:

> *Tyger, Tyger, burning bright*
> *In the forests of the night.*
> *What immortal hand or eye*
> *Could frame thy fearful symmetry?*

As she said the words, she patted the poem's rhythm on her desk. I'd sung enough hymns to know the pulse. I looked up. Anderson was staring at me. Or in me. I'd never said a word in class. I was certain she didn't know my name. But for the first time in years, I felt that drop in my stomach, that buzz between my ribs.

I was horrified. And strangely comforted, as if I'd been waiting for this moment, as if I could finally loosen my grip and relax my fingers.

> *In what distant deeps or skies*

> *Burnt the fire of thine eyes?*
> *On what wings dare he aspire?*
> *What the hand, dare seize the fire?*

Anderson balled her fist to beat her desk to the rhythm of the poem, giving the words the resonance of her rage. I felt it because, like Jared's, it matched mine. But there was something else in it: deeper, closer to the truth, closer to me than anger. The word that leapt to mind was *loneliness*. How could that be?

> *And what shoulder and what art*
> *Could twist the sinews of thy heart?*
> *And when thy heart began to beat*
> *What dread hand? And what dread feet?*

As it had so many years before, time shattered into vectors, heading toward sense in all directions. I saw words materialize along those filaments. The whole kit and caboodle started to revolve, a universe in script. I also saw a fine film of moisture on Caddie Anderson's face and felt a stir in my dick. Was this what set the heavens in motion?

> *What the hammer? What the chain?*
> *In what furnace was thy brain?*
> *What the anvil? What dread grasp*
> *Dare its deadly terrors clasp?*

Through some exquisite connection, some human contact beyond my chemistry brain and my fundamentalist self, words slipped into me. Not just under my skin, but into the hollow, hidden place in me. They made love to me.

Were they Anderson's words? Or Blake's? Did it matter? They were a terrible intimacy, emptiness made flesh, that blasphemous perversion of the incarnation of Christ and the promise of cumming. They filled what I'd glibly feared was a small chink between God and science, between the me who thought sex with Melody was wrong and the me who ached for it every night, between the self I was performing and some lost self, farther in, crying to get out.

I'd always been taught there was a God-shaped hole in me. I'd pictured it spleen-level and filled it with Bible verses. But it was a receptacle for words: the Old Testament prophets', Christ's, Dickens', the words in those condensed novels, and Blake's, too.

> *When the stars threw down their spears*
> *And water'd heaven with their tears,*
> *Did he smile his work to see?*
> *Did he who made the Lamb make thee?*

Words were what I'd been missing when I went silent in a folding chair at the back of the tent at Canton. When Mother kissed the top of my head and said I wasn't an orphan. When Melody jerked me off and I muttered yet another "thank you." Words, piling on top of each other, competing with each other, overshadowing each other. Words, cantilevered into their own heaven and mortared into their own hell. If I read enough, I'd always have the answer to *You don't even got the words for whut the hell you are.* Not because I had the right ones. Because I had all of them.

Caddie Anderson hit her desk louder and louder, a bodily pulse, the stuff of life.

> *Tyger, Tyger, burning bright,*
> *In the forests of the night:*
> *What immortal hand or eye*
> *Dare frame thy fearful symmetry?*

And then it was over. Blake's poetry didn't boil over the surface of my life. It stayed inside me. Later, it would freeze, expand, and shatter everything.

Anderson stood there, her hair plastered with sweat. She unlatched her eyes from mine and peered around the room. We were twenty minutes into the hour. I held my breath, as if for a revelation.

"Class dismissed," she said. She sat down, folded her arms on her desk, and rested her forehead on them. "Go and do what comes naturally."

No one moved.

She fluttered her hand at us again. "Get out."

I gathered my books and walked across the quad in silence, afraid if I said one word, they'd all spill out. The sun shone among the leaves, each one distinct in the carbonation of a spring day. Unexpectedly, almost as if I were being pulled by invisible strings, I veered to the administration building and changed my major to English.

Some people grow organically, slowly. I only knew how to do it by leaps and bounds, the old revivalist rhetoric made flesh.

"From chemistry?" my advisor asked. Her beehive was particularly alert. "You're not thinking this through."

She went at me for a long time, all about "the better investment of science" and "youthful indiscretions that lead to a life of misery."

"I did the same thing," she said. "I became an English major. And now I'm stuck here where I. . . ." She fanned herself with a file folder. "Do you know where you're headed, young man?"

I stood up, shook my head, and tried to say "yes." But I could barely hear her. I wasn't in Waco. I was standing on the slopes of Mount Nebo, looking across the Jordan River at the Promised Land. I could see an open prairie fit for homesteading. Blake offered me a deed and I walked into the emptiness to breathe the bracing air. And to start a new life. What could go wrong?

Years later, I wrote this story in the online memorial for Caddie Anderson's funeral. I said it was why I became a writer. But I'd abbreviated the plot, condensed it, sanitized it. That morning in her class, she made me a true reader, the sort who tries to connect heart and mind over words. She also led me into a tumultuous relationship with literature that would eventually become the most confusing union possible: a brazen fuck and tender lovemaking all at once, the sort of bond you can find in marriages that last long beyond any hope of success.

My Songs of Innocence

I'd changed course on a Wednesday morning. What about the next day? Or the following Tuesday? And all the months ahead? Secular conversions were hard. No sour-faced men in folding chairs waited to tell me what to do. And I didn't want anything else from Caddie Anderson. She seemed too self-assured. Or too nuts. I never took another course from her.

That fall, I signed up for eighteen credit hours of lit. I soon discovered that Baylor's English department was a fussy hothouse, *Brideshead Revisited* set in a terrarium. Spongy profs had grown their personalities to monstrous proportions. Their soil was the poet Robert Browning.

I heard his name so much, I thought he might have been buried nearby. But no, the professors hadn't stormed Westminster Abbey and pilfered the bones. They went for easier booty, scooping up the poet's paraphernalia at auction houses and cataloguing his literary remains in a cold, marble building: the Armstrong-Browning Library. A long-standing department chairman had funded the project through glad-handing, then put his own name before the poet's.

The library was more tribute band than arena concert. Upstairs were creaky floors, glossy reading tables, and monumental windows, touted as the "world's largest collection of secular stained glass." It was a strange boast for a Baptist university, but there were others, too. When I asked to see a curio cabinet laden with the poet's effects, the docent seemed on the verge of hyperventilating. "This cream pitcher! These stuffing spoons!"

Downstairs, things were more to my liking: linoleum floors, fluorescent lights, and workaday offices for the old dons who'd hightailed it to grad school on the G.I. bill after blitzing through Nazis' chests. They arranged themselves around the only good

German left, a hefty Frau who flashed a signet ring and spoke in a Wagnerian belt.

Actually, she was a central Texas native who'd gotten herself hitched to a title that went back to the Holy Roman Empire. Insisting on demitasse in the age of Mr. Coffee, she hunkered behind her desk, sipping Dixie cups of black sludge. Occasionally, she looped numbers around a rotary phone and bellowed into the handset, "This is the Countess in Waco. Does that mean anything to you?"

The rest of the faculty guarded the altar of literature by blowing out the candles. The Shakespearean was bent on knocking anything on his own syllabus. "*Twelfth Night?* We should have read *As You Like It*." The Enlightenment scholar took ten minutes to call the roll every class, muttering our names as if they were a surprise. "Scarbrough? You don't say." And the scholar-in-residence, a Prussian with a different pair of glasses in every pocket, giggled whenever he pointed out phallic imagery in a modernist poem. Even at Baylor, it probably got old.

I didn't care. The profs' quirks confirmed their irrelevance. I'd been converted by a poet, not them. Steeling myself against the disappointment I'd felt whenever I'd tried to belong, I told myself I was only here for the books.

Then I fell for Dr. Lewis Franklin, a true-blue, white-haired, Southern gentleman who'd gotten his degrees from Vanderbilt University back when it was the vanguard of literary studies. He started us out on William Faulkner's *Absalom, Absalom!*

"Read it slowly, consciously, self-consciously," he counseled, before tugging his tweed jacket into place and reciting the first, almost unendurable sentence by heart.

The words again moved around me: that long silence in the afternoon when Quentin Compson sits with Rosa Coldfield in her airless room, the blinds drawn for almost half a century. The dust floats in the hot, stale air; the wisteria outside offers a sickly perfume; her legs dangle off her chair with iron outrage. Then she slowly starts to tell him her story: jilted by her sister's husband, dishonored by a man too low for even her moral outrage, all of which is also the story of the South, its rage and defeat, its sin and damnation.

And I felt my innards again: less of a buzz this time, more of a drop in my stomach, like the passing glimpse of the emptiness from the top of the hill, the sheer thrill of a novel's opening.

I saved the book for the next day, an open Tuesday. I thought I'd follow Dr. Franklin's advice, take my time, and savor the prose. Instead, I gulped it down, first in an empty classroom, then upstairs among the Browning relics as the evening wore on, and finally in my VW under the wan interior light. I kept the windows open to the warm air and the sounds of the tree frogs.

My glove compartment was stocked with maps of exotic places I planned to visit: New York City, Toronto, Italy. But I was rooted in place. Rooted in time, too, with Faulkner's novel in hand. I plunged into . . . no, *through* the story of the plantation at Sutpen's Hundred and its tragic family. Unlike that morning with *Great Expectations* in Mrs. Marsh's class, I wasn't Icarus in free fall. I had no fear, no regret. Faulkner seemed to defy the rules, contradict all notions of grammar, and annihilate the sophomoric ways I'd read. I finished the book sometime in the dim reaches of the night, shut off the car's interior light, and let the darkness from the prim campus settle around me.

To my surprise, I didn't want to be alone with that miasma in my head. I needed human contact, craved it, as if the act of reading had pulled me so far out of my own body that I needed help getting back in my skin. Over those long hours, I'd separated from me: me reading me in Faulkner's words. Not an alternate me. Not a might-have-been, like with condensed novels. The real me, the same way I'd once found myself in the Bible. A solid *was*. Maybe even an *am*.

I walked to Melody's apartment. Her lights were off, but I was too impatient to head for a pay phone. I pinged her window with gravel until she peeped around the curtains.

She let me in and we crept to her bedroom. Having read a modernist novel in a single day, I felt strangely older, as if I'd lost my late-teenage bravado. But I felt shivery, too, like a pensioner in need of a shawl.

Melody's breath was stale. It matched mine. She undid my shirt, then started kissing my neck. We'd eased into making love, a step at a time. A refugee from the sexual revolution, having grown up in the '60s and '70s without actually having been in those decades, I had to get over a speed bump every time we fooled around. Should her breasts rub against my hairy chest?

There was a more palpable concern, too. We were careful not to call out or even jostle the mattress springs lest we get caught by her roommate, a Baptist Brunhild with a blonde ponytail. Students could get suspended for hanky-panky, even in their own rooms.

Melody flipped me over and straddled me. "Enough with the guy on top," she said.

I didn't care what position I was in. I wanted to be in my body but was still too far up in my head. My soul or my vision or some wordless part of me that I'd seen through Faulkner's novel came undone and settled above us, floating in the empty space that had once been filled with the orbital patterns of Blake's words. Aloft, I stared at Melody's smooth, pale back.

When I got inside her, I saw her shoulders and spine papered with the pages of Faulkner's novel: ragged, damp, and overlaid, like those glued-together pages of *Great Expectations*. I clawed at them.

"Take it easy," she said.

As we made love, the pages came unstuck, drifted up, and settled on my face. Not on the me under her, but on the me somehow above her. I could smell the mustiness, not of us, but of cheap, mass-market ink and glue. I came suffocating.

Afterwards, Melody fell asleep crosswise on the bed. I slipped out as dawn painted the room a warm pink. Looking for coffee, I meandered over to an IHOP on the edge of campus.

"Do you have espresso?" I asked the waitress.

She glared at me as if I were a Communist.

I chose a booth and looked out at Interstate 35, a concrete thread heading to Dallas and all I knew, all I wanted to forget. I'd heard the voice of the South in Faulkner's novel—and in Melody's and my lovemaking, too: mannerly yet satisfying, stagy yet true, Gothic yet honest. Without having to record the chapters on a clunky machine, I'd also heard my own voice in both: huskier now, throaty gasps, a tenor without a steady tone, hovering in the empty spaces between *Absalom, Absalom*'s sentences, between the me aloft and the me under Melody, in the airy gaps between my own ribs.

As I sipped IHOP's oily brew, I fused the experience of reading and making love into something all-encompassing about the South, my home. I'd been taught that Dallas was the westernmost outpost of Dixie. Dallas was cotton; Fort Worth, oil. Dallas had debutantes; Fort Worth, cattle. I'd been taken on pilgrimages to the Civil War battlefields where my great-greats had fallen in what Mother called "the unpleasantness." All this had been parked along my timeline before I came into it, so I knew Quentin's plea at the end of *Absalom, Absalom!* before I read it: I, too, didn't hate the South. Didn't. Didn't. If I said it enough, maybe I wouldn't.

Reading a great work of Western literature was about far more than just zipping down a timeline. It was about creating my consciousness. Or it was like a better version of the changing room mirrors at J. C. Penney. Rather than just letting me see the parts of me that didn't fit, the great books let me see the parts of me I couldn't see, that I didn't even know were there: the me who somehow spoke without the slightest trace of a Southern accent, the me who loved sex even though I wasn't supposed to, the me who found himself feeling more lonely after sex than before, the me who was still afraid of getting caught by the powers-that-be. I saw myself reflected in both the pages of the book and the events of my life—reading one, reading the other, of a double mind and a unified whole, the pages in the novel and on Melody's back forming some strange, redemptive overlay. Or maybe a chemical synthesis, a release of sexual and psychic energy that branded the marks of my split personality into a story I could call my own.

Scruffy, unwashed, stinking of sex and bad coffee, and so more like an English major than I'd ever been, I headed off to class. Before Dr. Franklin began, a frat boy in a faded sweatshirt asked him why Faulkner wrote the way he did.

"Like, I don't know what's going on," the guy said.

I wish he'd been wearing headgear. I'd have lunged for it.

Dr. Franklin was more patient. He looked out of the window at the live oaks, their limbs tinseled with leaves.

"You see those trees?" He spoke in a polished drawl. "I don't know how they got there but they sure are pretty."

Everybody laughed except me. I got it. Reading wasn't about what it meant, at least not at first. It was about what it felt like.

I waited for Dr. Franklin after class. "I need to talk to you," I said.

"They always do."

He glanced at my copy of *Absalom, Absalom!* I'd crimped so many pages that it looked as if the paperback had gotten wet and puffed up to twice its size.

"About the mess you made out of a great book?" he asked.

"Yes, no, all of them, the *books*," I said.

He nodded as if I'd made sense and led me down the hall past the Countess' open door.

"Heil, Hitler," he smirked.

His office was a shambles of loose paper: student assignments, drafts of his own writing, bills, bank checks, grocery lists. He cleared a space for me by knocking a pile out of a chair.

"You're the first," he said. "This semester."

I didn't know how to talk to an English professor. With the science geeks, you blurted out whatever was on your mind. I was titrating something in a sophomore lab once when an upperclassman stormed in and said, "All the sections of P Chem are closed and I've got herpes."

With these guys in the Browning cenotaph, I figured I should treat our time together about the same way I did when Mrs. Marsh invited some of us junior-highers for tea during study hall: smile a lot and breathe slowly.

"I'm asking for help," I said as a start.

Dr. Franklin fingered a chipped mug. "They always are."

I wanted to tell him about Caddie Anderson and William Blake, about my instant conversion to literature, about sex and reading on a Baptist campus. I wanted a father confessor—or a father of some kind. I hadn't spoken to mine much, mostly because he hadn't been outraged when I'd changed my major. He'd told me I was going to have to start living my own life. Frankly, I needed his outrage to make sure I was doing an outrageous thing. But Dad seemed to have mellowed. Which confused me. No, irritated me. No, maddened me. Maybe we were both changing in fundamental ways. Maybe it was better if the wedge of the great books came between us.

But not between me and Dr. Franklin. "I'm new to this literature thing," I said.

He smiled. "Thing. Yes." He paired his vowels into syllables. *Thay-ing. Yeh-us.* "You want my suggestions on what to read next?" He scrunched his lips to a wry oval.

I knew he was making fun of me, but I took him up on the offer. "Yes, sir. I want to read everything."

He blinked a couple times, then pulled out a legal pad. We set about making a hand-written list of British and American titles, mostly novels, short stories, and plays, along with a few long poems and a solid collection of small ones.

Dr. Franklin emptied the department's drip pot into his chipped mug and a second mug for me. We worked into the late afternoon. This was my first introduction to the Western canon: an old man in a dusty office on a warm afternoon, the day after Faulkner and sex, both of which might have been great fun yet were starkly ungodly, both of which contradicted the person I was while pointing the way to the person I could be. Maybe wanted to be. Certainly shouldn't be.

Dr. Franklin and I made a plan to meet once a week—not as an independent study, just on the sly, the way I liked it. For the rest of the fall and all through the spring, I completed my other assignments, then ran for our list like a goose to grain.

Dr. Franklin even called it my gavage. "How's the throat?" he asked. "Ready for more?"

I checked off three and four titles at a clip. I didn't go to department functions. I didn't schmooze with my new peers. I read Jane Austen's six novels on the side in two weeks. Practicing my skills from Sunday School, I memorized Shakespeare's sonnets in ten-poem chunks.

Dr. Franklin always asked cursory questions. "What was the best part?" "Why does that text matter?" "What's next?"

"Aren't we going to discuss it?" I once asked.

"My boy, the thing's the thing, to use your preferred diction."

Maybe this glide across literature, ice-skating over the canon, drew my obsession into a tighter spiral. Maybe my fundamentalist self craved some inerrant clarity in all those words. Mostly, I heard the siren call of the great books, their smiling, false hope. Reading is a safe thing to do on a dark evening. Skirt the snags and head for deep water. We promise you can always get back home.

The more I read, the more I yearned for William Blake. I took to reading his poetry in the ten minutes before class started, the fifteen minutes before I met Melody, the five minutes after we had sex and before I needed to take a quick shower to get out of her apartment before her roommate returned. Each time, Blake picked up where he'd left off, fashioning what I thought was a new way of seeing the world but which was really a more cocksure version of my old one. Blake was my kind of guy, a God-botherer who wanted out without actually getting out, who crafted an exit without taking it. He hooked me with my own hooks: tigers and lambs, innocence and experience.

I loved his words because of their dualism, or maybe their double talk, so easy for me to parrot. His poems spoke of this life and a better one, farther away, a place I could have been—which seemed to fit perfectly with my dreams. So much so that I didn't even notice when my brain started to crack.

One night, I sat in my car and recited Blake's poems as a benediction before driving to a dive bar to meet my buddies. We pulled chairs around a small table on a sticky floor and threw quarters in the jukebox to cue up Earth, Wind, and Fire.

The guys were wrapped up in where they were headed. Grad school. Law school. Some bank. But I'd gotten out of sync. I was a newly minted humanities major, just nineteen, already a senior by credit hours and nearing graduation with nowhere to go. That night, I was also headachy hollow, the way I got whenever I read too much.

"You gonna nurse one beer all night?" Clay asked.

He was a C-minus marketing major who sang bass in a church choir and screwed the minister's secretary on Sunday afternoons. None of us saw the contradictions. We were horny Christians, mouthing the pieties before hightailing to our girlfriends' beds.

When I didn't answer, Clay pushed it. "You still gettin' up Melody's skirt?"

Even with more books read, more words in the air around me, and more pieces of me inside the great works, I couldn't talk about what was happening in bed. I was both happy and unhappy when Melody and I made love, mostly because I couldn't get out of the airy space above us. Sex was more of a relief than a passion, as if her bed were a rest stop on the interstate, a place to dump my body, my trash, before my imagination carried on.

Which meant I was a terrible lover. "Done?" she'd asked the night before.

I looked around at the guys. "You're wasting your time majoring in business," I said. "Or math. Or chemistry."

I'd tried to lure them into my obsessions. I'd tried to recite Blake's poetry to five, four, then two of them.

This time, I broke into a sweat. "I will not cease from mental flight," I said, mouthing Blake like a Bible verse, "nor shall my sword sleep in my hand till we have built Jerusalem in England's green and pleasant land."

The guys shot each other glances. We used to be a great group, all josh and spin.

"The fuck?" someone asked. "What gives?"

This, I wanted to scream. I was hanging out with proto-corporate types, bullish on their careers, who also had no idea who I was. I'd followed my advisor's advice. I'd never told anyone my age. I never got carded. Bars were only too happy to take my money. But I felt young and old, as if I still couldn't make sense of my place in time. I was lost in every plot, situated on every timeline I read.

Without any way to explain all of that, I ordered the guys a round, paid, and walked out. I got in my car and drove out of town. I pulled onto the gravel shoulder of a long, two-lane road, no more than a gray ribbon across the moon-blue land. The sky was a star-studded bowl turned upside-down over the fields. These were the remains of the world after its end. The only words left were the ones in my head.

I got out and leaned against the hood. The metal was warm through my jeans. I breathed in the night and slowed my thoughts to a crawl so I could recite Blake's poems, so I could hear that voice that didn't change over time. I loved its pulse, the one Caddie Anderson had hammered into the dais. I could feel the friction. When I got to "The Tyger," I had a hard-on. That's when Blake came walking out of the dark toward me. He had curly, yellow-gray hair and a sallow face. He seemed hollow at the temples.

"I don't know why you called me," he said. "You're drunk."

I wasn't. And I wasn't afraid, just as I hadn't been when I saw myself hole-punched by plots or when I saw Melody wallpapered with a novel. I might have been creeping up to the edge of madness, but I'd been primed for this moment with New Testament verses. *Some have entertained angels unawares.* And if angels, why not a canonical poet?

"I'm buzzy with books," I confessed. "I read too much."

Blake furrowed his brows, then put his arm around my shoulder, as if he wanted to feel the warmth of my body.

"My son," he said, "if a thing loves, it is not necessarily infinite."

"Who said it was?"

He seemed to speak without moving his mouth. "I did. Remember?"

I wanted to tell him that I was still too innocent. That I hadn't slipped into his vaunted world of experience, the other half of his most well-known poems. That I was going to propose to Melody.

Without words, he insisted that ignorance wasn't the same thing as innocence.

I wanted to nestle against him, but his breath smelled cold and chemical, like the bags of ice in a 7-11 freezer.

"Once you get it all down," he promised, "*Beowulf* to now, you'll make sense of it."

"A Bible map of books?"

He laughed. "I couldn't have imagined you."

My only hope was that he had.

I woke up later, stretched across the car's hood. Had I had a dream? A vision? A prophecy?

I drove back to campus, the sky an untrustworthy pink. I went straight to Melody's apartment and woke up her roommate, who stared at me with blue, righteous eyes. I pushed past her to find Melody in the hallway between the bedrooms.

She was clearly concerned. "Your roommates said you haven't been home all night."

I wanted to tell her about Blake, about poetry, about his icy breath and warm embrace. But her face was too blank, too sweet. As I now saw it, too innocent.

Despite the outrage of Miss Baptist Scourge, I took a shower in their bathroom, then sipped coffee on Melody's bed while she got ready for class.

"You sure you're okay?" she asked as she brushed out her spiky hair.

I nodded. Maybe I should call my parents. And say what? I'm going nuts?

"Just a little hyper," I said.

"I can work with that." She nibbled my ear but told me I couldn't stay in her apartment. "You'll be under friendly fire."

As I walked back to my place, I tried to explain away the image of an old poet on a lonely road. Just beer, I told myself. And sex outside of marriage. Plus, not going to church enough.

But I knew I'd treasured my time with the poet. I felt like I'd finally settled among the great books. I delayed graduation until August.

"I have to keep reading," I told Dr. Franklin when I saw him the next week. His office looked the worse for wear, papers everywhere.

He narrowed his eyes and betrayed me. "Reading isn't a career," he said. "Maybe I was wrong about how you should do this."

No, I thought, still my favorite word as I got up to leave. I was wrong about you.

In what was already a pattern in my life, I treated him like a minor character and never darkened his door again. I avoided him in the hallways, never even went to my induction into an honor society because I knew he'd be there. But I kept at his list, reading indiscriminately, furiously. Willa Cather's prairie trilogy and all six of Christopher Marlowe's plays in one week. I couldn't get enough. To riff off Emily Dickinson—now I could!—my splendors were menagerie.

I saved the seminar on the early Romantic poets for my last course before graduation in August. I was all in for Wordsworth, Coleridge, and my precious Blake.

One June evening, in the hushed Armstrong-Browning library, I sat at a glossy reading table, poring over Blake's poem "The Divine Image," a meditation on how the mystic virtues operate in a world without the physical presence of God. I'd read it so many times, it had built a shrine in my flesh. I was a creaky docent, honoring my own relics.

> *For Mercy has a human heart*
> *Pity, a human face:*
> *And love, the human form divine,*
> *And peace, the human dress.*

I let my eyes come unfocused from the page and felt a chill in the cracks of my brain. A human form? My life had been about being something other than myself. About floating above my body. About fitting in, not getting caught, and not messing up—which all felt less human and more like what I called "holy."

Even so, I felt heavier, not lighter, more like a body, less like a soul. That night, there was no chatter in my ribs, no drop in my stomach. Instead, I felt the slight pain in the back of my right thigh, an old tennis pull. I sensed the crook of my elbow, the bend of my neck.

I could float above the words as long as I stayed a soul. A body needed a definite *where* and a *when*. But I'd lost track of time and space, mostly because I'd fed myself lines of poetry and performed my life among all that was still to be read—except for a few minutes in the arms of a dead poet. Even though Melody and I were now serious enough to string time in front of us and talk about marriage, I'd never woken up on a dark night and felt a human heart beating next to mine. We had sex and I went home. In fact, I was due at her place in half an hour. "I'll leave the door unlocked," she'd said.

Mercy has a human heart. I didn't know what mercy was, the sort that happens in love, where you give and take, forgive and forget, where someone holds your gaze before you wander off into bliss because you need it, deserve it. And because you'll come back.

> *Then every man, of every clime,*
> *That prays in his distress,*
> *Prays to the human form divine,*
> *Love, Mercy, Pity, Peace.*

Right then, I could have been anywhere else, preferably with Melody—and if not her (a terrible thought), with someone else. Anyone else. After everything, I was still interchangeable. There was a me suitable for every story: the guys at the bar, Dr. Franklin in his office, Melody in bed. I wanted to be none of them. I wanted to be holding someone, slipping into the deep stuff of life, reaching together for that elusive place called home.

It was hard to comfort myself with emptiness. But I could try.

> *And all must love the human form,*
> *In heathen, Turk, or Jew;*
> *Where Mercy, Love, and Pity dwell*
> *There God is dwelling, too.*

I looked up. Across the table at the opposite corner sat . . . Blake? I broke into a sweat. I thought for the first time, Books can turn the world into a lie.

But he was just an undergrad in a ratty Colorado T-shirt, reading a genetics textbook with his eyes at half-mast. I'd seen him around, mostly on the tennis courts.

"Hey," he said. "What are guys like us doing in the library on a summer night?"

I thought, *All must love the human form.*

Then: *What the fuck?*

Something happened, some combination of Blake's poetry and this guy, a mystical conflagration ignited beyond cause and effect, a link between an old poem and my heart. I felt I was finally reading literature and my life at the same time. The poem voiced him. And he, a guy I didn't know, embodied it.

The moment was not *real* in any sense of the word as I understood it. But it was literary in all the ways I'd come to love: symbolic, metaphoric, allegorical, changed with too much meaning for such a small spot of time. I wanted to take my clothes off and show this guy the bones of my body. Here, I wanted to say, pointing to them one by one. Here is where my story needs to live.

A tear slid down my cheek. Apparently, he didn't notice. "I don't think I've ever seen someone stare at a page for so long," he said. "I kept looking to see if you'd nodded off. Nope. Eyes wide open."

I could have swerved and saved myself. Instead, I became Blake incarnate, talking out both sides of my mouth, straddling the divide between fight and flight.

"It's nothing," I said. Lied, really. "And *nothing* is the direct object of the verb *to make*."

He cocked his head and laughed.

Stop, half of me thought, the rational half, the fundamentalist half. I loved Melody. I'd never once thought about a guy like this, never once imagined nattering on about a Blake poem while I got naked in front of him.

Wait, the English major half of me thought. Why don't you make a proper introduction to the guy you suddenly want in ways you think only an eighteenth-century poet can imagine?

"Mark," I said, extending my hand.

He smiled, tight lips over slightly crooked teeth. "Alex," he said, returning the shake. He held my hand a beat longer than any Texas boy should. "That must be some book," he said.

I felt that familiar drop, the top of the parabola, the zero-gravity float. I said the only thing I could. "It's poetry."

"You serious?"

"Romantic," I added.

"No shit? Like my mom reads?"

"I doubt it."

But I was wrong. Blake was whispering and wooing in my ear.

Alex and I played tennis the next morning. Melody and I met him for burgers a few days later. The two of them instantly hated each other. And I was flattered in ways I couldn't understand.

Then Alex and I moved in together for the rest of the summer term and the diverging plots of my life crossed and sparked like hot wires. In the ensuing apocalypse, books didn't catch fire. I did.

In the Resurrection, They Neither Marry nor are Given in Marriage

Late in that summer term, Melody called me over to help her write a class paper. "Otherwise, what's the point of sleeping with an English major?"

I walked in to find blank sheets of paper all over the dining room table.

"No draft?"

"No. Dinner."

She'd dropped the thermostat to meat locker and made a sticky, wintry casserole: pasta and ground pork with peanut butter, cream of mushroom soup, and jarred salsa, bubbling in a baking dish under Fritos and yellow cheese.

"How's Alex?" she asked, a sneer in her voice.

Anytime I wasn't with her, I was with him. I seemed to balance on a pin.

"Great!" I said. "Probably on the tennis court!"

She clearly didn't like my tone. "Let's eat," she said.

Well into a six-pack of beer, with a sweet smack on our lips, I started fiddling with the buttons of her sundress. She never wore a bra. Thank God for Methodists!

She grabbed my hand at the third button, the middle one, the key to all mythologies. "Not now," she said, nodding toward the front door. Any minute, her roommate might walk in.

I made for the button again. Heaven and hell, innocence and experience, Melody and Alex—I could make sense of it all.

Melody had another idea. "You need a walk."

"In this heat?"

She got her keys. I followed her out onto the deserted campus. Cicadas rattled in the trees. I may have yearned for the open road, but unpeopled scenes still freaked me out. The Rapture lurked in my soul.

We strolled the clean sidewalks. "How come we couldn't stay indoors?" I said, the sweat beading my forehead. "Air conditioning made God's country fit for fornication."

Melody sighed. "Speaking of other obvious things, haven't you always dreamed of a spring wedding? February, when the tulips bloom. We could...."

She knew I wasn't paying attention. I also hadn't formally proposed. "You don't seem very enthused," she said.

"You mean 'excited.'"

"God, English. Don't pick a fight. I'm just talking. I trust you know what to do. Besides, if we get married, we'll...."

I pulled my hand out of hers. I thought of Alex. I thought of Blake. I was doped with a gloppy amalgam of words and desires, the physical world and the imagined one.

Maybe she knew I was slipping away. She pulled me toward the edge of campus, toward a church just beyond Seventh Street, toward a scraggly oak at the back of the sanctuary. She squared her shoulders against the bark, pulled me close, and nibbled my ear.

"Say that Blake bit," she mumbled.

Although we read his poetry in bed, I'd never told her about seeing him on a country road. I knew his appearance marked something horrifying about my relationship with his poems, with all books—and maybe with Alex, too, although that made no sense. Despite having shoved so many words inside my head, I had none for what was happening to me. I was sliding beyond madness but telling myself I was the only serious reader I knew.

I couldn't stay in my head for long. My hipbones touched Melody's.

"Those who restrain desire," I said, "do so because theirs is weak enough to be restrained."

"This is why guys should learn literature," she moaned, unzipping my fly.

"Someone could see us," I whispered, as if anyone was listening.

She hiked up her sundress. "Don't talk so much."

I'd gotten so split between the me in the story and the me in my life that I only came when I was above us and under her at the same time. I glanced over her shoulder, hoping to see me in the air. Instead, there was Blake, peeping out from behind the sanctuary.

My knees buckled, but Melody held me up. I'd lost a lot of weight. Sex, a poet, a girl, a guy. None of this was supposed to happen. I did the only thing I could. I took my vision of the poet as a sign. While having open-air sex on a Baptist campus in the middle of a heat wave, the three of us mouthed lines from Blake's *Songs of Innocence* and *Songs of Experience* to each other. No, the four of us. Alex was in there, too. He was somehow beside me. Maybe inside me as I said, "My heart is at rest within my breast and everything else is still." As Melody said, "His dark secret love does thy life destroy." As Blake said, "You never know what is enough until you know what is more than enough."

When we were done, the poet rolled his eyes and stuck out his tongue.

Melody kissed me as I zipped up. "Did he who made the lamb make thee?" she asked.

I looked at the church, a brick monstrosity. Blake was gone, the light was long, and the guilt was staggering. "I'm not sure anymore," I said, trying to tell the truth.

"You okay?"

I nodded. Or lied. I was scared, but I told myself I was doing the right thing. I was making love to a girl, not a guy. Well, the wrong thing, really. Premarital whatever. But at least I was locked into this story. Everything else was just my overheated imagination, right?

"We're still going on that picnic next week?" she asked.

I nodded again.

She licked the inside of my lip. "Love that casserole. I'll see myself home. Call me. As if you won't."

Maybe not. The sex had left me more anxious than ever, even though warm tremors radiated across my back. *Shit, Blake,* I thought. Again. Twice now. And then Alex. Not once yet. Not ever. Maybe I should tell someone.

I couldn't. Not on a Baptist campus. And not with my understanding of how to handle this sort of thing. Resist the devil and he will flee from you, the Bible had taught me. Was Blake the devil? No, he was a kindly old man.

If I told my parents, they'd make me come home and feed me chicken rolls for the rest of my life. If I told someone professional, a minister or one of the campus counselors, they'd think *I* was the devil. Which couldn't be possible. I was still me: the affable, insecure, second fiddle. None of this could be happening. Or if it was, it shouldn't be. Like books. Like Alex: couldn't and shouldn't and wouldn't but was.

Maybe there are centered people who can handle the great works of literature off the bat. I wasn't one of them. I looked everywhere for messages, meanings, and signs. When I found them in print and hefted them onto the shelves in my brain, I collapsed under the weight. I'd been primed to live in a world of angels, antichrists, and demons. Then I learned something more terrifying still: the imagination is bigger than all the visions about it. There is no end to it.

I headed down Fifth Street through the heart of campus. I walked past Burleson Hall's pointy Victorian towers, which every brochure called "Greek Revival."

Alex and I had moved into the dorm. Our room was workaday, not fussed up, the sort of place I should have liked: twin beds nailed to cinder-block walls. I found it hellish. I'd thrown a square of red velvet over my desk lamp. Otherwise, our room was littered with my chapbooks and his jock straps, *A Room With a View* set in central Texas.

I stripped down and checked myself in the mirror. At five ten, I weighed less than 140 pounds, although I felt fatted and stuffed. The gavage had done its trick, even if I might be going crazy.

I grabbed a bottle of shampoo and headed for the showers, an open room with ten nozzles. I hung my towel on a peg and found Alex inside. Sudsy water ran down his chest.

He must have heard my footsteps. He stuck his face in the spray and shook himself clean. "Oh, hey," he said. "What's up?"

"Melody," I said, trying to tell the tale with one word.

"You get some?"

What was it with guys? Did they all need to make a story out of sex? Was I supposed to turn my life into an anecdote, rather than turning literary anecdotes into my life?

I stuck my head under the still icy water. It felt bracing. It felt like what I deserved. I lathered my hair, then started scrubbing my crotch.

Before I knew it, Alex was soaping my back. It was old hat. We took showers together all the time. After tennis, he'd throw me a towel and I'd follow him down the hall. We chose spots next to each other but stayed in our own streams. He washed my back but never my chest, my shoulders but never my face.

This time, I shrugged him off.

He went back to lathering his pits, humming a mindless tune.

I cupped my dick. The disconnect was too great. I liked Melody and we had sex; I loved Alex and we didn't. I'd read too much, probably the linchpin in this whole affair, an imaginative landscape that allowed for more possibilities than I could handle.

Alex shut off his shower. I heard him walk out. He never dried off. He dragged his towel behind him, leaving a wet trail.

I stayed behind, nudging the water hotter to see how far I could stand it.

By the time I got back to our room, Alex was blasting Bach's *Christmas Oratorio*. Butt-naked, with a Bic pen in hand, he pretended to conduct, bringing up the winds, shushing the horns. He didn't play an instrument, didn't know a quarter note from a quarter tone, but he loved baroque busyness.

I slipped on a pair of cut-offs. My pale skin was blotched red from the shower.

I watched Alex's every move. He'd been a quarterback in high school. Second string, but it counted. His shoulders were wide and supple. I hated him.

In the middle of one chorus, he gave his performance a satisfied nod and flung himself onto his bed to start his homework. He held a bio-chem book in front of his face.

I stopped his record, purposely dragging the needle in the vinyl.

"Watch it!" Alex said. Smiled, really. He never cared about anything.

I put on one of my albums: Christopher Cross. I stretched out on my bed, one ankle over the other. My ribs arched from the cave of my stomach. I rehearsed the lyrics to "Sailing" until I could say something that made sense.

"You ever want the world to end?"

He didn't look over the book. His hairless legs were long and sculpted. "Can't see a thing with that red shit over the lamp."

"No, seriously."

"Okay, sure."

I thought I could risk the truth. "Just the two of us," I said. "Nothing outside."

He laughed into the binding. "Did I tell you I got a date with Jackie?"

Was he going to play it this way? I could, too. "I thought she hated you," I said.

"This?" He pointed to his chest. "I'll even put up with Melody. You want in? Dinner?"

She wouldn't want to double-date with him. "He'll never grow up," she'd told me. I hoped not, but he could be pretty obtuse.

So I said, "Man has no body apart from his soul."

Alex put his book down. "What?"

"*The Marriage of Heaven and Hell.*"

He rolled his eyes. "Here we go."

Melody was patient with my bookish obsessions. She listened to me read chapters aloud, even memorized some poetry with me. Alex was at best half-interested, mostly bemused, sometimes even irritated. Yet I felt an almost overwhelming need to parade my literary self in front of him. I was terrified I'd see Blake when I was with Alex, although I'd actually seen the poet when I'd made love to Melody. I couldn't explain any of that, but I could explain Blake's poetry.

"His great hope," I said, "is that everything'll end up where we're one thing, not divided anymore, our desires and actions in harmony. He thinks we'll even give up marriage. We'll just love anybody we want." I sat up and pushed my shoulder blades against the wall. "I want that."

Alex looked away. "Who doesn't want that?"

"No, I mean I want to see where life leads. To see how it ends."

I was so close to the truth I could almost smell it. But I'd fallen for the ploy of literature. I read the great books because they trafficked in the trappings of truth, in aphorisms and insights, wishes and their fulfillment. Then they pulled off a linguistic switcheroo. They made me think *Yes, that's it,* and robbed me of my voice—because to say what I meant, I had to ventriloquize them, just as they demanded.

Alex chunked his textbook onto his desk, scattering papers everywhere. "And how are you gonna make all that better-world shit happen?"

"I'll ask Blake."

He narrowed his eyes. "You'll do what?"

"He can tell me how he did it."

"Damn." Except he drawled it out: *Day-yum.* "You gotta cut this shit out."

"I know. But Blake can give me some advice."

Alex got up and walked to the mirror. His dick jostled against his pubes. "You know you're bizarro," he said. "But that's probably why I . . . why we live together. What do you really want to do?"

"I guess I'll read a little more, maybe go out for a beer."

"No, I mean always." He fronted me, his face a tragic mask. "You read all the time. It's crazy."

I didn't hear it as a betrayal, as I had from Dr. Franklin. I heard it as "Congratulations!"

"How much have you slept?" Alex continued. "Two hours a night?"

"I'm not reading now."

He picked up a pair of white briefs from a pile in the corner. "Yours?"

"I think so."

He put them on, as well as his own T-shirt. He started to leave but wasn't done. "I'm serious. What do you want to do after Baylor?"

"What you said. Read all the time."

"No, answer the question. What's your future?"

We'd been at this long enough that my record had stopped. The needle scratched in black nothingness. My voice turned small. "We'll go somewhere and get an apartment."

"We?"

I spoke the ultimate dualism. "You and me."

"No," he said, once my favorite word. "I'm going to grad school at Minnesota. What are you going to do?"

"I should. . . ." I looked up at him and grinned. "Minneapolis or St. Paul?"

He shook his head. "You've got two weeks until it's all over. First of August, we put on the mortarboards and say good-bye to everything we know." He walked to the door. "I'm going to the lounge to watch some TV. I'll save you a place on the couch."

Was he gay? I don't know. Waco had one gay bar downtown: an unmarked door under a single light. I'd gone several times with my drinking buddies, never Alex. We weren't grossed out or titillated. We were the new liberals, the coming globalists, like Victorian tourists in India, seeking the curiosities.

The floor wasn't sticky like our dive's. The air held the lemony tang of disinfectant. Most of the patrons were women who rode motorcycles. The few men wore the Baylor, Oxford cloth-and-khaki garb. They played darts in the back.

The bartender was a slow-spoken man with rounded eyes. Clay loved to shoot the breeze with him. They even bonded over ABBA. Once on our way back to campus, one of our bunch started to toss out some slur and Clay cut him off. "Shut up. The hell do you know about life?"

Fair enough, but the joint wasn't for me. The drinks were made in a blender. I preferred beer or bourbon. Sure, I loved Alex— probably like a found penny, a cheap lottery ticket, a cute quirk. I didn't feel anything for the guys playing darts.

Even now, I don't have the words to explain Alex. *Love* is how Blake would have put it. Jesus, too. But I'm ventriloquizing them. What I felt was beyond the marrow: cellular. By becoming a two-sided soul under the tutelage of a prophet-poet, I didn't *get in touch* with my homosexuality, as the '70s lingo would have put it. I got in touch with my loneliness. They weren't the same thing, despite what I'd been taught. Loneliness was farther in, the sticky creosote, not just from the fires of reading, but also from the dead embers of my adoption. I'd traveled through life without seeing my face reflected in anyone else's. No one looked like me. But Alex—obtuse, fucked-up Alex, a guy who didn't know what he wanted even when he wanted it—was the best mirror I'd ever had, better than any book.

And still it wasn't good enough. I was coming to the chilling understanding that I would always go through this world on my own.

In the end, I relied on Blake's poetry to give me the words to explain all this. Then this eighteenth-century poet failed me, not because he couldn't imagine a twentieth-century relationship between two guys, but because no poem, no novel, no piece of literature could sum up my experience, our experience, human experience. Problem was, every book tried to, offering a balled sphere of time, beautiful on the inside but really just the false hope that this piece of writing was enough. That it made sense of the world. And—here's the heart of the insanity—of me.

After Alex left, I pulled out my copy of Blake's poetry and played magic Bible with it. Back at Pastor Daniel's church, whenever someone had a problem, one of the sour-faced men would suggest opening Scriptures at random and reading whatever came to hand. We could always make it fit, the words a cosmic solution. Psalm 90:16—*Let your work be manifest to your servants and your glorious power to their children.* Which clearly means, "Don't take the night shift!"

But I couldn't make sense of *I asked a thief to steal me a peach* or *Does not the worm erect a pillar in the mouldering church yard?*

I gave up and sat on my bed, the wall now warm behind me. What's your future? As a fundamentalist, I'd counted the days, weeks, years until the end: maybe a decade, tops. Back in the days of the Canton flea market, there'd been only one possible string of events, shot out of a sunny eternity past, zipped across history through crucifixions and Christmas shopping, and bull's-eyed into another, sunny eternity. I'd wanted to hang the ornaments of my life off of it, a garland of everything I knew was right and everything I'd done wrong.

Now my problem wasn't the multiple timelines of many plots. It was what had happened to them all. The second bull's-eye, the future, had disappeared, so the lines had come unstuck. They dangled around me like torn wires, like a Texas street after a tornado. I'd also missed my seminar paper deadline.

I didn't blame Blake. Or books. Not yet. I blamed Caddie Anderson, Dr. Franklin, even the Countess. Worse than false prophets, they had tossed torches into a fathomless cavern and left me spelunking without any intact safety lines.

I was still stretched out on my bed but with the lights off when Alex got back. He stank of contraband booze. He slid into his bed without a word.

I didn't move, trying to be still enough to hold my bones in place.

Sometime in the small hours, he got up, crossed the gap between our beds, and took me in his arms. I felt the warmth of his skin. He rocked gently back and forth. I smelled the musk of his chest. I'd never felt safer. Not even with Blake. But this time, I felt something else, stranger yet. I'd never felt sadder.

Alex stroked my hair, looked out the window into the night, and simply said, "Mark." My name, the only one I had, conferred by court decree. Maybe not really me, yet me nonetheless.

I drifted to sleep against him and woke the next morning long after he'd nestled me into my pillow. There was nothing more. He'd left for class.

I skipped mine, bought a bottle of Jack Daniels, and drove out into the country, barely visible in the glare of the August sun. I drank half the booze, somehow made it back to campus, and went to Melody's apartment.

"What happened to you?" she asked. "You smell like my grandmother."

I muttered something about my term paper, then spent the afternoon passed out on her couch. Later, I called my prof to spit out some incoherent blather about "Tuesday, latest."

That evening, I staggered back to my room, hoping I'd missed Alex. He was headed home for the weekend, but I walked in just as he was throwing some of my underwear in his satchel.

I hadn't washed my hair since the day before. I looked fit for skid row.

"What happened to you?" he asked, a bad echo.

"Blake," I said this time, as if that name explained anything.

Although Alex seemed in no hurry to leave, I bum-rushed him out to the parking lot and pushed him into his Camaro. He chunked a cassette of the Brandenburgs into the player and started to conduct.

"Wanna watch?" he asked.

I smiled. "No, thanks."

"Your funeral."

Exactly, I thought.

He revved the motor and pulled away. "Do the things I wouldn't!" he yelled.

Count on it.

My timeline lacked a real beginning. I couldn't do anything about klieg-lit home movies. But I could give my story an ending. I could kill myself. I had Valium stashed in a bottle in the medicine cabinet. How many pills did I need? Waco was no Haight-Ashbury; Baylor, no valley of the dolls.

Still, getting the stuff had been easy enough. Back in the fall, I'd gone to the on-campus health clinic when I felt a deep ping in my leg after tennis. The thin white-coated man, all beak and blink, had nodded and said, "Take one a day." He gave me ten.

I tried them over a couple of weeks and liked the chill. In the spring, I went back and complained about my course load.

"English?" he said, staring at my chart, not me. "I see." He offered a full bottle with three renewals.

I should have told him that I'd read so much poetry that I'd fallen for a guy while seeing a dead poet and having sex with my girlfriend because I needed to split my soul in half to come. The doc would have let me mainline the stuff.

For now, I had six pills left. Were they enough?

I shaved, took a shower, and drove to a strip mall. Texas boys are supposed to be bulked up on beer and barbecue: barrel chests and flat butts. I looked like the love child of Freddie Mercury and Billy Graham. Nothing fit—until I tried on a pair of rusty hip huggers from the discount rack.

"Can I get away with these?" I asked the clerk. "They're really out of style."

She stepped close. She smelled of cigarettes and Aqua Net. "I had a nephew like you," she said. "He got over it and put on some weight." She grabbed the belt loops and yanked the pants into my crotch. "Army," she said. "Trust me. It'll help you."

"I'm buying clothes for a funeral," I said, pushing down the waist.

She nodded. She worked Friday nights at a Waco department store. She'd probably heard it all. "You'll need a suit."

I didn't buy one. I also didn't write a note. I was already gone, lost in plots I didn't make, didn't want, didn't know how to get out of. William Blake had cracked open my ribs and poured in words that gave shape to the loneliness of a cold bed, the loneliness of never seeing me in the world around me, the loneliness I believed was my lot in life.

Back at my dorm, dressed in my new duds, I cupped the pills in my palm. They should at least burn bright in the night. Shit, they were chalky blue, the color of my eyes.

I put on Dan Fogelberg's *Netherlands* and looked in the mirror. Whoever looked back at me toted around a startling chunk of fear. I could see the strain in his eyes. He seemed to be mouthing something. His lips were pale, gray.

Could I be friends with him? Could I make love to him? I did the only thing I knew. I whispered Blake's poetry.

> *And I made a rural pen,*
> *And I stain'd the water clear,*
> *And I wrote my happy songs*
> *Every child may joy to hear.*

Liar! No one wanted to hear what I had to say. I was about to be graduated with an English-degree-by-mistake. Baylor was a persnickety place. The old grammar rules held. I couldn't graduate myself. I could *be* graduated. But I could kill myself.

I looked again. Dammit, Blake was staring at me. I saw the white hair, the sad eyes, a prophet-poet anticipating death. He started to say something. I leaned closer.

Tyger, Tyger, burning bright.

I let out a yawp, that most unpoetic expression.

The guys next door were apparently having a late-night Bible study. I'd heard murmurs of "Jesus" and "sin." One of them banged on the cinder block. "Quiet down. We're praying."

When I looked in the mirror again, there I was, that fatted skeleton. I saw the waste of a life narrated with the wrong voice. I took one pill and felt it trip down my throat without a lick of water.

"I loved you," I said to myself, as if it mattered. I wasn't gay. I hadn't fallen for any of the guys in high school. Why had this happened? Was it the fault of literature? Or just my sinful nature?

I took a second pill.

"Did you love me?" I asked him, me, Blake, somebody, anybody.

I was screwing a girl and wanting to sleep with a guy, maybe not as a euphemism, maybe not even to have sex with him, just to fall asleep in his arms because something in him seemed like something in me, the same way something in books seemed like something in Melody, the woman I craved when I wasn't obsessing over Alex.

I took a third pill.

I'd stepped away from the words of the Bible and found nothing in all the others. Was that the whole . . ?

And then, yes, a swerve, a miracle, worthy of the best fundamentalist, based on that one word: *whole*. It was the shadow behind all those condensed novels, the promise of the missing pieces I'd been searching for. I didn't have to get trapped in this story. There were other timelines, right? Whole ones. If I wasn't at home on this one, find another.

I tossed the remaining pills down the drain and turned on the water in an epic thrash.

The Bible was the book I'd always known. Hadn't I already learned this lesson with *Great Expectations*? Who cares? I could act like a pulp plot, circling back to repeat a former scene. It didn't faze me. I could only make sense of my life by treating it like a book anyway.

I wrenched up my hip huggers and pulled *The Norton Anthology* off the shelf. I got more books, even my copy of Blake's poetry, thatched with my notes. I walked down the hall and tossed them in the bin near the showers. I congratulated myself on my resolve. Ages ago, I'd stacked those cassette tapes in my closet. This was a better purge. I carted away several more armloads.

I looked at my few remaining titles. Oddly, I felt a little sorry for them, tipped this way and that on the shelf. I could throw them out anytime. Later, I'd pack them up and take them home. I'd wait years to fulfill the courage of my convictions.

One thing was for certain: I didn't have to give up books. I could press the line of time back into its spot in the future by turning from the volumes that had given me a voice—but were killing me—to the Bible, the book that had done nothing worse than silence me.

With its words, I could figure out why I'd had some sort of break on that country road, why Blake had walked out of the night, why I'd used another guy as a mirror and wanted him in ways that made no sense. I could figure it all out by analyzing the only book that was singular and pure. Mine was indeed a literary quest. Now, the right kind.

On the spot, I decided to go to the same seminary that had stamped out Pastor Daniel and those sour-faced men, an inerrant-Word-Of-God, better-in-the-original-Hebrew-and-Greek-than-in-English school that just happened to be in Dallas, my hometown. Like most committed readers, I mistook narrative coincidence for fate. I told myself I was going home.

I knew the next few days would be rough. They'd take every lick of self-help advice I could tell myself. Then I'd have the rest of my life. All this traveling around, this questing, and home lay where I thought it had. I could arrive where I'd started and know the place for the first time. And be done with it.

What I didn't know was that William Blake would do me one last injustice. In his poems, he'd led me to believe that I could leap from innocence to experience with a running start. But I was a guy born at the tag end of the Baby Boomers. Like Bill Clinton, George Michael, and Rob Lowe, I was about to find out that I could slip back to innocence any time I wanted. I could fall again and again just to justify who I was.

How to Get into a Fundamentalist Seminary When You're not Sure What You Believe

Step 1: Break up with your boyfriend.

He'll be driving back on Sunday evening, so stay out late to miss his arrival. Put on Baylor Oxford cloth and your new hip huggers, then drive to your favorite dive bar. Sit alone. Nurse beer after beer. Mutter to yourself, even when your buddies come over to see if you're okay. Wave them off but buy them a round. Tell yourself you finally understand the meaning of an empty gesture, one without literary ballyhoo. Call this "clarity."

By the time you get back to your room, your boyfriend will be lying on his bed, wearing tennis shorts and that ratty Colorado T-shirt, the one he wore when you first met.

Lurch tipsy to your desk and fall into your chair. Unbutton your shirt to show him what he's missing, the hollow concave of your chest.

There'll be a little package waiting for you. It'll be from your girlfriend. "Found it in our mailbox," he'll say.

Rip it open. A 24K gold pen, engraved with your name. Not a line from a silly poem. Not a future wedding date. Just your name. Which feels more and more like who you are.

She'll include a couple of racy photos. Don't look at them. Shove them in one of your few remaining books, *The Complete Works of Samuel Taylor Coleridge*. There's no need to get sentimental.

Realize your boyfriend is staring at you. Say something about working on your seminar paper. Feel the cold, clean air on your skin, in your mouth, between your ribs. It'll toughen you up for this conversation.

"Hey, what's with the retro jeans?" he'll ask.

Say: "Not much."

"They look good on you."

Say: "Yes." Make it clipped.

"You okay?"

Say: "Never better."

He'll cross the room and touch your shoulder. "You want to go watch some. . . ."

Say: "I need to work."

He'll Steve Martin it—"Well, excuuuuuuse me"—then flop back on his bed.

Nod but don't look up. You did it. You ended the relationship. He's so stupid, he didn't even notice.

Turn back to your term paper and rewrite something small, manageable, maybe the opening paragraph. The words are important. Is Blake's poetry *overwrought* or *beside the point*?

Your ex will soon fall asleep. Wad up the red velvet square on your light. In the glare, notice a few acne pits on his forehead. Congratulate yourself on being able to enumerate his flaws. You'll want to congratulate yourself a lot more often now.

Step 2: Break up with your girlfriend.

Remember: holiness is not one of the great works of Western literature. In some ways, it's their opposite. It's a blunt force, easier to wield.

Keep your promises and go on that picnic you've planned at a local park overlooking the Brazos River. Pick her up with Kenny Loggins playing so loud on your car stereo, neither of you can say a word.

In the park, choose a spot that's back from the cliff and under the live oaks. Spread out the backpacking blanket you bought in your freshman year because one of your buddies said, "Trust me: you'll need it with that girl."

She'll have a copy of *Let's Go 1980*. You've been planning a trip together. It was just the beginning of the plans you had.

"Should we start with London?" she'll ask.

Shrug. Male bravado goes well with righteousness.

"I mean, how important is Venice?" she'll ask.

Tell her you never wanted to go to Venice. Or London. Or anywhere. Lie a little. What can it hurt? Then tell her you two need time apart.

She'll look confused. "How much time?"

Say: "Forever."

It's not a lie. It's what you've got in spades.

She'll start to rage. "After the other day? Behind the church? After we . . ?"

Explain it. "I've decided to devote my life to God."

Not exactly, but close enough, words that obscure more in Texas than in most other places. At least you're speaking in your own voice. Or the voice that works. Try to hide how happy you are.

She'll get up and walk to the cliff's edge. You'll hear her say "fuck" a few times. It'll be decades before you'll learn that she's been off the pill for months, that she's pregnant, that the next week she'll drive more than five hundred miles to New Orleans to abort the child you never held in your arms, the one that never got a chance to be adopted, all because Texas is not a place for a modern woman. And because you were too righteous to notice the truth.

For now, wad up the lunch in the blanket. Toss the whole bundle in a bin. You didn't realize breakups could be so easy. Thank God you didn't buy that ring.

Don't get cocky. Stay focused. Call her back to the car. Dial down your attitude but apologize like a regular guy. "I'm sorry if you're hurt." Don't emphasize the *if.* You're trying to do this the easy way.

On the drive back to campus, don't pop in another cassette or turn on the air conditioner. The relentless August heat will blow in the windows. Enjoy the silence.

When she gets out at her apartment, don't drive away. Wait for something. You're all about signs. Portents and wonders. The whole Bible thing.

She'll give you the finger.

Nod. The Lord our God is one God.

Step 3: Lie.

When you call the seminary, you'll discover they have rolling admissions, but you need a rec from your "overseeing pastor." You haven't exactly been a regular churchgoer. William Blake, after all. Sex, too.

Your friend Clay is still having that affair with the church secretary. He'll be down the dorm hallway in summer-school shame because he flunked the last course in his major. Wait until you can hear the high-pitched whine of the Bee Gees behind his door. Knock, walk in, and jolly him up by pretending to listen to him.

"Then she wanted me to take us to that motel in Salado," he'll say. "You ever been there? They got stuffed shrimp."

Laugh and laugh. Now's your chance to play the regular guy, although this is the tricky part, despite the idiocy. Nod toward his Farah Fawcett Major poster. "Who wouldn't want a piece of that?"

He'll chuckle. Or commiserate. It's hard to tell with guys. Anyway, his guard will now be down, so this will be the moment when you'll ask him to get you some of the church's stationery. "Two or three sheets."

He'll wonder if you're in trouble. He'll press a little.

Look away, then tell him the whole story. Tell him you almost killed yourself. He's the only person you'll ever tell. Sometimes, the truth is necessary to get what you want.

"I was in love with two people, Alex and Melody," you'll say.

"We all wondered why you moved in with him," he'll admit.

Keep telling the truth. "I don't think I have the words for who I am."

He'll try to find some for you. "Like that bartender over at the . . . you know? The guy who likes ABBA?"

Shake your head. One more truth. "Not at all."

Clay's a decent guy with a limited imagination. You can work with that. He'll reason you want to go to seminary because "they probably have a lot of guys like you."

Say: "Yes."

When you get the stationery later that day, use an old typewriter in the dorm's study hall. The "e" will stick. It'll make the rec look real.

In front of a blazing sunset, drive downtown and mail your application at the box outside the main post office, an extra step you think makes this whole business look official.

Then drive out into the countryside. Park on a country road and wait for the stars. Wait for another sign. No poet will come walking out of the dark. Consider *that* the sign. You'll be accepted within a week.

Step 4: Get Through Graduation

Maintain a rough truce with your roommate. Was he ever really your boyfriend?

Finish your term paper. Go with *beside the point*. It's a hack job. C-.

Pack up. Look at your remaining books. They're like photos in an old album. Nostalgia. Nothing more. Put them in a box but throw out everything else: cards, mugs, dried-up boutonnières, all the notes you've ever taken in every English class.

Spend the remaining time making cassettes. They don't get scratched like records. They're supposed to last.

To prove it, offer Alex your turntable.

"You sure?" he'll ask.

Say: "Consider it a graduation gift."

When you shake hands over your diplomas, he'll lean in to hug you.

Say: "We're not like that."

He'll furrow his brow. "Like what?"

This is why you hate him. But put on a good face. Say: "Let's keep in touch."

What's one more lie when you're offering it in the service of the truth?

Head out to the strip of I-35 concrete that leads back to Dallas. Just north of Waco, put in a cassette you made from that Christopher Cross album. The songs will remind you of what you've lost.

Smile. Good riddance. You know where you're headed. You don't even need to read the signposts.

Hebrew in My Underwear

The only do-overs are in novels. The only sequels, in the imagination. Life spins on—inexorably, unforgivingly, redemptively. The best laid plans don't just go awry. They get caught in the whirl.

I was trying to escape it. I needed to believe my path was straight. Partly because I'd been raised with the Bible map of history. And partly because I-35 led from all I'd lost to all I knew, through nothing more profound than the sun's glare against the sky's blue. And through my beloved Texas prairie: a steer at a fence, a windmill on the horizon, an American emptiness that had symbolized redemption for the likes of me ever since the Pequots dragged the first Puritans into it. I even chucked that Christopher Cross cassette out of the window and cued up Christian rock on the AM dial. If I wanted to marshal my newfound tools of literary analysis and drop a plumb line into the Bible, I needed fewer distractions.

I'd gotten mixed up in too many books, too many lives, too many beds. I needed to embrace my identity: loneliness. I reasoned that the sheer number of voices in my head—Melody's, Alex's, and especially the ones from the great works of Western literature—had led me to see a dead poet on a country road.

Look, I told myself, you know what you have to do. Blame yourself. Smash your tape recorder. Forget your birth mother. Declutter and purge.

With a tight grip on the steering wheel, I eased off the interstate in West, Texas, a Czech settlement. I was after kolaches: squares of yeast dough with a fruit paste spooned in their centers. I wasn't hungry. I was determined never to be hungry again. But my family had been stopping here for years. I reasoned I should start doing everything I'd done before. Maybe there was a way to pray myself back to virginity, too.

I drove by the new bakeries in gas stations and turned down a two-lane road toward a wood-paneled joint with dusty curtains and rickety four-tops.

The waitress was aproned and withered, with oversized dentures and teased hair. She wrote down my order ("two cherry, one apple") although I was the only other person in the place. She brought the kolaches on a paper plate along with a coffee I hadn't asked for.

"Cup's on the house," she said. "I was about to make a fresh pot."

She sloshed coffee on the table and handed me a wad of paper napkins. "Take care of that, will ya?" she said, walking back to the register.

Holy God, this all felt right. It had to be the way back to sanity. And to holiness. They had to be the same thing. Otherwise, I was out of answers.

"You from around here?" the waitress asked, flipping through a *Cosmopolitan* on the counter.

I didn't want a conversation. I didn't want to monitor her voice in my head. So I tried to shut her up with politeness, a Southern ploy. "Just headed to Dallas, ma'am."

"Tourist," she muttered under her breath.

No, I belong, I wanted to say. But the kolaches were warm. I dipped a cakey corner in the coffee—just as I'd done when I was a kid, dipping it into Mother's coffee.

The waitress brought my check, scrawled on a green stub. A buck ten. She also handed me a brochure for the world's largest fruitcake factory.

I pushed it away and gave her my last two dollars, another purge. "Keep it," I said.

"Mr. Big Bucks Dallas," she replied.

Her attitude, her hair, her gait as she walked to her magazine—they all reminded me of that clerk at the department store when I'd picked out clothes for my own funeral. At the time, I'd noticed the slightest graze of something sharp along my skin. Now only two weeks later, I felt the cut more deeply. It was the deft scalpel of irony, the ghastly notion that the present was no more than an echo chamber for the past.

Among all the things I'd done, what if I were doing over the wrong ones? What if my life was making fun of me? Dammit, I didn't want another existential dilemma. I wanted cake. And the confirmation that I was right.

Like every truth-teller, I didn't understand irony, no matter how many profs explained it. Saying one thing and meaning another? Expressing an essential absurdity? Whenever I tried to be ironic, it sounded mean.

Once, Melody teased me about my clothes. "I'm dating a guy who still struts around in hip huggers," she said.

I told her a little anorexia wouldn't hurt her either. We didn't speak for a week, not until I ate a quarter of a chocolate cake in front of her to prove I was kidding.

How could I get through life if I couldn't take things at face value? If I believed God's world was a symbolic landscape waiting to be interpreted, how could I tell which parts were hollow resonances? Worse, which were the jokes?

Although everybody hailed the great works as a goldmine of irony, I'd nixed the notion and read them straight through. I had no idea which words deserved what weight, which ones were more jagged than the others. No one did. That's why English classes had been so nuts. All those endless debates. Everything was a matter of interpretation.

Not the Bible. God's Word was unsullied, every inerrant word equal to every other. Irony was a liar's game, double-speak. Mostly, a proliferation of intents, voices in a text, the sin that almost did me in.

I banged out of the café's door, drove to the interstate, and kept in the right lane as passing semis buffeted my Beetle. Despite my commitment to loneliness and my good-faith attempt to become who I'd been, I'd touched the lip of the bowl again, the edge beyond which nothing made sense.

But here was the difference. The Baylor gavage had done its trick. Words filled the spaces in me. Yes, there were voices in there, too. Those I had to silence. And I knew how. I had to disassemble them into their parts, into more words, which in and of themselves were neutral and couldn't be weighted—at least, until they got toggled together. Then they could feel like an anchor, a cold mass of forged letters, the fluke caught between my ribs.

I had no other options. I'd lost faith in professors like Dr. Franklin. I hadn't spoke to a minister in years. My family was still happy in splendid isolation. And I'd been trained to distrust psychoanalysts. "Me-generation charlatans," Pastor Daniel had called them. Then he'd muttered, "Jews"—although his anti-Semitism made no sense. We believed the promises to Abraham and his descendants were as good today as millennia ago. Jews were the chosen people; Christians, the addendum. How could "Jews" be a sneer?

It didn't matter. I couldn't go in for analysis, if only to keep from disappointing everyone again. Dad's answer to life was "Go to work." Mother's, "Don't think so much."

The best way forward was to make my way back to the original words. On that drive back to Dallas, I decided to limit my seminary studies to the Hebrew prophets. They had long been the architects of what I believed. They were the progenitors of Blake, too. In fact, with Homer, they were the poets who started the great works of Western literature, who began the ages-long process of straightening out the lines of time by writing them down.

I needed to make my way to the burned-out center those naysayers and soothsayers had created, to find the kilns they'd used to fire up their visions of the future. If I sifted the ashes, I might be able find the real treasure: a different ending to my own story, one in which I stayed alive. Or even harder, stayed myself. By which I meant, who I'd been, not who I'd become.

I reached Dallas's chain-link suburbs afire with monastic zeal. Ahead lay a starched, white-collar business center, the perfect place for a spiritual cleanse. In 1980, the city buzzed with the thrill of the future, which we evangelicals thought was the same thing as "now." Four states had rescinded their votes for the ERA amendment. President Carter was a hypocrite; candidate Reagan held prayer breakfasts. Dallas was little more than a shopping center with parking on the perimeter. I'd never get distracted in this tidy metropolis.

Back at my parents' house, I tested my resolve and denied all comforts, even those from the past. Mother tried to fatten me up with chicken rolls. I pushed them around my plate. Lies, I thought. Or irony. It was hard to tell the difference.

My parents seemed glad I was going to seminary, a proper venue for a kid preacher. Dad dropped some money in my account, a sign of middle-class approval. He probably wouldn't have been so generous if I'd told him about the last year and a half.

I had no intention to. I didn't want to ruin my new start with the story of my mistakes. Which meant I needed to keep a vice-like squeeze on the air at the back of my jaw.

The day before classes, I parked between the lines in an empty lot and walked across the treeless quad. I strolled by a concrete monolith that looked like a giant tombstone. Dallas corporate-speak had invaded even a school devoted to God's word. The monument was labeled *Our Mission Statement*. On the side facing the street, it proffered hope: *Touching Lives With Scripture*. Its reverse, hidden from the public, voiced a sterner ethic: *Preach The Word*.

I was on my way to meet my advisor, assigned by a lottery. I strode into an institutional building, a strip mall of righteousness, streaking the linoleum with my cowboy boots. I knocked on an office door and introduced myself to a bald, grinning, affable man, all cheeks and crow's feet. Cotton Mather at a patio party. Jonathan Edwards in seersucker.

His desk was scrupulously clean. His bookshelves felt right, too. Volumes were in perfect order, many grouped by color. See, the quirks and kinks of this world didn't matter. My mission statement did, although it was backwards from the seminary's. The sterner motto faced the street: *Turn yourself into who you are*. On its hidden back: *Find your way home*.

I had a few more hidden things that belied my intentions of starting over. My remaining volumes of the great works of Western literature were in a box on my car's back seat. And I'd tucked Melody's 24K pen in my suit pocket.

Students were supposed to wear a tie on campus. I sat down and wriggled to get my collar straight. I'd just turned twenty. I was trying to seem older, the right age for grad school. Yes, I'd lied to get into seminary. But it was all in the service of the truth.

My advisor must have sensed something wrong. A Calvinist, he was nonetheless avuncular made flesh. "Where is the Lord leading your heart?" he asked in what I would come to know as the school's preferred diction.

"To the text in the original languages," I said. "I'd like to start learning Hebrew."

He suggested I wait until my second year. "Why don't you start out on easier stuff?" He mentioned systematic theology.

I thought back to earlier versions of me. The me who'd fingered apart the living room sheers as my buddies played football. The me who'd taken a nip from a flask at a freshman dance. The me who'd watched a naked guy conduct Bach with a Bic. At best, those versions of me were fractured, split open.

Words weren't. At least, not the ones spoken by God through his prophets. And if one of those guys were to stroll toward me on a country road in the middle of the night, I'd at least know I was among the Lord's appointed saints and angels, who could come and go as they liked.

Besides, I've always been in a hurry, always wanted to get where I was going the minute I started out. Given my upbringing, I understood, gravitated toward, and even craved the beginning and the end, the Garden of Eden and the apocalypse. The middle was harder. Confusing. Mixed up. In other words, life. Which meant Melody, Alex, Blake, suicide, and a psychotic break.

Those fears must have fused with my hopes for holiness and fired up my eyes. I held my advisor's gaze. He filled out the necessary forms.

I began learning Hebrew through Isaiah, the grandest prophet, major in every sense of the word. At the center of his epic vision lay a future that included the Messiah and a redrawn geopolitical map, as well as a new heaven and a new earth.

I felt something far better than my cheap, orgasmic response to Blake's poetry. I felt nothing at all—because my work was rational, a construction site. I swore I heard the thwack of mortar and the clink of bricks as I pored over vocabulary flashcards, ate soggy sandwiches, and sat at the back of classrooms. And not just because I was translating a text, rather than reading it. I was treating a book seriously, analytically, and academically.

Which meant I finally saw the point of words. They weren't self-expression. They weren't tools. They were bricks. Bricks in the wall a book built, the dividing line between "what is" and "what might be." My life was here, Isaiah's was over there, and Hebrew lay between us.

Words were safety. Sanity. A sure way to keep "is" untainted by hope. Hope lay on the other side of the wall. I trudged to class on the still-hot days of October as Isaiah entered the royal court to change the course of history. I house-sat in any home I could find while the prophet shifted the politics of the Fertile Crescent. My car broke down because I couldn't afford an oil change; he zapped divine symbols into this mundane world: Wonderful Counselor, the Mighty God, the Prince of Peace.

I couldn't go crazy. I couldn't get into trouble. I now understood the almost incomprehensible manifestation of reading's quantum mechanics: the expanse of proliferating, alternate universes on the other side of the walls that words create.

I didn't have to live over there. I just had to hold the wall. It was enough to pitch my ladder against it, peer over it once in a while, and know that clear meaning, sense, and purpose were on the other side of the text, those bricks. I could then live my life testing them. Admiring them. Polishing them. Was that a lonely task? Yes! Thank God, the giver of words.

Years later, I met a guy who gave his life to another wall. Cloistered in a Manhattan studio apartment, he read *Anna Karenina* in endless loops. Besides a leather-bound copy of the novel, he had a red chaise, a grand piano, seven white T-shirts, seven pairs of jeans, a winter coat, and nothing more. He survived off trust funds, canned tomatoes, and limp pasta.

He didn't work. He'd never been in love. He'd passed the state department exam in Russian and submitted papers to academic conferences as an independent scholar. Once, late, after we'd shared his meager meal, I asked him if he thought his service to this tragic novel was worth his loneliness. He tightened his lips and told me to get out.

I didn't get to perch on my ladder for quite as long as he did. Few do. Toward the end of the term, Alex called me up.

"I need to see you," he said.

His voice was soggy soft. Maybe I should resist him. Or the past. I wasn't sure which. Then I thought of my new understanding of words. Of the wall and my cordoned-off life. I reasoned I could prove to him how far I'd come, how different I was.

We met in a shopping mall parking lot on a humid night. He'd washed out of grad school and moved back to Dallas. There was some family trouble: his sister, an older guy. He told me the story in pieces: his failing labs, her pregnancy. He started to cry and I shuddered. I'd once fallen asleep in his arms. How could he have changed so fast? How could he have become a human ruin?

His pain robbed me of all the words except the Hebrew ones for love. אהבה. רחמ. חסד. I'd just written a position paper on that first one, *chesed*, in Isaiah 40:6. "All flesh is as grass and all the godliness thereof is as the flower of the field." Except the word wasn't *godliness*. It was *chesed*, a hard, phlegmy *ch* belying the softer truth. Love in the context of faithfulness. Love based on a covenant. In other words, the ability to stay true to your promises. *Chesed* is as transitory as a daisy, but it's the most godly thing we humans can do.

Could I hold onto my promises? The ones I'd made to the seminary not to drink, dance, or engage in premarital "congress"? Or the ones I'd made to myself to stay out of the ironic fracas of life?

That night, I decided to test myself. Living like a Bedouin, I didn't own a stick of furniture. I invited Alex to the place where I was housesitting, a red-brick four-bedroom owned by a childless couple who'd gone to Europe for a month. He jumped at the chance.

We went through half a bottle of bourbon. I thought of my promises to the seminary. I liked the rules as much as the next guy. They lessened my worries. Because of them, I could risk a lot. And the ladder I'd pitched against Isaiah's text-wall had an unexpected benefit. It made me brave, especially when I came off it. After all, I was headed right back up. No wonder so many ministers get caught with their pants down.

"Did you love me?" I asked.

Alex nodded and looked away. "But not like you think."

He told me he might move to California and start over.

"Nobody starts over at our age," I said. That is, twenty or twenty-one. What did I know?

He looked at me, his eyes at half-mast, like that first night in the Armstrong-Browning library. "You did," he said.

The ice jingled in our glasses. It had gotten late. We were talking about nothing real: Bach, Baylor, and Reagan's election.

"You want to stick around for old time's sake?" I asked.

Alex shook his head. "I can't."

He did. He spent the night on a pallet next to my bed. "To be near each other," he said.

I couldn't stand the game we were playing. I couldn't stand not to play it. I put on my PJs. He slept in his briefs. I turned off the light. He rolled over and went to sleep.

I didn't. I heard his breathing in the small hours, that rattle of a bum septum. I didn't hate him. I didn't love him. I felt nothing and credited it to what the right words could do. What the true prophets could do. What the wall could do. I didn't even feel irony's slice. It never occurred to me it might run like a fault line underneath everything I was trying to build.

I had an early morning appointment with my advisor. I stepped over Alex, showered, and left, but not before inking him a note. *Dinner tonight?*

When I got back that evening, he was gone. He'd crossed out my message and written *No, thanks* below it.

I never saw him again, although I tracked him down on social media a while back. He looked wan, his smile stretched thin, horizontal. We didn't become cyber friends. And not one of the prophets' words could make my last moment with him fit any of the others in my life.

That day, my advisor had called me in to ask why I wasn't attending any classes except Hebrew. My case was so dire that he dumped the preferred diction. "What's up?" he asked.

Didn't he know how important the prophets were? "I can't make my way through Isaiah 53," I stammered. "Do you know there's this pronoun shift? The suffering servant goes from being *him* to *them* in Hebrew. I mean, we think it's about Jesus. But how's *he* suddenly *them*?"

My advisor cleared his throat. "Maybe you'd like to teach at a seminary?"

"Me?" I asked. "A Hebrew prof?"

Could I become a saintly Caddie Anderson in male drag, looping a classroom, whispering prophecies into students' ears?

He smiled and nodded. He'd solved me. "Let's make that happen," he said.

I downshifted my course load to work on a proper translation. I was twiddling with revelation, diagramming God like a sentence, doing my best not to notice that Isaiah's book was farcically complex. Almost every sentence headed one way, only to be turned aside, rethought, and refashioned in mid-stream, a massive study in misdirection, probably edited over centuries.

Even my Hebrew prof thought the whole thing was, yes, the Word of God, but written by many men over several generations.

Maybe even, he dared suggest, by women. "Otherwise, it's nuts," he said.

"You think like the liberals," I called out from the back row.

I didn't mean it as a partisan attack. I wanted to save myself. He was discounting the only author who mattered, the one I was doing my best to straighten out. I slipped my translations under his door each week. We communicated through marginalia.

He craned his neck to see me. He was a lanky cadaver with hollow eyes. "Scarbrough, you haven't been listening," he smirked. "If there's just one writer, he must have been a maniac." He paused for effect. "The sort who would try to read *Moby-Dick* in Sanskrit."

As with Dr. Franklin's explanation of Faulkner, everyone laughed. This time, I was furious. Because my prof didn't understand. Because he'd mentioned one of the lying works of Western literature in the middle of a seminary class. Because I was afraid I was the brunt of some irony I couldn't understand.

I walked out and worked harder. The guy couldn't fault me for trying.

I survived on beef jerky from 7-11. I lost a few more pounds. But I felt secure on my feet, even if I was so thin I could barely stay awake in the library. In the prime of male sexuality and starkly celibate, I called myself "lucky."

But books are liars, even the holy ones. No matter how little I weighed, the iron anchor in me weighed more. I'd put my faith in words, the heaviest things, gravitational wells in our spin through space. They're strong enough to break up anything that gets near them. Relationships. Holiness. Even the best ladders we pitch against sense. I didn't know it yet, but my salvation would be to control the fall.

Not everyone's so lucky. My *Anna Karenina* friend's trust fund dried up and he lost his apartment. The last time I saw him, he was warehoused in a Manhattan homeless shelter. Sitting on a filthy cot, he looked through me, not at me, and offered his terse assessment of his fate, mixing up his tenses in insanity's fracture: "I was somebody who takes books seriously." The next day, he disappeared into the city, never to be seen again.

Late in the fall term of my second year, I was trying to get to school in an unexpected crush of Saturday traffic. The Rolling Stones were playing the Cotton Bowl, touring to promote *Tattoo You*.

Alex had had a collection of Stones' albums. When he wasn't Bic-conducting Bach, he strutted around to "Honky Tonk Women" in my underwear. He was a liar, all churn and spin. I cursed both him and this bumper-to-bumper time-waster.

The seminary library was almost deserted. Across one side of the vaulted space, plate-glass windows looked out on the bare quad. I had a big table to myself and pored over a tough bit the cadaver expected by Monday. The God of Israel announces that Egypt and Assyria, the worst of the Gentiles, are his chosen people, too.

> *In that day, Israel shall be the third with Egypt and with Assyria, even a blessing in the midst of the land, whom the Lord of Hosts shall bless, saying, "Blessed be Egypt my people, and Assyria the work of my hands, and Israel mine inheritance"*

I hated this passage. God was supposed to be a whirlwind of judgment. He raised up nations to smack down Israel. When he'd had enough, he commanded Israel to smack down those nations. He was vicious and tribal, like a high-school cheerleader, the same way I wanted to be with my own life.

Except I didn't know that God was also the master of irony, wrecking my saintly consistency. On a dime, he called for an end to the fighting and named Israel's enemies his children. Suddenly, things weren't a matter of here and there, this side and that. They were us together, Gentiles and Jews, a blended family, beyond blood.

Although I could attest that adoption was no answer to life's problems, it was definitely the hope in and under these words. "Comfort ye, my people," the prophet says. For a few verses, the wind shifted. I didn't trust it. No one on a ladder does.

As I tried to bring Isaiah's prophecy into English, I could feel the Stones thump my chest. The concert was about a mile away. Its licks bounced around me: no Jagger or Richards, just Wyman and Watts, bass and rhythm.

They made a strange thing happen. At first, it was nothing more than a prickling sensation in my fingers, poised over the page. The tingling flowed up to my head and collected in my brain, as if Jared's old carotid was working again, as if my thoughts were turning effervescent.

I began to yearn for something . . . for someone . . . for the safety of a person. Not anyone from Baylor, not Melody or Alex, but a person only books can create. Was it a he? A she? It didn't matter. It was a human voice. No, a human form. I could see a shadowy shape through the page, across the hot sands, beyond the Hebrew words.

It wasn't Isaiah. Or Blake. It was someone dimmer who'd always been there, someone I'd known all my life, since flannelgraph Bible stories and *Dick and Jane* books, since condensed novels and *Great Expectations*. I saw it, him, her: the narrator, the one who tamed the words and corralled any irony they might create.

The Hebrew cadaver had been right. Even if this prophecy was split in pieces, a narrator steadied the whole thing. Could I become a manifestation of this presence? Could I become a voice like that? Maybe I could even reach the top of the wall and call out to the world, though not with my voice, fallible and fractured as it was. Instead, I could continue the work of editing the prophet. Or anything I would read. I could parrot the words on the page, transforming myself and everyone I knew into the children of God. Was that the way out? To make the world fit a story, one story, as I became a narrator formed from the words of one of the original narrators?

By now, the Stones had become more than licks and thumps. I could hear the lyrics. I conjugated Hebrew verbs in my head, waiting for the music to Doppler down.

But the Stones were insistent, an id to my literary superego. The letters on the page began to gyrate. מ with צ and י, ר with ם, round and round, all to the riffs in "Start Me Up." Those letters danced with that shadowy figure on the sands. Ancient symbols strutted around in *my* underwear, whirling in endless gyres through the thick pulp of a sacred text.

Like Jagger, the Hebrew characters were absurdly sexy. They fucked their way into other texts, other stories, everything I'd read, that first sentence of *Absalom, Absalom!*, those Blake poems, my story. Those letters had created the words of the great prophet *and* the ones I'd used to wall off the most important things in my life. Worse yet, they and they alone created the very narrator who then turned around and forged them into sense, as if God had made Adam and then Adam returned the favor and made God. Unwittingly, I'd fallen over the wall and into a quantum literary reality again.

This time, I saw the ruin of my faith, not of me. It was and always had been a matter of privileging some words over others. Religion was irony at its core, a matter of assigning certain weights to certain words. Which meant that redemption was out of God's hands. It was a narrator's job.

My vision that day was the companion piece and fulfillment of the one I'd had in Caddie Anderson's classroom. Words were the fields of the Lord, the playground of meaning. And now I knew they were the foundation of what I'd tried to express to Melody, to Alex, even to Mother when she told me Pip was an orphan. They were the basis of love, of *chesed*, the thing more holy than loneliness, the physical manifestation of everything I wanted.

As the Stones played on, I lost one cardinal virtue, faith, but gained another, the one that lived on the other side of the wall, in the world that books create: hope. Not in an abstract future. Instead, in the ability of words to make the promises that could become love. In their ability to create the narrators who create our world on this side of the wall.

I merged with the narrator and danced with the Hebrew letters. With the Stones in my ears, maybe in my body, I was on both sides of the text's wall, here and there, in the world and out of it. Innocence and experience, men and women, cadavers and God—if I tamed the words, I could do more than tell my story. I could bridge the contradictions in me, live on both sides of the wall, and embrace the duality of my being, the strange bipolarity of my true self, a fractured conundrum I'd never once seen in the great works of Western literature but that I'd caught sight of in Alex.

And maybe in Melody. Or somehow in both of them at once. Maybe, if I worked hard enough, I could ease out of the dislocation I felt every day of my life and vanish into the best story, a story that wasn't about me but was mine nonetheless. After all, the best sort of narrator was a disappearing act. Like my birth mother.

I was slipping toward the lip of the bowl, back toward insanity, maybe an even more precarious drop this time, with music by the Stones. If I'd taken my new hope as far as I could have, maybe should have, I would have ended up a mumbling wreck on the streets. But thank God, the prophets, the poets, the words, or something I still didn't understand, I was saved the only way anyone can be.

"Hey, steady," a voice said as a hand flattened the text in front of me. "You okay?"

I looked up, half expecting to see Isaiah. Instead, it was Thaddeus, Thad, a fellow seminary student: married, staid, several years older, with floppy hair and ebony eyes.

"We're in a library," he said. "You have to be quiet."

"I am quiet. I'm just. . . ."

Thad bent closer, dropping his voice. "You were yelling. We all heard it."

Sure enough, the few other guys in the reading room were staring at me.

"You're saying some mishmash of English and maybe Hebrew," he said. "*Qumee oree I hear him kawbode I see him.* Something like that."

I couldn't tell him I was enrolled in seminary but now put my hope, not in God, but in craft, the narrator's skill.

"I'm fine," I said.

"Doesn't seem like it," he said. "Let's go get a . . . a. . . ."

I wanted to scandalize Thad and be done with him. "A drink?"

No soap. He laughed. "Right. How about just some air? A breather."

We'd chatted a few times in the hallways. Raised Greek Orthodox, an atheist for a long time but now an evangelical, he'd been a Kent State student during the riots. He'd rushed to the side of Jeffrey Miller, shot through the mouth and bleeding out on the sidewalk. Thad had darted off for help, just out of frame as the Pulitzer Prize-winning picture was snapped.

I thought of Pastor Daniel and his glee at the massacre. But Thad was a better man, trying to find a good cause in a bad world. He'd already told me he didn't think those students got what they deserved. I'd soon discover he didn't think I had either. He was a more compassionate Melody, a more comprehensible Alex. But all that lay in a future no prophet could see.

"It's Isaiah," I explained as I got to my feet, scattering loose pages around me. "And the presence behind the words. I can't get my head around it. Him. Them."

"Around what?"

Why did these sorts of things happen to me in libraries? I decided not to lie. "Around everything," I said.

He clearly didn't believe me. "You want to talk?"

"I've got a lot to finish before I can. . . ."

"At least there's a good soundtrack," he said, nodding toward the concert.

I shook my head. No more contradictions. If I was going to become a narrator, I needed my characters pure.

Thad shut the Hebrew scriptures on the table. "Let's get out of here."

I gathered my things and pointed downstairs. He seemed disappointed but followed me to a basement conference room. I scattered my notebooks in front of him.

"What gives?" he asked. "People don't do that."

"Take the text seriously?" I started pacing. "They should."

"But they don't. Are you in trouble?"

"I hate the wall."

He raised an eyebrow.

"Or the ladder," I said. "But I don't want to come down."

Thad grabbed my hand. "Just say what you mean."

I couldn't. Where were the words? I shook him loose. The only help was in front of me. I sat down and chose a sheet scrawled with my notes. "What do you make of this passage?"

He bit his lip. "Are you sure? Because I think you were trying to tell the whole library something about you, not about Isaiah."

I wanted to ask, Is the deepest irony that the universe is just a void to be filled with the stories we make up? That we're all really orphans, adopted by the narrators we find or create? Instead, the Hebrew letters helped me say, "Of course, I'm sure."

Thad and I went to work, trying to figure out the intricacies of a twenty-five-hundred-year-old prophecy in a language far distant from our own, for a religion far distant from our own, in a way that could only bring the text into our lives and steady the ladder against the wall that divided the world into halves—until one of us, maybe, could climb up and become a squatter on top for the rest of his life. People build homes on walls. All the time.

The Stones still thumped the library. With Thad, I was better at tuning them out. I didn't yet know that their music was part of the disconnect built into everything, the stuff that's so ironic, so split down the middle, it can't hang off the neat lines of time we narrate. It falls off our official stories to make us who we are after we run out of words. If you want to find us, any of us, just read between the lines.

But at that moment, I only wanted what the great books promised, the remaining cardinal virtue, greater than the hope I'd found. By that I mean "love," that most bookish word. It turns the rest of the words into the best promises and dares to keep them in the middle of the cacophony on our side of the wall.

Funny thing is, I was about to get it. I was about to find *chesed* because of the very text I was trying to translate out of its irony and into mine.

The Prophecies of Love

This is how *chesed* works:

A few months later, Thad and I were driving back to Dallas on a two-lane strip of concrete south of Waco. Above us, the sky was stuffed with cottony clouds, although not one seemed to cast a shadow. If this road wasn't the same one on which William Blake walked out of the dark two years before, it was close enough—except the light was bright, the windows were down, and the breeze came in plush gusts.

Thad and I had spent the morning in the no-stoplight town of Lott, shopping at The Fair, a strip of false-front, spaghetti-Western buildings that made up the world's largest shoe outlet. I'd bought a pair of gaudy yellow sneakers, a knock-off of the coming punk wave. Thad had thrown new work boots onto the back seat. He was barefooted, his jeans rolled up. I'd stopped at a 7-11 and gotten us the necessary provisions for a Texas road trip: Big Red sodas, Hershey bars, and salted peanuts.

We'd needed an excuse to get out of Dallas. Thad had a demanding church job. His wife worked long hours as a nurse. I'd taken to selling men's clothing at a department store. To make ends meet, most of our classmates loaned themselves out to the pharmaceutical industry, which prized human subjects in the early '80s. Almost every guy on campus had a tube that snaked out of one nostril and into a sterile bag in his suit pocket.

Thad had a second job, too. He kept me sane while we worked on Isaiah's text. Whenever I got near sanity's lip, raving about the real meaning of some Hebrew word, he pulled me back to the center, to the ironic safety of deeper waters—that is, the many interpretive problems in the prophecy. The little faith I had left was in those words. And maybe in him. The words could call into existence other worlds, maybe this world. Thad could help me call into existence the narrator of the story I was telling myself. So he and I had become that strange human twofer I'd once tried to speak to Alex: you and me, a one-line poem that dares the promise of who we are.

That day, we rode in silence until he asked me what I was going to do when we finished our translation.

I looked toward the horizon. Why did people always want to know where I was headed?

"I'm keeping my options open," I said. "Uncle Advisor wants me to consider Aberdeen. Best Hebrew department, apparently."

"Jump on it," Thad said. He had a leather satchel between his feet. He reached in and pulled out a flask. "How about a nip to celebrate your status?"

With an echo of Melody's words on that bridge my freshman year, Thad's scared me witless. Did these callbacks happen to other narrators? Did other people try to stay upright when their story folded back on itself? Or did they lurch this way and that, waiting for things to settle down?

"You drink?" I asked him, seemingly calm.

He shrugged.

"What would the powers-that-be say?"

"I don't care," he said.

His rakish act bugged me. Part of being a narrator was making sure something was at stake at every moment. "Okay, what would God say?"

Thad took a pull from the flask, side-eyed me, and told me not to judge. "Isn't that in the Bible?"

He didn't wait for an answer. I couldn't have given him one.

"Listen," he said, "I know what keeps me steady."

Me, too. My Isaiah narrator constructed the text so that mercy was always followed by judgment. The last verse of his hopeful prophecy was a forbidding hellscape.

> *And they shall go forth, and look upon the carcasses of the men that have transgressed against me: for their worm shall not die, neither shall their fire be quenched, and they shall be an abhorring unto all flesh.*

Knowing that grace was a gaudy coverlet for damnation, I forgave Thad his faults in what I thought was a particularly godly way. This world is still a dumb show, I told myself. He tried to save his friends at Kent State but can't save himself.

"Oh, don't go silent on me," he said. "I'm not going to get sloppy drunk. Yet. But who doesn't have secrets?"

I looked him dead in the eyes. "They're overrated," I said.

Thad and I had momentarily switched places. He was using me as a marker for the limits of his behavior. I'd become the prophet in his wilderness. The breeze felt hotter.

"So I still want to know what's up after Isaiah?" he asked.

I gave it one word, naming the next major prophet. "Jeremiah."

He cocked his head. "I mean settling down. Don't you want . . ?"

I raised my hand to stop him. True, I was decades before Instagram, turning my life into a story rather than living it, figuring out how to narrate my life as a sequence of events that explained me, that didn't just happen to me. But I wasn't quite that far gone yet. I still believed I had to make sure that I saw other people, not as characters, but as fallible humans, even when I refused to let them slip off the timeline I made for them.

No problem, I told myself, just go with what you know. "This open land," I said, looking out the window. "It's everything I love."

He fingered the flask. "More. That's what I was going to ask. Don't you want more?"

The pastures were smeared in light. "So settling down and wanting more are the same thing?" I asked.

He nodded. "For most of us. My hunch? Not for you."

"Look, I'm going to spend my life working on the only text that matters."

"Yeah, you with the words."

I was irritated. I hadn't forgiven him as much as I thought I had. "And where is God if not in the words?" I asked. "Where do we find Him except in the sentences that string out after someone encounters Him?"

Thad closed one eye to find the vanishing point on the road ahead. "Everybody's gotta love something."

I knew that he and his wife had bought a small tract home. They were talking about kids. They were a romance plot in straitened circumstances. I knew, too, that he was trying to make me fit into my own life. If only for that, I loved him. Melody, Alex, Dr. Franklin, Mother and Dad, even Isaiah and Blake—they'd all tried to adopt me and make me fit into theirs.

Still, he was too cavalier. "You came to a seminary that's all about the inerrant Word of God and you'd rather not lose yourself in it?" I asked.

He winced. "I get it. We should learn Hebrew, Greek. But what it does to you. . . ."

"Me?"

"Anyone." He didn't finish the thought. Maybe he couldn't. "Check out those cows?"

"Longhorns."

"You're a model of precision."

"Thanks," I sneered.

"It wasn't a compliment."

I didn't think it was. We weren't communicating, even though we were talking about things so close to the truth.

Under them, I felt a weird nostalgia for the Baylor gavage, for the sheer hope of those undergrad years, when the answers had seemed just out of reach. What happens, I asked myself, when you're trying to be the narrator of your own story but you keep ending up at the start of it?

Thad didn't wait for me to figure it out. He launched into a hypothetical story about a teenager who walks into his church. She's in some jam, sexually active, thinking about killing herself.

I shifted in my seat.

"Does she really care about Isaiah?" he asked.

"She should!"

"Boilerplate inerrant-word-of-God stuff. But forget her."

"You brought her up!"

He took another pull from the flask. "My point is, you want a perfect world. A world of verbs and nouns. You know you're going to end up by yourself, right?"

Mostly, I wanted to go back to the quiet comfort of two guys driving a country road. "Prophets are desert creatures," I said.

"Maybe, but you're not a prophet."

It stabbed me. Because I wasn't. Because I wanted *him* to be one. And he wasn't.

Thad took another hit from his flask. "Which brings me to a bigger question," he said. "Why don't you go to church?"

I'd spent two years at an ultra-conservative seminary and never joined a congregation. I told my peers I hated the smugness, the glad-handing, what everyone called "fellowship." But I couldn't tell Thad my secret: I said I wanted to believe in the words of God; but I now hoped, at the end of my studies, to touch the silence on the other side of them. The silence of the desert sands. The emptiness without the music of the Stones. The silence that ringed my story and held it together. The silence of my birth, a story that didn't start with a baby's cry.

I also didn't want to be cross-examined. "Church is not why I'm in seminary," I said.

"And you think drinking's a problem? Listen, you should try the one we go to."

Ah, the pitch. They were all proselytizers. I'd been one once, too.

Thad worked at one of the first mega-churches in town. They were ramping up with electric guitars and slide projections of hymns. He told me they'd agreed to let a director come in and mount a full-scale dramatic production to attract new people.

"Young people," he clarified.

I was twenty-two. He was barely thirty. And he was talking about something far removed from Pastor Daniel, from county fairs and swap meets, from sour-faced men and folding chairs. It was the coming wave. It sickened me.

"We're going to do a musical," he said. "You're a tenor, right? What do you say? The director's weird. Worked in New York. Good Christian, though. Maybe you should audition."

"What's the play?"

"*Godspell*."

Outrage was still safe. "For God's sake, no! I hate musicals. They're as fake as *The Wizard of Oz*. Besides, that sort of production is probably pretty serious. Probably involves dancing. Believe me, I don't dance."

"Doesn't matter," he said. "You need a life."

I smiled at him. We'd settled into a place I knew. Not home, exactly. Just one guy telling another sentences that approximated the truth. So I risked a fragment from my past. "Asshole retard," I said.

"Huh?"

"*I need a life.* What does that mean?"

"Sounded good, right?" He knocked open the glove compartment. "And it might explain this."

He pulled out a snapshot of Melody. She'd stuck it in the card with the gold pen I still carried. She was smiling and topless—or almost so, her shirt open to her navel, no bra in sight, her breasts round and wonderful. I could still taste them.

I stammered something about needing to clean out my car. Thad didn't let me finish. He pulled out a second snapshot. Alex, in that ratty Colorado T-shirt. He'd scrawled soapy drivel on the back: "What symphony should I conduct for us?"

And one more thing: a 3 x 5 notecard under a paperclip that held the shots together. "Stay true to your promises," I'd written in her ink.

I'd put that bundle in my glove compartment on the first day of seminary. Two years later, the three of us were still unreliable narrators.

"You shouldn't leave me in the car while you get the snacks," Thad said.

I revved the engine to 80 mph. The wind grew deafening.

Frankly, I was more embarrassed by the picture of Melody than the one of Alex—which I couldn't explain, which made me madder.

"That's all over," I said.

"That? Or those?"

"Don't try to corner me! She was my girlfriend. He's the guy who, a friend who. . . ."

Thad waved me off. "Don't lie. I made it through the '70s on a college campus."

"I'm not lying!" And I wasn't. "I'm trying to tell you. . . ."

But I couldn't finish it. I didn't have enough models yet to be a proper narrator.

Thad patted his flask. "You're doing that thing you did in the library. You're not talking about anything that matters."

Then he reached over and brushed the bangs off my forehead. It was the smallest gesture, the most caring thing that happened to me in seminary. I had no idea what would happen next. Would Thad tell me he was my long-lost brother? Would he rip the sky open and make Isaiah walk out into the world in front of us?

Instead, he said the thing I thought I'd mastered, the thing I needed to hear because I hadn't mastered it: "Hey, no sweat, buddy. I forgive you."

"You can't! I haven't done anything to you."

He smiled. "People don't behave. That's the business we're in. And you're driving too fast."

I didn't dare stop. All I wanted was to tell a story that proceeded in a straight line from where it started. Or a story that ended *as* it started. A balanced story like Isaiah's, apocalypse to apocalypse.

Before I could say anything else, Thad helped me out by turning back into a fundamentalist. "The good news is that salvation is not found in how people behave. It's found in what they believe."

"What does *that* mean?"

He stayed calm and righteous. "That Jesus can help you figure a way out of yourself, Mark."

He silenced me by using my name, that piece of me that was and wasn't me, that always sent a chill up my spine. He shoved the snapshots and the 3 x 5 card back among all the old maps to places I still wanted to go. Everything got bent and torn. Then he slammed the glove compartment closed and turned to face me.

"These sorts of dramatic productions would be professional everywhere else," he said. "But our church is in Dallas. The bar's lower."

For the next hour, he wore me down, not with cheap knocks about the city I called home, but with his own story. He told me about his addictions, his failures. After Kent State, he'd been in rehab for years. Nothing worked. He patted his satchel where he'd stashed the flask. "I've come to accept my damage as fair trade," he said. "Maybe it's not how everyone does it but it's how I do it."

I started to say something about AA.

"Spare me. It's not my story." He held my gaze. "What do you say? *Godspell*? I just want you to settle down, find a home."

"A home?"

"A church home. What'd you think I was talking about?"

For the first time in years, I felt that sharp drop in my stomach, the emptiness before the roller coaster hill. I thought I'd gotten rid of it with my new role as the narrator and a hyper-rational respect for the text I was translating, even if the letters sometimes danced in my underwear.

Instead, I gained a new understanding of that sensation, that drop. It was the long view into the silence around me, maybe all of us. It wasn't the thrill of a new plot, first-chapter jitters. It was the stillness of space without metaphor, irony, or any other narrative device. It was the glimpse before a story starts of all that could not be told, maybe should not be told, certainly would not be told. I'd once thought that words could fill the hole in me. I had no idea that they could also push back the emptiness around me so that it didn't press quite so close.

By the time we got to Dallas's southern suburbs, Thad was in his cups. He blathered on about how he and his wife wanted children.

"Little bits of me in the world," he said—which only made me feel worse. Which further loosened my resolve.

So the next weekend, maybe to humor Thad, maybe to humor myself, probably because I'd come to see him as the only sort of savior I'd ever get, I put on those yellow sneakers and sang "Learn Your Lessons Well" in what was called a "worship space." It stank of new paint. Professional spotlights hung off iron bars. Narrow windows looked out onto asphalt.

The director was noticeably short, Alfred E. Neuman in spandex. He had an overbite and a terrific sense of his own centrality. I told him I was in seminary, in case classes conflicted with rehearsals.

"Fair theology," he said, gazing to my right.

He asked for my monologue. Thad had told me to prepare something that wasn't from the play. "He'll be less likely to detect your missing acting chops," he said.

So I walked up on stage and recited Isaiah 60:

> *Arise, shine, for thy light has come; and the glory of the Lord is risen upon thee. For behold, the darkness shall cover the earth, and gross darkness the people.*

I savored the words. They were sweet, not like honey, more like the subtle aroma underneath the char on a strip steak off the grill.

The director jerked his hand aloft to stop me. "More," he said.

I got louder, and the words tasted better.

> *But the Lord shall arise upon thee, and his glory shall be seen upon thee. And the Gentiles shall come to thy light and kings to the brightness of thy rising.*

I felt my pulse calm. I was in control of it. When I recited a text I knew so well, I felt like myself, the only person I'd ever been.

The director interrupted me again. "Much more," he said. He made a gesture as if he were cupping his intestines to bring them out of his mouth.

I didn't want some guy in Lycra to get in the way of Isaiah's words. So I hollered,

> LIFT UP THINE EYES ROUND ABOUT AND SEE: ALL THEY GATHER THEMSELVES TOGETHER, THEY COME TO THEE!

I thought that might get rid of him. Instead, he said, "Perfect. Now I'd like you to watch me sing."

"Watch you?"

"Tut, tut. Patience."

He leaped onto the stage, tripping over folding chairs in a sprawl of can-do optimism. Before he got to his feet, he launched into an *a cappella* version of "Day by Day."

This time, he motioned me down. I bent over. He kept singing and motioning. Soon, I was sitting on the floor. He motioned some more. Finally, I was lying on my back, looking up at him as he sang. I had no idea what he wanted. I must have looked fish-faced blank.

He stopped midline. He beamed at me. "Wonderful!"

This is how I ended up spitting out the prophecy I thought would save me in an amateur production of *Godspell* at a burgeoning megachurch while attending a seminary that debated whether rock-and-or-roll came from Satan. I put on a suit, went to classes, worked on a passage, typed it up, slipped it under the Hebrew cadaver's door, took off the suit, sold men's clothing at a department store, left work, put on sweats, and rehearsed a musical that started with verses from my prophet and ended with the Messiah's funeral dirge.

The only constants were Isaiah's words: *Prepare ye the way of the Lord.* They felt like the script of the story I was living. Or perhaps the story I was living felt like a convincing set of fragments linked by this prophecy. I wasn't off the wall, against it, or even in two worlds at once. Instead, the text fell to pieces as the Bible was force-fit into Broadway, as Broadway was force-fit into the Bible, and as the prophecy faded to camp.

We actors weren't expected to do any complicated choreography, just grapevines, box steps, and cross-body leads. I found I could repeat steps in a row, which was sort of like dancing if you were a chemistry geek who became an English major only to end up in seminary and then a musical.

On opening night, the director gathered us backstage. He puffed out his cheeks, sighed out his breath, and waved it around the room. "I free you to become who you are."

He shouldn't have said that. My born-and-bred clumsiness set in. Most likely to trip on a flat floor, after all.

The first number was a pastiche of easy steps and static tableaux. On a high riser through most of the song, I had to hold one person after another in a freeze for four beats before they moved on, all the while belting out the prophecy I'd come to adore and misunderstand: "Prepare ye the way of the Lord."

As the curtain went up, I felt my ankles sway. I tried to hold my position. I needed to grab the arm extended toward me to complete the movement, to pull her onto the platform with me and hold our freeze. "Prepare ye the way of the Lord."

I started to slip back, off, down. A trained dancer, she took a graceful step behind me, put a hand in the small of my back, and righted me.

Miranda was ridiculously sophisticated. She'd choreographed professionally, then landed a job in the new world of software development. Ross Perot knew her by name. She and I had been out to dinner after rehearsals, sometimes with the whole troupe, sometimes alone.

I turned to give her a thank-you nod before she moved on to the next riser.

"Prepare ye. . . ."

She winked and I fell in love—for the first time in my life without clumsiness or hesitation, without tripping or stalling, all while spitting out Isaiah's prophecy at full voice.

A chain of interlinking texts gave me a new story, one I could play for the rest of my life, what all the great works of Western literature promise: love, the sin in the tragedies they tell, the hope of the comedies they unfold. I stayed upright, the wall fell down, and the world opened up. Isaiah's words predicted my future, lost their power, and brought Miranda and me together.

The best thing about the day after the walls of Jericho fell down? You could stand in the middle of town and feel a breeze.

The Parson's Tale

Thad came backstage after the last performance of *Godspell*. "I told you this would be good for you," he said. "You just needed to find the right . . . her."

Sitting on a stool in front of a mirror and wiping the rouge off of my cheeks, I also watched Thad's reflection as he yakked around the cliché of *I told you so*. Like everyone else, he wanted to be the narrator of a romance plot.

As if on cue, Miranda walked behind us. She was in an '80s black leotard, her hair blow-dried without any aerobic-video frizz.

"Hey, babe," I said, comfortable in my skin, a twentysomething out of his fears and into the middle of his life. "Here's the guy who wants the credit for us."

Wordless as she often was when she first met someone, ferociously independent everywhere except in her private life, she sized Thad up with expressionless eyes.

He wasn't cowed. He was still proud of himself. "A simple 'thank you' will do," he laughed.

"Not yet," she said, holding his gaze. "Give it time."

Which was what I wanted, too: time, the thing I'd been afraid could escape me.

A year ago, I'd have said that the Christian ethic was "Love thy neighbor." But I'd had it wrong. "Love thy neighbor as thyself," Jesus said, another narrator with the words of the prophets in his mouth. Why didn't someone tell me it was so easy to do both?

Miranda kissed my head. "I'll see you in fifteen for dinner?"

Thad watched her walk away. "And I'll see *you* later this week," he said without looking at me. "We're still moving on to Jeremiah?"

Now I held my own gaze in the mirror. I had no doubt what I was doing. "Sure thing," I said. "I'll call you."

I didn't. I stopped going to classes at seminary. Occasionally, I picked up my mail and scurried away. I never officially withdrew.

Thad probably phoned a few times. I wouldn't know. Those were the days before caller ID, even before answering machines. He did leave a few notes in my seminary mailbox. "You sure everything's okay?"

I ignored them. I'd taken the story Thad wanted to tell and made it my own. Which made it easier to dismiss him.

I saw him one last time, getting out of a Ford Pinto across the seminary parking lot. The sun glinted off a pharma tube snaking out of his nose. He waved and called out something. I pointed to my ear, shook my head, got in my car, and drove away, bequeathing him my role as a minor character, someone who should have gotten a better ending but vanished into silence as the tale coalesced around me.

The silence *in* me was another matter. Apparently, it hadn't been about Blake. Or condensed novels. Or some word wall those texts built. No, Isaiah had been right: it had been about love, or the lack of it, the universal reason for the human voice: *l'amour, die Liebe,* ἀγάπη, the tonic chord that grounds the story and predicts its ending. It was the subject of almost everything I'd read at Baylor, Shakespeare to Faulkner, Austen to Joyce. And of course, Robert Browning and his wife, Elizabeth Barrett Browning, whose marital assets filled the library.

And irony was no longer my bogeyman, especially after *Godspell*. I understood it and love in the same way I read: I could never see to the bottom of it. Even so, I had no worries because I had the right voice to tell the story of who I was. Everyone straightens out the swirl of the universe. Everyone puts story first. Me, too.

And I could because Miranda's hand stayed in the small of my back. She was boarding-school polished yet part of the tech wave. She called herself "a feminist with poise." She wore pearls, even when shirtless. When she wasn't coding, she read George Eliot and Anthony Trollope. "For fun," she said.

I didn't know you could. I'd gone at books with a Puritan fervor. Now my life meant as much as the great works, mostly because it matched them. I could finally read whatever I wanted and not fear that the flood gates might open and drown the world.

Although I was still homeless, crashing at housesitting gigs or my parents', I went back to Dr. Franklin's gavage list. At Dallas libraries, I checked out the obscure titles I'd missed: Lord Byron's *Beppo*, Herman Melville's *Omoo*. I moved the box that held my remaining great works into my parents' garage.

When I stopped by one day to rummage through the titles, Mother asked, "You sure I shouldn't throw those out?"

She was now prone to contractions, slower in her judgments. Her oldest son kept restarting his life, banging from despair to contentment. My brother was nearing his teenage years. She was past fifty and facing adolescence again.

"Can you keep storing them for a while?" I asked her. I put a couple volumes in my backpack and headed out to sell clothes at the department store. "I think I'm going to keep reading them."

I did. I also decided to go to grad school in English. Not yet as a career choice. More to justify reading.

I wanted to stay close to Miranda, so I enrolled at a satellite campus of the University of Texas, an office park of higher learning set in an empty field north of town. The faculty was a surprisingly smart set. Some with fancy degrees hadn't gotten tenure at grander places. Others with less prestigious degrees were well published and on their way to those grander places.

I told myself I might as well follow the advice Blake had offered me on that country road. I wasn't even afraid of him anymore. I'd worked his appearance into the story of my past. He'd told me to get the sweep of the canon down, so I enrolled first off in a Chaucer seminar. And like almost every English major at one point or another, I tumbled headlong into the open pit of medieval lit. Miranda and I spent more and more time together as I worked through *The Canterbury Tales* and drafted my seminar paper on The Parson's Tale.

Familiar, literary voices washed over my brain. They were no longer terrifying—partly, as I've said, because Miranda had ahold of me. But also because *The Canterbury Tales* wasn't a complete work. Left unfinished at Chaucer's death, it was actually a book of books, an anthology of stories.

Thirty or so pilgrims rumble down the road to Thomas à Becket's shrine. To pass the time, they agree to a tale-telling contest and offer pious or filthy or even smarty-pants stories to win the prize, a full meal in a world whose moral arc is bent toward starvation. Just as the pilgrims near the cathedral town, an impossibly good man steps up to tell the last story, to give the book its swan song. Promising a "merry tale," the Parson recites a treatise on penance, the longest piece in the book—and not a story at all, more like a slag heap of medieval theology.

My seminar paper argued that *The Canterbury Tales* was a system of interlocking frames. What was amiss in one story was only noticeable when the reader saw it in the frame of another. To be honest, that thesis was pretty shopworn. But I claimed that since the righteousness of the Parson's Tale came *after* all the bawdy stories, orthodoxy was the new heterodoxy. Or the frame was the true picture.

At least that's what I hoped. I'd slept with a woman but been in love with a man. I'd talked to a dead poet and watched Hebrew letters gyrate on a page but was now reading whatever I wanted to. Miranda and I were already hosting dinner parties. The last storyteller made everything right. I'd rounded the bend and seen home.

One afternoon, I stopped at a jewelry store on my way back from class. I toted the heavy volume of Chaucer's complete works in my backpack. I could feel its weight on my spine. On scholarship money, I could afford half a carat.

I wasn't cheap. I was medieval, afraid I'd be crushed by debt. I thought I'd keep the ring for a few months.

That night, Miranda and I were fooling around at her apartment when she climbed on top, as Melody once had. Instead of launching into some dream vision, I noticed that Miranda's bedspread was cheap and scratchy against my shoulder blades. I sighed in relief. You're reading and being sexual again, I told myself, but in your own body because of the woman you love.

We were both starting out, although I was starting over, too. I was younger than Miranda but strangely older: twenty-three but four years out of college. I was pounds underweight, looked like a teenager below the neck, but already had folds in the corners of my eyes from reading too much.

Miranda didn't seem bothered by my contradictions. She was lithe without being skinny, the most beautiful person I'd ever seen. She sat out by the pool in her apartment complex just enough that her skin was the color of the Texas prairie in August.

She said, "I like it when you. . . ."

"You want to get married?" I asked.

She laughed a soprano lilt. "It's the wine talking."

"No, it's me."

Surprised, she got off and lay down next to me. "I assumed you'd, we'd, I'd."

"Don't assume."

"Apparently not."

"So it's a 'yes'?"

"I assume so."

We didn't make love that night. Even at our age, we were too excited by our changed status. And we wanted affirmation for reasons neither of us could have explained. So we got dressed, drove to my parents' house, and woke them up. They hugged us in their robes, although Mother looked as surprised as Miranda had.

"Men and women," Mother said, toasting us with iced tea and daring a sentence fragment or two. "The eternal mystery."

We went back to Miranda's and snuggled up. I loved being alone with her, just our two voices, coming into plainsong unity. If I noticed that familiar drop in my stomach every evening when she walked in after work, I chalked it up to seeing the start of our story together. If I occasionally felt that buzzing between my ribs when she was gone for hours in the middle of the night to fix software malfunctions, I told myself that we had the rest of our lives, that she'd soon be back to put her hand in the small of my back.

A few weeks later, we flew to see her family in St. Louis, hoping to repeat our Dallas scene with its genial toasts. But Miranda's parents didn't play along.

They fronted a sprawling Italian family. Her father, the first to go to college, had forced his way into top city contracts, then into society, sending his children to the best private schools and buying a house in the tony section of town despite anti-immigrant covenants. He'd festooned his home with his civic awards and photos of Miranda in debutante white.

Although she'd joined the evangelical church where we'd put on *Godspell*, her parents were aggressively, genetically Roman Catholic. They weren't happy with the changes in her life—of which I, the humanities grad student, was the chief.

Her father took the family to a downtown restaurant with darkened windows and white tablecloths. He wore a crisp linen suit and an open-collared shirt. I had on Britannia jeans and a faded Jimmy Carter T-shirt.

The line stretched down the block, but he ushered us past the crowd. We walked in to Puccini arias and huzzahs from the bar. We were shown to a table in a back room. Miranda's father didn't need a reservation for a party of fifteen that included aunts, uncles, and cousins.

They all wanted to get to know me. Mostly, they wanted to warn me. "You treat that girl right."

A cheap, bumper-sticker Jesus fish out of water, I reverted to my Southern manners. Mother had taught me that if someone else was paying, I should order "down." When the waiter got to me, I asked for the fettuccine alfredo.

Miranda's father shot to his feet. "What are you saying?"

I repeated my order.

He bashed his fist against the table, rattling the glasses until the room fell silent. "You trying to embarrass me in front of my family? You think I can't afford meat?"

I looked down at my jeans. The red cross-stitching seemed to glow. I thought I heard a sound like the tide going out: a sizzle in the sand. What story was I telling myself?

"You pay attention to me," her father said.

I looked up.

"You order the veal chop."

I blushed and nodded.

"No, I want to hear you say it."

"I'll take the veal chop."

The waiter asked me how I wanted it cooked.

I looked at Miranda's father.

His face relaxed. He smiled. "Any way you like it."

"However's best," I told the waiter.

The room's din crescendoed back to a roar.

This was hardly the Chaucer fantasy I'd wanted: no merry tale-telling on the way to a saint's altar. But before I could get too worked up, Miranda leaned against my shoulder. Her hair was soft and cool. She smelled like everything I wanted.

"Dad's testing you," she whispered. "Just be yourself."

When her father ordered a martini, I did, too. But we never got on a better footing. Her parents hated me, partly because I had no money and (as they said) "no future." Partly because I was a Protestant and (as they said) "not a Christian." But mostly because they only knew one story: America, rags to riches. I didn't fit it.

A week later, we were back in Dallas, and I was in Miranda's living room, working on Chaucer's Franklin's Tale. I needed to write a small paper on its place in what was known as "the marriage argument."

About a hundred years ago, a Harvard don identified three of Chaucer's tales as a thematic unit about wedlock. Another scholar soon added a fourth. Someone else, a fifth. By this point, most of *The Canterbury Tales* had been lumped into the marriage argument, because most of the pilgrims tell stories about a husband bound to duty, a husband dead drunk, a husband picked by the gods, a husband killed by the gods, a husband too old, a husband too randy—husbands, all. I might not have fit Miranda's parents' stories, but I was about to fit into the sum of the pilgrims' tales and enter my own version of the marriage argument.

Except I heard hard words flung around Miranda's bedroom. "Shit." "You." "Never." I closed the book on my finger and crept down the hallway.

Miranda was sitting on the bed, halfway out of her work clothes, her back to me. I could see the tension in the angle of her fingers as she held the phone's black handset to her ear.

Her mother was yelling so loudly, I could hear her words in the receiver, a tinny amplification of rage. She told Miranda that a marriage only counted if it was officiated by a priest. She made sallies into their heritage, their struggle for acceptance. Then she said that as of this moment, she didn't have a daughter. She should have given Miranda up for adoption. She hung up mid-sentence.

Without moving, slowly, almost imperceptibly, Miranda started to cry, a ghastly exhibition of control and fear.

I took the phone away and held her. "I get it," I said.

She had few words. "You can't."

I said something about being adopted. About looking for home. About knowing what it was like to have it and not have it at the same time.

We lay back on her bed. She cried a little more, a dull whimper.

"I may not be strong enough to hold us both," she said.

It was the first time I realized she knew what she was doing with me.

I tried to quiet her. And comfort her. I started touching her, holding her. We stripped down and started fooling around. We wanted to taste another body in a world that hurt so much.

We were soon in a furious romp, with rumbles in the bed slats. I pushed myself to a monstrous sweat. In six months, I had to be ready for three hundred guests, my family, my friends, a tux, a wedding dress, a dance band, a rented historic mansion in downtown Dallas, a break from the past, and the start of the rest of my life, almost the ending the Parson promised. Yet Miranda now had as much to lose as I did.

Suddenly, I yanked my head up from her crotch. I was bawling like a baby. Not Stoic tears. Great hiccups of despair. At first, they were the sorrow from realizing my search for home wasn't the lonely path I'd thought. It was Miranda's journey, too. Maybe everyone's. I couldn't escape the abyss by asking Miranda to steady me because she was trying—like me—to make it to *the end*, to contentment and peace.

Then my sobs turned into something deeper: the inchoate, inarticulate wail that I wasn't the narrator I pretended to be. That's when I fell off the bed.

Miranda jumped down and started rubbing my back as I curled up on my side.

At last, I thought, the real story can begin.

"My mother's always had problems," Miranda said, trying to find a way out. She was on surer footing now, trying to comfort *me*. "I should have told you. I meant to. Mental. Institutional." Her hand made small circles along my spine. "We'll figure out how we can. . . ."

I swallowed hard. Truth-telling can be contagious. "I was once in love with a guy," I said.

Her hand stopped. It was warm against my skin. "What's 'in love'?" she asked.

How could I explain? Could I tell her I fell in love with William Blake or Alex or some weird combination of the two?

Instead, I said, "I tried to kill myself."

She stayed silent.

"I'm like *The Canterbury Tales*," I tried to explain.

"What?"

"A bunch of unfinished stories."

Reading Chaucer's masterpiece, I now saw myself as a pilgrimage of stories, all trying to be heard in a world whose moral arc bends toward silence. In one of the great works of Western literature, I could hear echoes of the half-finished stories inside me. Not some might-have-been. Or even a "was." Oddly, and truer, too, an "almost is." Much of what's in me, maybe in all of us, was as incomplete as *The Canterbury Tales*. I no longer needed to read to see all of myself. The pieces were enough. The half-told tales. The truth in fragments.

Admittedly, the unfinished business of a failed suicide attempt was easier to tell in the early '80s than some of my other stories. Miranda's hand started to move again.

"You tried to kill yourself because you'd slept with this guy?" she asked.

"No."

"Did you want to?"

"I don't know."

"You don't know?"

"I couldn't tell."

"You either did or you didn't."

"It wasn't like that. It was about. . . ." I thought about falling asleep in Alex's arms. "I'd wanted to see myself in books for so long. Then there was this guy who sort of looked like me. As lost as I was. As alone."

"And that's it?" Miranda asked. She sounded more determined, corporate.

"Not really," I said, telling the whole truth.

"Did you sleep with him?" she asked again, more flatly, maybe even sure that my problem was just another she could solve.

"You mean, um, sex?" I stammered. "No. Not at all."

We were trying so hard. How could it take so much effort when we were so near the beginning—which also felt like the end? Ladies and gentleman, I present to you Mr. and Mrs. Scarbrough.

Her hand kept moving. "We'll get through this," she said.

"How?" I asked.

"Because we love each other."

She'd answered "why." But I'd asked a harder question, a narrative one.

What else could she say? It was long before *Will and Grace*. Sure, everyone knew a gay man, especially in the South, some two-bit Uncle Arthur who led people around an antebellum mansion and lectured them on the importance of the Jefferson cup. But there were no gay couples at work, church, next door. Maybe in San Francisco or New York. But in Dallas? Miranda would have to tell her parents that they'd been right. He's not for me. He's a. . . .

Except I wasn't. A rumble in the slats, after all. I loved her in the depths of my being. Down where I'd laid my hopes in boxes, she'd made a home. Everything I'd read pointed to her. Everything I'd experienced, too. Melody, Alex, all the novels and poems—they were rehearsals for Miranda. More than that, in some quantum confusion, they were echoes of her. Fragments of her.

We got back up on the bed and held each other. We stayed like that until dawn, well on our way to morphing our doubts into our passions.

"I can't make a mistake," she said.

"I won't let you. By God, if women had written the stories, we'd see things differently."

She shook her head. "What are you talking about?"

I was ventriloquizing Chaucer. His complete works sat on the bedside table next to me. I reached over and put my hand on the cover. It felt smooth and cold. It felt true.

Miranda, however, reached down and held my dick. Maybe to do the same thing I was doing when I put my hand on Chaucer's book: to make sure we were who we said we were.

"We can make this work," she said.

Her touch felt so comfortable, so far from loneliness. I wanted to tell the story right. "We can make this work because we want to," I said.

She nodded.

"Need to," I added.

"No, you went too far. We can walk away right now."

"Do you want to?" I asked.

"No. You?"

"No, I don't think so."

"Think?" she asked.

It's not what I meant. I wanted to say something about sex and stories, about ambiguity and truth, about the narrator and the way even the best stories escape him. But I couldn't go that far. I didn't trust the ground under my feet. So I buried my face between her breasts and said another truth. "I love you."

She pulled in closer, although it was a hot Texas morning. "Me, too."

"I'll keep my word," I said.

She let go of me. "What?"

"It's Arveragus."

She was silent, uncharacteristically so.

"Chaucer," I said.

She rolled onto her back. "You never give up." But she was smiling. This was the easy part. "Okay, tell me," she laughed.

I did, even though I thought we were going to make love.

In the Franklin's Tale, Arveragus goes off on a knightly quest, leaving his wife alone. She begins to obsess about the black rocks that poke up offshore. What if he is shipwrecked on his way home? She hires a young student who knows magic. She promises him anything he wants. He casts a spell, the rocks disappear, and her husband comes home. No more worries, except the student demands payment. "You said I could have anything—and I want you." She fights him off for a bit. Then her husband almost forces her to go to bed with the guy to keep their honor intact.

"The highest thing a person may keep is his word," Arveragus says.

"That's the best marriage argument I know," I told Miranda.

It was, because it brought me full circle. It expressed the medieval equivalent of חסד, *chesed*.

I knew our plot's conclusion, even if the filament of time was still wound around the present. We would get married and set up an enviable life. I would become a committed academic, trapped in libraries at night, my passion for books unchecked. Miranda would become a success in a time when women weren't welcome in the boardroom.

For now, it was enough to love her. And to love Chaucer. I bound the three of us in a tight embrace. I fell asleep with my head on her chest and rumbled down the long road to the journey's end: a feast ahead, the famine probably behind me.

Geoffrey Chaucer in Kalamazoo

Holy hell, if some combination of *The Canterbury Tales* and Miranda had helped me negotiate the stories about love without losing my mind, then the great works of Western literature weren't walls that divided the world into neat parts *and* divided me from everything I wanted. They were foundations. I could build anything on top of them. I could fit into any story. That is, be anyone. And be myself. Which still seemed like two ways of saying the same thing.

That spring, I took an independent study to further develop my paper on The Parson's Tale. I worked with Dr. Olivia Keller, a commanding presence who'd churned out a nineteen-hundred-page dissertation on The Knight's Tale, the first story in *The Canterbury Tales*. On the side, she also hacked out articles on Ryan O'Neal's sex life and Kenny Loggins' hair for *People Magazine*. She was bird thin and (unlike me) staunchly single.

"I'll need your paper two weeks before finals," she said. She was skipping out to attend the world largest hootenanny for medievalists, held in Kalamazoo at Western Michigan University. She mentioned a few panels that were still open.

Was that a hint? Should I submit my seminar paper? Miranda goaded me on. She'd already broken glass ceilings. "Why not?" she said.

I took her advice. I also thought about how Chaucer had wormed his way into the court of Henry IV after the coup against his patron, Richard II. And I fudged my cover letter, making a vague claim about "grad school." I wasn't a Ph.D. candidate. I didn't even have a Master's. But I reasoned I had a good shot at a professional conference for tenured types because no one writes about The Parson's Tale.

I also didn't tell Dr. Keller. I told myself all this academic stuff was a subplot in my brave new story with Miranda.

I got accepted to a panel a few weeks later. I left the letter in Dr. Keller's box. I kept telling myself she'd be pleased with my bravery. Or ambition. Maybe just with me.

She was furious. She summoned me to her office, the Texas heat glaring in the windows.

"The hell are you doing?" she asked, her blue eyes piercing mine. The smooth moles that colonized her neck and threatened her cheeks seemed to darken with her ire. She hammered me with all the things that could go wrong. She called me a liar, the most unkind cut, especially if I could put my hand on *The Canterbury Tales* and make Miranda understand who I was in bed.

I stammered out an excuse. "You didn't tell me I had to be a . . . to have a. . . ."

Dr. Keller softened under my inarticulate blather and flashed a wry grin. "You're not going to get away with pretending to be someone you aren't. You don't even know Latin."

"I know Hebrew."

"Oh, good, because Chaucer didn't."

"I once pretended I could dance."

She squinted at me. "What the hell are you talking about?"

This: there were lots of ways home.

Dr. Keller wouldn't have understood that. She was too busy having a good time at my expense. "Dammit, we're all stuck at this Harvard on the highway. . . ." She took a deep breath and stacked papers together. "Okay, listen, I've got a big interview at this year's conference. I'm gunning for a better job in Minnesota. The Chaucerian died. Medievalists don't die. Not routinely. I don't want my peers to think I'm skirting the rules with you."

I wanted to say, This story isn't about you. Instead, I said: "You won't even know I'm there."

A few weeks before my wedding, I deplaned at a two-gate regional airport and took the shuttle to a campus overrun with habits and cowls. Their inhabitants knocked around hacky sacks and listened to The Clash on scratchy cassettes. Like me, they'd read too much and missed their undergrad years. So they showed up on campus for their dream sophomore experience: to discuss St. Thomas Aquinas by day, then get wasted and throw up on the quad at night.

They were serious scholars playing around. I was playing around at being a serious scholar. I spent the afternoon holed up in my dorm room, a spare cell. I'd fused literature and love but still felt out of sync. I should have been congratulating myself. But I missed sessions and went to bed early.

The next morning, hunger forced me out of my hiding place. I was no longer good at waiting days between meals. I called this "emotional progress."

The long, dark cafeteria was appropriately medieval. It horked up overcooked, mushy fare with a funky aroma. I filled a plate with mealy pancakes and limp bacon, then picked a corner table to watch the cassocks and wimples.

Unfolding my napkin, I bowed my head to pray. Whenever I felt out of my depth, I still went through the motions of piety, even if my prayers sounded like modernist poetry, a pastiche of fragments and clauses I'd once believed.

That's how I missed her entrance. Or maybe she appeared out of nowhere.

"You can't be saying the paternoster," she laughed.

She was a small woman, maybe five-one, in her early thirties. Her sweatshirt featured a sequined, bucking bronco. I would soon discover that she was the embodiment of medieval lit and my best gatekeeper to the canon since Dr. Franklin. She would lead me to read as widely as I ever dared and teach me how to harmonize the plots in my head.

All that was the future. For now, I was speechless.

"Speak, sweet bird, or I know not where thou art," she said, quoting one of Chaucer's tales. "You want company or not?"

My mannerly upbringing came to rescue. "I'd be delighted." I motioned to the chair across from me.

"Yep, I hear the South in your mouth." She plopped down and stuck out her hand. "Alphonsa. It's nun. Or ex-nun. You can't be a nun when you've got a lover who's a lady. Or maybe you can. Damn modern world. Anyway, Alphonsa. Immy to my friends. Call me what you want."

People form quick friendships at conventions, but she didn't even stand on that ceremony.

"Let me guess," she said. "A Protestant? You're going to piss off half the brothers here. Okay, the girls call me Immy. As in Alphonsa of the Immaculate Conception. At least, the ones who haven't taken a vow of silence."

She roared with laughter. Was that a joke? Like almost everyone else in the Middle Ages, she was a Christian in every way I could never be: ironic, detached, crusading roughshod over the world.

She pressed on without a breath. "I don't really know why I kept the name after I left the order. I was born Jean Holtz. You can call me Jean if Martin Luther has you by the balls. Or John Calvin. You look like the Calvin type. Oh, say, you got the bacon. Don't get the bacon. Is this your first time? Of course it is. What are you writing on? Don't tell me. Chaucer."

She brooked no manners, a force almost as raw as Blake, but more sardonic and therefore—as I was coming to understand after spending so much time with Chaucer—more human. I never once smelled the fires of the apocalypse on her. She didn't want to save me. At least, not yet. And I didn't need saving. At least, not yet.

"I'm giving a paper on The Parson's Tale," I said.

Immy looked aghast. "Why?"

"Why? Because I can. Or want to."

"Which is it?"

I didn't answer. "Don't you want to know my argument?"

"If I have to. Man, I used to love the ones about straight people fucking. Miller's Tale, Merchant's. Morbid curiosity. But I'm glad someone's working on the Parson. No Catholic would." She shoveled up gobs of scrambled eggs. "Grad school, right? Or are you some baby genius with tenure? I hope not. What are you writing your dissertation on?"

Had she already found me out? "Probably not The Parson's Tale."

"Do tell." She chewed with her mouth open. "What else you got?"

Mostly, a story she didn't fit, although I wanted to be closer to her by the minute. "I had a fling with William Blake once," I said, trying to find common ground.

She wrinkled her nose as if at a bad smell. "Oh, the this-then-that thing called you. Right." She crossed her arms. "Okay, you did it with Blake. And you lived to tell the truth."

"You're closer to the truth than you think."

She hooked a thumb into her sweatshirt. "Nun, lesbian. Comes with the territory."

Was I living *The Canterbury Tales*? A nun and I on the way to some place better? If so, the best thing was to keep talking, like the rest of the pilgrims. "I was once in a production of *Godspell*."

"You're killing me."

"But I wanted to get back to books. I've always had this weird relationship with words."

She stretched out her arms to take in the room. "Club, meet you. Enjoy the day."

Despite her bravado, I recognized the loneliness in her eyes. She'd chosen to eat with a guy she didn't know. Maybe she was too much for most people, but she was exactly what I needed when I needed it. Was life really a plot? Why didn't this feel like any other I'd been in?

Immy launched into gossipy details about the conference: who got tenure where, who was sleeping with whom. I didn't recognize a single name. But I wanted to know more about her, to find a treasure at the bottom of all this overflow. What if she was my birth mother?

The notion was bats. She was at most ten years older than I was. But I'd always hoped my birth mother would appear out of nowhere and demand an immediate connection.

Immy circled back to books. "God, I hope you weren't one of those louche English majors. Sweetie, let me tell you about what I've read while you look at my dick."

I laughed to stop her. I didn't want *that* conversation. "Honestly," I said, "I can't seem to have a thought without its having been in a book."

"Now we're onto something."

"But once I met Miranda. . . ."

"Your dissertation director?"

"My fiancée."

Immy ran her hand through her hair and deadpanned: "Your fiancée? How?"

Now I quoted a line of *The Canterbury Tales*. "Whan that Aprille with his shoures soote. Does 'how' really matter?"

"Morbid curiosity."

"Okay, well, I'd been to seminary and. . . ."

"Say no more."

"We're getting married at the end of the month."

Immy whistled a long note. "Okay, tell me the marriage argument."

"The Wife of Bath is a feminist," I smirked, offering the name of one of Chaucer's pilgrims who tells a complicated tale about a woman's place in medieval society.

Immy didn't take the bait. "No, she's not. The Wife of Bath's a liar. You boys confuse the two. Listen, you do what you need to do. There are hundreds of ways to be married. It's only individual couples who don't think so. Promising love is the hardest thing we do."

I gasped. There it was: חסד, *chesed*.

Immy didn't notice. She was too busy making fun of me. "Should I go on spraying you with clichés or do you get the point?"

I'd spent so long trying to control the words in every conversation that I had no idea how to handle one with Immy. "At least she's a Catholic," I said.

"The Wife?"

"No, mine to be."

"And who am I to judge?"

"She's not a Catholic anymore."

"Please be an atheist. Don't tell me you're getting married with those bouncy Jesus songs. Would it kill you people to do a nice *Agnus Dei*?"

I nodded.

She tsked. "What do her parents say?"

Another thing I didn't need to explain. "They're not coming to the wedding."

Immy rolled her shoulders. "I wouldn't either."

"That's not nice!"

"And you're not my child." She must have sensed my hurt because she added, "Sometimes, we have to take a stand for what we believe in."

I tried to be brave, to make sense. "I'm not getting married to take a stand."

"No, you're not, Mr. Parson's Tale. You gonna eat that?" She stabbed at the bacon on my plate.

"You said to skip it!"

"To leave more for me! Shit, you're easy. This is going to be a great weekend. Here's the deal. I'm a choir director."

She named a liberal arts college. She specialized in polyphony, the intricate tapestry of melody lines, the forerunner of the grand fugues Bach would write.

"I'm conducting a concert," she said. "Well, I told you it was a concert so you wouldn't freak out. It's a mass. Come to the rehearsal in the morning. Hey, when's your paper? I'll come to your session. We should hang out."

Yes, we should. She could be my academic beard. I wouldn't need to worry that some prof might find out I was faking it. That I'd only recently read all of *The Canterbury Tales*. That my renewed reason to read the great books was my impending nuptials. Or was it the other way around? I could get married *because* I was reading again?

Point was, it didn't matter. Every answer fit. Relieved, I headed off to a day of sessions. Maybe I still believed in God. Maybe grace did get poured into this world through the most unlikely channels.

The next morning, I went to Immy's rehearsal and sat in a wooden chair against the cathedral's back wall. The choir launched into complicated polyphony. The music started with one voice, then added another, and another, layering the next on top of the last, no voice dominant. I had to work to hear the lines, as if the music were an amalgam—all the parts, distinct; the voices, separate.

I could feel the music around me, in me, in *The Canterbury Tales*, a book that celebrated individual voices. All the storytellers fell together in a great mash-up, making one work from their separate tales. Like me with Miranda in bed. Like Immy with her failed vows and successful career. The answer to life's muddle was not to be a narrator. I should have paid closer attention. To Chaucer, yes. But even to the writers and editors of Isaiah. The answer to my fears, doubts, and joys was to see them as pieces of many stories. To be lots of narrators. No life was one plot. I could keep all of them in balance by treating them as polyphony, a tale of tales.

After the rehearsal, I hung back and waited for Immy. She was fussy, distracted. "Working with amateurs," she said in the noontime warmth. "They want to. Mostly, they can't. I've got six ringers and a bunch of old academics. I'm pushing notes uphill."

I didn't say much. Polyphony swirled in my head. It made sense of Chaucer. It made sense of me.

Immy wanted to change before coming to my session. She said she'd meet me at my room in twenty minutes.

I walked across the workaday campus. So many voices, I thought. The whole canon of Western literature was a library of voices. Interweaving. Plural. Ever-changing but one thing.

I'd long thought I had to pick a voice and call it mine. But life was harder, deeper. For the first time, I thought, I should be an academic. An English prof. A collector, a narrator of the narrators. Someone who could let the voices run free. Who let them interact with each other. Who reveled in the play of consonance and dissonance.

I'd never met a prof like that, but I told myself a life in books was naturally polyphonic. As my life had to be. So many distinct parts, separate voices. I didn't have to choose. I wasn't the boy for every story. They all could fit in me.

I got into my suit, a narrow black one from years before. I stuffed my paper in my backpack. The Parson? The ending? No way! Life was among the storytellers.

Immy knocked on my door as the phone rang. I picked up the clunky receiver, stretched the cord, opened the door, and heard Miranda in a panic. Wedding plans had run afoul.

"The caterers lost their liquor license," she said. "What happened to hiring the best?"

We were paying for our own reception. Well, she was paying for it. She'd cashed out her savings for a grand soirée. I was contributing what I could. Mostly, I handled the details.

"I'll take care of it when I get home," I said, trying to *there, there* her.

But she stunned me speechless. "We can't back out now."

Despite my craving for the middle of things, I was suddenly scared, as if I'd just heard her Parson's Tale, her own ending.

"Who said anything about backing out?" I asked, motioning for Immy to sit down. "Miranda, I. . . ?"

"Say it!" Immy called out.

"Who's that?" Miranda asked.

"Someone I met. An ex-nun."

"Oh, great. She probably smacked my hand with a ruler once. Did you tell her about us?"

"The whole thing," I lied.

"She's going to say I shouldn't marry you."

"She already did. First time we met."

Immy reached over and put her hand on my knee. "Tell her what else I said."

I smiled. "She wants me to tell you that we sound like the perfect couple."

Immy frowned. "I never said that."

Even so, I went on, spinning another tale. "She said we have to take a stand for what we believe in."

Immy nodded. "It's called the grace of God," she said, again loud enough for Miranda to hear.

"It is not!" Miranda barked. "It's harder than that. On top of everything, caterers. How am I going to tell people?"

"About the booze?" I asked. "Don't worry. I'll hire a. . . ."

Miranda sighed. "I mean, about why my parents aren't there."

Finally, something I knew. "To tell a story," I said, "just start at the beginning."

Immy shook her head. Liar, she mouthed.

I glared at her. "Or that's one way to do it," I said to Miranda. "You put it together piece by piece."

Miranda had had enough. "Yes, I know. I didn't mean 'tell people.' I meant make it right, make *me* right. We're barely hanging on financially. I have to go. Call me when you're done."

I put the receiver back in its cradle.

"You don't get to see that shit in a convent," Immy said. "I guess now's as good a time as any. I'd like to give you something. For your marriage." She pulled a slip of paper out of her pocket. Scrawled across it in a crabbed hand was this:

> *Life is so short, any skill takes so long to learn, any attempt is so hard, any victory is so sharp, any joy slips away so quickly—by all this I mean love.*

I looked hard at her. "Why?"

"It's sexual, you know?"

"I don't."

"Fine. Just pray it. Every day."

I had no idea I would. "I'm late," I said. I slipped the paper into my jacket pocket.

Immy scowled. "You don't have to thank me."

"You wrote that?" I still hadn't read enough to know.

"Sure," she said. "Don't lose it."

I didn't. I carried it down the aisle at my wedding. Eventually, I found a silver Victorian pillbox for it. I folded the prayer into a lozenge and tucked it inside. It became my relic, a sacred way to ball what was and what will be into the middle of one of the many stories of who I was.

For now, we had minutes to get to my panel. We ran a bit, walked a bit. "Thank God for sensible nun shoes," Immy huffed.

I made it to the room just as the session was starting. I scrambled to the front, knocking askew folding chairs. My paper was up last. I had time to catch my breath.

Dr. Keller came in right before I was introduced. The leader of the panel had been shocked at my minimal credentials. He said something about my "grad work," rather than my dissertation. I stepped up to the podium. Immy beamed. Dr. Keller lowered her eyes.

"With The Parson's Tale, *The Canterbury Tales* comes to a satisfactory close," I said.

I didn't believe my argument anymore, but I could say those words, another unfinished tale. In truth, conclusions were just a fancy way of talking about a world without stories, about silence. But even Chaucer's book wouldn't end. Here we were, still talking about it.

I'd found something better than Blake's poetry or Hebrew roots, better than a long drive across the Texas prairie. Stories exist for their characters. Maybe that's the ultimate marriage argument. It's a test of your character.

Afterwards, a couple of Chaucerians came up and asked where I was studying. Dr. Keller scooted to the rescue. "He's with me," she said.

A short woman with severe hair squinted at me. "What are you writing on?"

Dr. Keller caught her arm. "He'll decide when he gets into a Ph.D. program," she said.

"Let's talk."

She started to lead the woman away, then said in a stage whisper to me, "Wisconsin. Good money."

Later that night, as I walked to Immy's concert, I tore my conference paper to shreds, dropping the bits in street corner trash cans. I didn't need to keep something I didn't believe in. I could indulge in a minor purge and lose one voice when there were so many more.

The cathedral was packed. I sat in that same wooden chair. Again, the music covered me, a tangle of lines. I heard *The Canterbury Tales* in it, counterpoint in print, voices interweaving, commenting, disagreeing, on the road to a holy shrine that held the hope of the afterlife, a mystical presence in this physical world and not the damning silence of time's lapse.

What grand fun to set out on a spring morning and talk about love! To tell tales of men who aspire too high, roosters who do the same, bed tricks and bets that end in bed tricks, the good life and the better one. This great chorus of talkers wound down to my Parson, but he couldn't tame them. They were the choral strains of life. Vocal exercises, the chords and intervals of meaning.

Here's how I loved Miranda. Sometimes, when I emptied the dishwasher, she passed behind me, casually running her finger down the curve of my butt. Later, stretched out in bed, I turned over and grazed her crotch with my hand. Impromptu touching. Finger exercises, the chords and intervals of affection.

In a few weeks, she'd walk down the aisle to crashing arpeggios. There'd be a large wedding party but not her parents. Mother and Dad would sit on the front row and look at me with peace in their eyes. Miranda and I would promise outrageous things that would prove us liars. I would cry. She would stay calm, self-assured.

We wouldn't make love on our first night married. We'd fall asleep against each other and drive the next day to our honeymoon. We'd spend the night at a roadside motel in Amarillo, Texas. We'd make love there, the first time as a married couple. It wouldn't go well. I'd give up trying to come. If we'd have listened, we'd have heard the gears of the plot we were constructing. Instead, we'd say we had forever to try again.

We'd drive on to a national park, as much as I could afford. We'd hike for a week, then come home and start a life together, start what happens after the marriage argument: a final year in my Master's program, her ascent up the corporate ladder, another paper at Kalamazoo, and a slow slide down the timeline of life.

She was going to give me a story that explained who I was. I was going to give her one that separated her from her family. And we were going to make a new one together. It was all irresistible, the essence of coupling: a polyphony of plots that kept coming together so pilgrimage of life could go on and on.

In the cathedral that night, the choral voices flowed toward consonance, unity, singularity. Then they split apart, distinct, articulated, an entrance here, another there, a hymn to the many stories that make up who we are and the many ways we tell our one story among the others. The music was glorious and redemptive. I wished it would never end. Then it did.

The Last of the Mohicans

Madison, Wisconsin, was surely hot once in a while: July, the first of August. I only remember it as frigid and bleak. In the 1980s, the lakes downtown still froze into solid sheets. Somebody plunked down traffic cones so commuters could drive across parts of the white expanse, rather than around it, one of the many examples of a can-do, you-bet Scandinavian spirit befitting the icy floor of hell.

Olivia Keller had worked out my fate. I'd come to the university for my Ph.D. thinking it was the next leg of my quest through the great books. I didn't know it was the polar terminus.

On the shore of one of the lakes, the English department was garrisoned in the top floors of a concrete block of a building that looked like a set out of the later, low-budget *Planet of the Apes* movies. The place was a walk-up outpost, some Midwestern Checkpoint Charlie in the no-man's-land of tenure attrition. The graying office-squatters held the line against grad students and assistant professors zombified by French literary theory.

The old dons could have kept their powder dry. The battle was lost, but not in the way they feared. The department had long been funded by an undergrad English requirement: fourteen or fifteen sections of introductory lit per semester, each class chock full of hundreds of sophomores with at least half a dozen teaching assistants per prof. In the year I arrived, a gaggle of science and ag deans decreed that any university class even vaguely literary could fulfill the basic requirement. The money that supported the old guard dried up overnight, done in by "The Rhetoric of Fashion Magazines" and "German Comic Books: Then and Now." Adjuncts began to replace retiring faculty. The number of Ph.D. seminars dwindled, even as their membership bumped from eight to fifteen and beyond.

The lone medieval offering quickly filled and closed. So on the first day of a new life that seemed to be signposted by publish-or-perish, tenure, and retirement, I got gobsmacked by budget woes, a late start in line, and maybe the promise of a little more Faulkner before I lost myself forever to Chaucer—probably the only set of conditions guaranteed to fuck up your life. I enrolled in "The American Project" with Dr. Tom Prescott.

Before classes began, he stuck his syllabus in our mailboxes with a note scrawled in his shaky hand: "No sessions the first two weeks so you can read it."

His reading list had about twenty titles, half of which were standard American fare: *The Last of the Mohicans*, *The Portrait of a Lady*, *The Great Gatsby*. The rest ranged across British and even world literature: *Jane Eyre*, *Crime and Punishment*.

Some grad student dropped Prescott a note asking what "it" was, which title we should read first. He photocopied that note for each of us and scrawled a single line across it: "The syllabus, lads!"

Twenty books in two weeks. Prescott was my kind of guy.

I arrived at the first session a few minutes late. A fine, frozen, mid-September mizzle spattered the windows. My peers were wrapped in threadbare coats and scarves. I was in creased wool pants, a white shirt, and a brown check blazer. Miranda had secured a corporate transfer to Madison. We'd come to a Ph.D. program with professional movers and a comfy per diem. The first Gulf War was on and grad students were marching in the streets at night, while I was unpacking bone china and cut crystal.

Everyone in the seminar was jammed at the far end of a white laminate table. The chairs at either side of the head were empty, so I chose one. I said a very Southern "hello." No one answered. I didn't know a soul. I'd been holed up in the library with Prescott's list, a contented reader.

After about fifteen minutes, a scarecrow kid with wild hair asked, "How long do we give him?"

As if to answer the question, Dr. Prescott shambled in with the fetor of unwashed wool. He was a doughy sixty-something whose chest sloped to his paunch. His hair shot out in Toscanini puffs; his teeth were rimmed with his lunch. He carried a beat-up copy of *The Last of the Mohicans*, as well as *Madame Bovary* and Kierkegaard's *Fear and Trembling*, neither on the syllabus.

Prescott dropped the books at the head of the table and backed his chair up against the door, possibly to bar the exit. Then he sat down, leaned forward, and put his hands on his rumpled trousers, the proper pose for his question: "If you saw Doctor Zhivago, Jane Eyre, and Mrs. Dalloway hitchhiking on I-90 east of town, which would you pick up?"

No one said anything until the scarecrow asked, "Aren't you starting with *The Last of the Mohicans*?"

Prescott blinked like the Mad Hatter, reared back, and hollered, "Have it your way, lad! *The Last of the Mohicans* predicts the 1894 Pullman Strike! Natty was the forerunner of our first socialist presidential candidate, Eugene Debs!"

Actually, no. The novel's an American classic set during the Seven Years' War and written almost seventy years before the labor unrest Prescott had mentioned. Truth be told, even its historically-based battles at Lake George, New York, are little more than a cheap backdrop. The book's real business is Natty Bumppo, the consummate American frontiersman and Cooper's elegy to an already-lost, don't-tread-on-me past.

"Young man," Prescott said, fixing his rheumy eyes on me—probably because I was the student nearest to him, although I'd like to think he knew our fate. "What did you think when you first arrived at Fort William Henry?"

I shifted in my seat. I didn't know his game yet. "I think Cooper's trying to. . . ."

"Who? No, you. What did *you* think when you got there?"

"I've never been to. . . ."

"Haven't you read the book?"

I'd come to learn that he meant, Haven't you memorized it? But he didn't wait for my answer. "There shall be no turncoats! Onward to World War I!"

Natty was apparently the forerunner of that, too. Or at least of Georges Clemenceau. Really, Natty was a catalyst, not a character, pushing Prescott beyond the facts, maybe even beyond the fiction, out into the open expanse of the human imagination.

Prescott seemed to tent in Bumppo's world. Or maybe Bumppo homesteaded down the street in Madison, because Prescott saw no difference between our world and *The Last of the Mohicans*—or in fact, among any of the worlds in the books he loved. Madame Bovary tented in upstate New York, too.

True, these were the last days of the freaks and crackpots warehoused in English departments, the tweedy nuts who couldn't find their cars in otherwise empty parking lots. Even so, Prescott stood out. He was an American original, as bonkers as Henry Ford or Theodore Roosevelt. And all that I'd hoped for.

Prescott soon launched into a diatribe about the Missouri Compromise.

"It's not about a state. It's a fulcrum! Pay attention to this Senator Danforth!"

And somehow about baseball.

"Because he's our national shortstop! The pop fly lands in the Midwest. Saint Louis is second base. But all of you knew that!"

His ravings were bound together with Cooper's vision of the frontier. Prescott sank back in his chair and recited a passage from *The Last of the Mohicans*, his creed from a place where the difference between "is" and "might be" was irrelevant:

> *I've heard it said that there are men who read in books to convince themselves there is a God. I know not but man may so deform his works in the settlements, as to leave that which is so clear in the wilderness a matter of doubt among traders and priests.*

"Don't you see?" Prescott pleaded. "Cooper's writing about Danforth's Missouri. Well, not Missouri in a novel set before the Revolutionary War." He let his eyes focus on the windows, not the fallow fields out on the horizon. "Cooper's writing about the idea that becomes Missouri."

My peers pulled their scarves tighter. They had little patience for his reconnaissance mission into the wilderness of meaning.

But I did. Ever since I'd been tricked into thinking *Great Expectations* was just grammar, ever since I'd renewed a failed relationship with the great books by obsessing over Isaiah's words and studying Chaucer to make my way into a polyphonic world, I'd been on the lookout for a prof like him. He was to become my last and greatest "voice crying in the wilderness." Not a competing voice, nor a compiling one. He was all of them at once, a Stones concert and an early Renaissance mass at the same time and in the same room.

My search had been a mad one . . . yes, mad. Is there any other way? A mad search for the fullness of time that can loosen the vice of the tick-tock and sound the call for a rapture, maybe not into heaven, but at least into this present moment. Although I still didn't have a real beginning, I could narrate a bunch of tales that made up the past. Although I'd lost my apocalyptic notion of the end of everything, I still knew the future: married, Miranda. All that mattered now was, well, *now*. I could follow Prescott's scouting and walk securely into what so defied me: our Einsteinian logjam, the present moment, made of all that had come before and all that would come after, all that had been read and ever would be.

Sure, Prescott went too far. But how far is too far when all that is—or as he would have put it, "the truth, dammit, lad!"—was at stake? He strode the crosshatch of timelines and never worried about falling between them because they kept proliferating around him, reinforcing each other the more he read.

That semester, I settled in to a familiar routine. I started reading widely, following up on hints Prescott dropped in seminar, the names of American authors I'd never heard: William Gilmore Simms, Charlotte Lenox, Nathaniel Ward. Books that only experts read, that define the literary canon by its margins.

By mid-semester, Prescott was onto Edith Wharton, although he still kept bringing the discussion back to Natty Bumppo. Somehow, Lily Bart in *The House of Mirth* was a rewriting of Rosalind from Shakespeare's *As You Like It*, if—and only if—the whole thing had been sieved through James Fenimore Cooper.

"Which brings us to the American Football League," he said.

I heard an exasperated sigh from the woman next to me. "Has he no shame?" she asked.

Rona was a formidable presence, all spiky hair and wiry glasses, a second-wave feminist given to ironic interpretations and the grapefruit glaze of Nina Ricci perfume. She had a boundless intellect and scoured Madison's rag shops for vintage Chanel. She was also a department celebrity: on decent grant money and a fixture at academic conferences. Her desk sat next to mine in one of the faceless T.A. offices.

Just a few days before, Prescott had burst in, pointed at her, and said, "Bring your blunderbuss to class this week, lass."

She'd told him quite clearly to "fuck off."

He'd chuckled and stalked away. "Atta girl!"

In his canonical brain, she'd confirmed her role. By this point, he had one for each of us. He'd fused us into various fictional characters, as if they, not we, sat in his class. Blond and blue-eyed Rona was none other than dark-haired Cora Munro, whose miscegenated past threatens to ruin American history from the get-go in *The Last of the Mohicans*.

Prescott must have heard her disbelief about Cooper and football. He slumped back in his chair and said, "Okay, let's have Cora tell us what she felt when Uncas saved the girls."

She felt outrage. "We'd rather talk about the play of discourses in the novel! I mean, can't we come up with a single, cogent interpretation of just one book?"

Prescott stared at his crotch, waiting for her to come around.

She did. We all did. He was inescapable. He was the only truly irredeemable individual I ever met. He was obstinately himself, not in need of a resurrection, a new heaven, or a new earth.

Rona sighed. "I knew the French fort was no place for an English woman."

He shot up in his seat. "Exactly!" He turned to me again. "Natty. . . ."

Because I'd somehow become the supreme woodsman and forest guide. I, who'd hiked in the national parks as a kid and mostly remembered them for their decent signage and good ice cream. I was the Deerslayer, the Pathfinder, Leatherstocking, *La Longue Carabine*, Hawkeye, me.

"Natty," he said, "when you found Cora dead, did you feel history had ended?"

By now, I'd gotten the hang of his style, his freedom. I turned to Rona. "Why don't we ask her, since she's sitting right here?"

He didn't seem to credit my playing along as he had hers. For a moment, he looked at me as if *I* were insane. Then he picked up his ragged copy of the novel and shook it until loose pages sifted onto the table. "If you don't push a book into your flesh, you have no right to teach it, lad. Books belong in your spit."

Yes! I'd always come at the great works with the heart of a zealot, thinking *The Canterbury Tales* or Blake's poetry offered the right way to see the world. Or that they were "right" in some fundamental way. But Prescott showed me that the great books were an imaginative wilderness, a vast overlay of plots on plots, poems on poems, the sedimentary layering of meaning on the flat floor of civilizations long gone. He was content out in the expanse—digging through the layers, mixing them up—because the point was not *how* the great works built solid ground under his feet, but simply that he could stride across it.

I stayed after class to ask him a question about my seminar paper. He threw his arm around my shoulder. "Do you really want to know why Fort William Henry is important?"

Was this a quiz? I shook my head.

"Then you leave tomorrow," he said. "You have a car, right?"

"Oh, well, I can't.... I have to...."

"You need gas money?"

"No, I'm.... My wife is a...."

He glanced down the hall. "We let women in here, too. Next the homosexuals." He slapped my back, then tromped off to his office. "See you when you get back!"

I never went to Fort William Henry, but Prescott didn't follow up. He could barely recall our encounters from one day to the next. I forgave him because he and he alone turned the great works into what they should have been all along: a rupture in my continuum that revealed not the multiverse around me, but the one *in* me as a committed reader.

I started jonesing for books as physical objects. I never had before, maybe because I didn't grow up with a home library. I had those few volumes left from my Baylor purge and a few more from my Master's program. Before the semester started, I'd neatly lined them on snap-together shelves in my home office, a corner room in an Art Deco saltbox. Here it is, I'd congratulated myself, thumbing the spine. *The Complete Works Of Samuel Taylor Coleridge*.

It wasn't enough. I took to buying the books for every English class, grad or undergrad. At home, I opened them one by one, pressing my nose against their spines. Paperback classics were the best: slightly pulpy but sweet, not cloying, hints of vanilla tempered by late winter leaves. Academic presses went for astringent glue, pungent but bracingly clean, like my palms after Miranda and I made love and I washed up. Small presses published contemporary poetry with a bright, peach-tinged aroma, studded with the vinegary hints of early spring.

I quickly ran out of space and started stacking books in corners, piling them in towers. One day, I tried to feel their weight. I stood in the middle of the room, stretched my arms into a T, and imagined balancing the titles in my palms. I quivered with the tension along my spine. The pain would be clarifying. Beautiful. Hordes of words in the pans of my hands.

I swore I heard my forearms crack. I yelled, dropped everything, and came to myself.

Why had I let Blake leave me on that country road? I'd been so close to *the truth, dammit, lad!* So close to touching the ineffable mystery that lay underneath the words.

Clearly, I was still too weak. But I knew what I had to do. I had to follow Prescott onward. And I had to keep Miranda near me. With her, there was no danger of madness or suicide in the face of the great works.

I went downstairs, pulled out a grill pan, and started dinner: seared salmon and a chopped salad. I'd taken over kitchen duties because my schedule was more flexible than hers. Plus, eating was something like reading: more in, more in.

I'd started putting on weight, which surprised me. I was now 180 pounds, more than I'd ever been. I loved the feeling that my body was no longer an addendum. It, too, seemed rooted in this bookish now.

A key slid into the front door. I could hear Miranda set down her briefcase and hang her coat in the hall closet.

"Hey there," I called. Every time I heard her, saw her, even thought about her, my relief was exquisite, as if I'd been holding my breath. She was the remainder in my elegant equation, what was left after the great works summed up the world. She was the person who loved me. And she was as inescapable as Prescott—although she was and always would be redeemable.

She came into the kitchen, her pumps clicking against the floor. We kissed without another word. I told myself we didn't need many.

After she opened a bottle of Pinot Noir and poured herself a glass, she picked up the bookstore sales receipt from the counter. I never hid my purchases from her. I wanted her to see them. She made them real.

"You bought more?" she asked.

I nodded, happy. The anchor's iron fluke was outside me now, standing in the kitchen, smiling. I could follow Prescott's lead and push myself into a bookish mania because I could cook dinner for the person I loved.

She held her glass to the light. The wine glistened at its edge, shading to a deeper darkness. I loved watching her assess things: size them up, resize them to her scale. If Prescott was the most committed reader I ever met, she was the bravest person. She managed hundreds and pulled down six figures before it was a cliché. At cocktail parties, she walked right up to CEOs, high-powered attorneys, even the governor of Wisconsin. She extended her hand and stared them dead in the eyes. She could also force troublesome accounts into the black, sometimes ruthlessly, although she was never ruthless with me. If anything, she was quieter at home, more likely to duck her eyes. She gave ground to me, the bet she'd taken despite her parents' warning.

"We're going to have to build a library wing," she said.

"You're serious?"

She smiled gently. "No. Just confused. Where does it all end?"

"End?"

"When will you have enough books?"

"Don't worry," I laughed. "Grad school only looks confusing from the outside."

We kissed again. We had it all. We were made for each other. I couldn't drift away. And the massing gravity of those books upstairs held me in place. I never felt that hollow space in my gut anymore. Contentment and loneliness *can* be the same thing, I told myself, refusing for once to let two tales run simultaneously.

"What are we doing tonight?" Miranda asked, thumbing through the mail on the counter.

I peppered the fish. "The usual. Reading."

"I've got a breakfast meeting tomorrow." She worked sixty hours on an easy week. "I need to be in bed early."

"Not me! I need to get through Frederic's *The Damnation of Theron Ware*." My desires were out in the open. It was freedom for a fundamentalist kid.

"Well, don't stay up too late," she said. "I'll miss you." She looked off, beyond me, her green eyes momentarily glazed. "Let's go to bed together some night."

"Tomorrow!" I lied.

But I got antsy in the evenings. I didn't want to waste time. In the small hours, I read on and off, then stared at my new books. There was an endless supply: reams of paper, vats of glue.

Not everyone was enthused. Toward finals, Rona confronted me in the hallway after class. "How can you sit there and defend that asshole Prescott?"

"Aren't prophets indefensible by nature?" I muttered, unsure for reasons I couldn't name. He'd just praised me as a reader of "infinite perspicacity."

"Who the hell believes in prophets?" Rona laughed. "And what the fuck was he doing with Frederick Douglass?"

Prescott had recently turned to Douglass's second autobiography, *My Bondage, My Freedom*. It's the longer story of Douglass's escape from slavery and his work to become one of the world's great orators. Prescott had had a wild notion that each chapter represented a battle in the Revolutionary War.

"Don't you see?" he'd called out. "His chapter *The Runaway Plot* is the Battle of Kings Mountain. *Introduced to the Abolitionists* is the Siege Of Yorktown!"

"Pure balderdash," Rona said.

"But inspired balderdash," I countered.

She pulled her wire glasses down her nose. "Have you lost your mind?"

"Done that," I said, breezier now, on familiar territory. "This isn't that."

"Well, no matter what *this* is," she said, staring at me as if she could read my thoughts, "you're his pathfinder. You better get him back on track before we lose him."

A true believer again, I didn't believe her. "How can he get lost when he can head in any direction he wants?"

She pushed her glasses back in place. "Hey, that's cute. You care about the guy."

Not really. Not in any standard way. But I've always been attracted to quirky types. They seemed like the best books—that is, an interruption of someone else's plot into mine, some node of another reality that had the power to sidetrack whatever I was doing and make it grander. I saw Prescott as a tangible "x marks the spot" in the divergence of timelines.

After finals, he stopped me in the hall and pressed the book list for the exams in the American area into my hands. It was four pages of single-spaced titles. "Stop fooling around," he commanded.

I stammered something about Chaucer and another paper at Kalamazoo.

He wasn't listening. "The world's all before you," he said.

How could I not walk into it? For one thing, Prescott was parental without being my parent, another in a long list of almost-right stand-ins. And despite his Ahab-like megalomania, he seemed to have all the answers. I withdrew from the medieval seminar, and he crowbarred me into one on Henry James and Henry Adams.

I became his teaching assistant, too, in an American lit course for majors. We met in his office before his lectures. The room was monkishly stark: a beat-up desk, a metal chair, not a book in sight. Despite having a view over the lake, he kept the blinds closed. His class materials were jumbled together in supermarket bags that he brought from home. We never once discussed student papers or exams. Instead, he gave the literary equivalent of a pregame pep talk, if the coach were talking to himself in a mirror.

"We'll first capture them with the sweep of American history. That should take ten minutes. Help me remember Ansel Adams, Scarbrough. Just call out his name from the back. Then I'll bring them back to the book. And baseball. You can't understand literature without baseball. And the buffalo. I'll bet you've forgotten the buffalo, Scarbrough."

As he ranted, he drummed his fingers on his desk, sounding out the only real contents of his office: empty booze bottles. They stood like soldiers in the deep drawers and lay on their sides in the shallow ones. Even the pencil drawer held rows of airline bottles. As I read in the T.A. office in the late afternoons, I sometimes heard him gather up an armful, plod to the bathroom, and toss them in the bin. Later, I'd spot shards of glass on the floor. But I never once saw him drink.

I'd heard the bottles the first time I'd been invited to one of these pre-class harangues. I was shocked, of course. Yet Prescott's was a maximalist ethic, brooking no protest. You were with him or you weren't. And he never made me work at ignoring his problem. He was an easier version of Thad: tipsy without Jesus, true without the Bible.

That day, Prescott was five minutes late for class. He reached into the grocery bags to grab up sheets of notes. He also pulled out five or six paperbacks, not a one of them assigned.

"To the ramparts!" He called, then paused on his way out and patted my stomach. "We've got to get you back in shape, lad. My God, you're pudgy."

My physical change seemed to descend in waves, folds of flesh layered one after another over my bones. I told myself I was more and more of this world, my feet on the ground. I ate as much as I wanted. I read as much as I wanted. Life was about the fulfillment of desire, right? Which was the basis of every plot, the cause of every tragedy, the hope of every comedy.

Prescott didn't need me in class. He came into his own around cowed undergrads. He hoisted his feet onto the desk and free-associated with literature while spitting out bits of the tuna fish salad he'd had for lunch. He set seventeenth-century Puritan sermons against Chekhov short stories. "Don't you see? The AFL-CIO!" he trumpeted. Louisa May Alcott's *Little Women* against the poetry of the Beats. "That's how you get Julia Child!" *The Great Gatsby* against the Federalist Papers. "And so we come to this Bill Clinton fellow!"

I hoped things would go on like that forever. Then, late one frigid February night, I got a call from the department chairman. "When's your class with Prescott?" he asked.

"I'll see him tomorrow."

"You won't. He's been missing since late Monday."

"Missing? What does that mean? Lost? Sick? Dead?"

"All fine ideas. You need to track him down."

Prescott had pulled off his vanishing act in the fading days of the private life. There were no cell phones. I couldn't contact him on a whim.

But he could get to me. The next day, the phone rang in the T.A. office. Rona picked it up. We'd become better friends, but she still didn't cotton to Prescott. She had two kids in a struggling high school. Her grant money had recently been cut in half. She made up the difference waiting tables. She straight-armed the receiver at me.

"Chingachgook on line four."

I jumped up. "Where are you?" I asked, breathless.

"No time to talk!" he hollered.

I pressed the phone to my ear. "What's that noise?"

"Trucks. What do you expect in North Dakota?"

"Where?"

"Minot. Why not Minot? That's the tourism slogan. I've almost caught up with them."

"Who?"

"Whom. Don't wait for me."

The line went dead.

I rushed to the chairman's office for privacy. He sat wordless and grim while I made harried calls.

It took me that night at home and most of the next day back in the chairman's office to track down Prescott in a flop motel. He was surviving off vending machine sandwiches. Apparently, he and some theorist grad student had had a donnybrook because Prescott insisted that all American literature recapitulated the Lewis and Clark expedition. Washington Irving was Nebraska! Nathaniel Hawthorne was North Dakota!

Unable to win the argument, Prescott went straight to his car and headed west. He packed nothing, planned nothing. He didn't even have glove compartment maps. He'd gotten off-track in Bismarck and headed north by mistake.

I was determined to get him back. "Just go south to I-94," I said. "Then head east. You'll eventually hit Minneapolis. Call me from there."

"Not on your life!" he cried.

The next day, he phoned from a truck stop in Montana. "Scarbrough, you like Twain! Get out here!"

With the lines of communication dead, I had to take over his course. Still a traditionalist at heart, I tried to carry on in some sort of order, some version of the timeline of American literature. Plus, only a year away from being a medievalist, I was still playing catch-up.

One night, I was awake as usual in the small hours, trying to get through James Fenimore Cooper's *The Prairie* before I had to teach it at 11:00. The book was the third of the five Leatherstocking Tales, but the last in the timeline they laid out. *The Prairie* told the story of Natty Bumppo's death, far from his home in the East Coast forests, riding a wagon across the Midwestern prairie like a ship captain on an ocean of grass. Here was the world I'd craved on those Texas drives. Except it now held the corpse of its most iconic hero.

151

I stopped reading. I heard a threat in the plot. What if the great works were nothing but a cemetery? What if, like the graves of my Civil War kin, they memorialized only their irrelevance?

Miranda came into my office sometime after five, the sun a faint hope in the Wisconsin dark. "Just checking on you," she said.

It was bitterly cold, an icy dawn. I had a blanket around my shoulders. I shook Cooper's novel at her. I wanted the pages to fall out. They didn't.

"I have to finish," I said.

"You want me to make some coffee?" Doubt seemed to ring her eyes.

I shook my head, strangely wordless.

She walked behind my chair and put her arms around me. I sank against her. Of all the people who'd ever tried to care for me, she did so unreservedly, as if I were the one real human in her world of bottom-line problems.

Even so, I couldn't let go of my fears. What if life was a limitless expanse? What if it truly was the prairie I'd loved? What if there was no gradient change to the horizon? What if this now was just one moment that led to the next and the next and the next, each one like every other one until they petered out in exhaustion? I'd never get home. But I was home. Which made no sense.

Miranda kissed my forehead. I could smell the lingering, lemony scent of her shampoo.

"Come to bed," she yawned.

Wasn't now enough? The marriage argument was resolved. The two of us were becoming what I'd hoped: respectable.

"I'll be there soon enough," I lied.

I watched her almost sleepwalk to our bedroom. I felt safe because I trusted her to hold me together. Every couple I read about did the same, even the ones who failed at it. True, Natty Bumppo never got married. But I wasn't Natty Bumppo, no matter what Prescott thought.

That morning in class, bleary-eyed and punch-drunk on coffee, I piled a mound of books on the desk in front of forty undergrad majors, relaxed my new bulk onto my hips, and channeled Prescott. I compared Cotton Mather to Geoffrey Chaucer, claiming the old Puritan's sermons were actually a story cycle. I called Cooper our literary Napoleon, an imperial consciousness that failed in the too-wide expanse of the prairie, our Russian steppes. I told them *Moby-Dick* was probably better in Sanskrit. I finished with my pulse racing, a divine intoxication.

Three weeks later, I carried a load of midterms into Prescott's office. To my shock, he was standing there, breathing heavily.

"There you are!" he said, as if I'd been the one who'd been missing. He fell back into his chair. "What'd I miss?"

His disciple now, I didn't skip a beat. "I did Jonathan Edwards, Cooper, Hawthorne."

I'd taught *The House of The Seven Gables* without first finishing it. My own coursework was demanding; my seminar papers reaching fifty, sixty pages a pop. I'd read the first three chapters of Hawthorne's novel and let free-association take care of the rest.

"We're up to the Civil War," I told Prescott.

He nodded, uninterested. "All as it should be. You don't need me."

"I wouldn't say that."

"I know. *I* did." He fiddled with the exams. "These done?"

"Of course." I knew he'd never look at them.

"So you got them through Cooper? Which book did they read?"

"You set *The Prairie* on the syllabus!"

"Ah, lad. You can't resist your story."

"It's not my. . . ."

He looked crestfallen. I recognized his despair, that feeling of having found a book that could hold a part of me, only to have someone dismiss it. So I pulled a Cooper quote I'd memorized out of the basement of my soul.

> *The tree blossoms, and bears its fruit, which falls, rots, withers, and even the seed is lost! Go, count the rings of the oak and of the sycamore; they lie in circles, one about another, until the eye is blinded in striving to make out their numbers; and yet a full change of the seasons comes round while the stem is winding one of those little lines about itself; but what does it all amount to?*

Saying these words felt wonderful, like reciting Bible verses in front of my childhood church's tent at swap meets. Or like holding vast swaths of Blake in my head to mutter to myself in the long stretches of the night. Sometimes, the web of texts is too much. Sometimes, you just need a thread.

Prescott closed his eyes, sighed out a boozy breath, and said, "Go on, Scarbrough. Please."

He was testing me to see if I knew the novel as well as he did. But there was more. He'd again found himself where he should be. He was back home. I thought I was, too. So I went on:

> *Then come the winds, that you cannot see, to rive its bark; and the waters from the heavens, to soften its pores; and the rot, which all can feel and none can understand, to humble its pride and bring it to the ground. From that moment its beauty begins to perish. It lies another hundred years; a moldering log, and then a mound of moss and earth, a sad effigy of a human grave.*

Without opening his eyes, Prescott stood up, a signal for me to go. He was stock still, his face calm, its creases relaxed. Like a death mask, the struggle over.

"Natty," he said, "I love you."

I reached for his arm. It was the only time I ever touched him. His skin felt cold and scaly.

"I hope so," I said.

He didn't seem to hear me, didn't move another inch. His eyes were blurry and gray.

I walked out in silence, my soft-soled shoes barely making a sound.

This was home: to fit the tales I loved. I strung their timelines across the void—like telephone wires, lines of communication that settled the wilds. And they gave me what I wanted most. Prescott, yes. A purpose, of course. But mostly, Miranda.

I no longer needed to roam the American expanse. I didn't need to wait under the stars for a dead poet to step out of the dark. I'd eventually travel beyond Prescott, into his real hopes, not his drunken failures. I'd become the true Natty, a literary frontiersman, living this plot and then that one, whichever suited the moment, a bodily incarnation of the polyphony of the great books and so what I thought was the redemption of time itself, the past and future bound up into the only thing that mattered: now.

I thought the great works of Western civilization let me make sense of the crazy, oracular, and fallen life I'd built for myself, even as it started to be strafed by time and its most cunning minion, sex.

By All This I Mean Love

Although Prescott continued to ride a cavalry charge through my brain, I treated him like Caddie Anderson and never took another course from him. Maybe I was afraid. Maybe I didn't want to ruin what *had* happened with what *might* happen. Maybe I was still enough of a fundamentalist that I thought I'd lose everything if I got too greedy.

I stayed his T.A., however, until he finagled me a position on staff. By my fourth year, I was teaching American lit to English majors, just as he did. I had a private office with a window that looked out to the fallow fields on the horizon. I bossed around my own teaching assistants.

Prescott didn't fare so well. The herd of graying profs was thinning fast; the theory quants, taking over. Most afternoons, he sat alone in his office, slumped in his chair. Then he got the most damning accolade: emeritus. After that, I rarely saw him. The distance between us felt good, like ecstasy or grief, neutralized by time and distance.

Plus, I was almost thirty and more settled than ever. Miranda made more money than we could spend. We'd started using "summer" as a verb. And I filled a noted role: the dusty, academic yin to her corporate yang. All of which meant I no longer needed to justify how and why I read with the stomach-churning turbulence Prescott brought to our every encounter.

I lived the great works, usually in my head, often in my mouth, and sometimes in my body. My bones seemed at different angles whenever I taught Dickinson or Whitman, Faulkner or Fitzgerald, as if the weight of their words deformed my posture, my whole physical aspect.

Or maybe I didn't live them so much as they somehow lived me. Not just in me, but—how could this be?—actually me.

I'd moved beyond reading with a "what's next?" mania. I now *re*read—for teaching, yes, but for pleasure, too. I didn't need to find myself on the page. I read the great works again to see who I'd been, where I'd been, who I still was. The great works now felt like echoes, reverberations in a cathedral after the music's done. I even read Blake's poetry once in a while, just to feel what I'd felt a long time ago—as if time and I were one thing in the words but separate things in life.

These pristine visions of literary selfhood started to fall apart in a library, as any prophet could have predicted, if I had any left in my life. Over four days, my story got smeared with chaos—the thing that every novel or poem tries to straighten out, that none of them can comprehend, and that destroys the this-then-that plot all of us try to tell ourselves.

Late one winter Friday, I was nestled in a cage-like cubicle in the stacks at Memorial Library, the warehouse of research arcana on the Madison campus. I was bent over, folded into, maybe lost inside a paperback copy of Henry James's *The Portrait of a Lady*, reading it for the third time in about a year.

I walked the line of lawn that extends to the river at the back of the Touchetts' superbly English home. I heard the rattle of silverware on trays, the bustle of activity that marks the ritual of afternoon tea, that opening moment in the novel when the glow of light settles into the words. I felt a tingle of surprise—still, after so many times?—when Isabel Archer appears out of nowhere, standing at the back of the house, facing the family and daring them to come to her, the fearless American woman in their midst.

I closed my eyes and recited many of the sentences before I read them, waiting for that gentle pull at the heart of James's art, the deeper draw into the murk of human emotions that he almost, but never completely, clarifies.

I'd thought I'd never get here, never be a professional reader, someone who read his life out of books and into the world around him. Melody and Alex had once tried to. . . .

I shook myself back to James's novel. Dammit, the past. The muck that ruined a great book. It was one thing to see it in a work of literature. It was another to have it sully one of the greats.

The actual page in front of me wasn't all that clean, either. Those of us in the American lit area circulated our books among each other.

We underlined passages and linked up cross-references, wrote comments on the text, wrote comments on those comments, argued, pontificated, and thus proved ourselves grad students.

My copy of *The Portrait of a Lady* held dozens of voices beyond the original novel. Most were marked in the margins; a few, scrawled wholesale over paragraphs. The book was a monstrous fugue, thicker than polyphony: my voice, Rona's, others', some who'd gone on to academic jobs, many who'd dropped out, and behind them the narrator's voice, maybe James's, certainly the ur-words, the novel itself, all part of the same page.

Heated exchanges unfurled in the blank spaces at the ends of chapters. Updates sprawled under some of the comments. *Or so I thought until I read Heidegger.* And more: phone numbers, grocery lists, *1 1/2 pounds pearl onions, pick up the dry cleaning on Thursday, the last frost date for planting in Madison is May 15th*, all the stuff readers write in books because they're the paper at hand.

Among the words, I could see Rona's fine pencil marks in block print. She occasionally threw a barb at me. *Caspar Goodwood? James names a character after a hard-on? Shit, Mark, you guys.*

None of the voices harmonized. The narrator's pulsed alongside theirs. And mine alongside theirs. And theirs alongside each other's. One of the great works of Western literature was a hodgepodge. A mess. Sometimes, I couldn't even read the original text, hidden under scratches, smears, and an absurdly stupid pink highlighter. It all reminded me of those glued-together pages in *Great Expectations*. Except no one was trying to save me from this mess. James's novel had become a blank canvas for some sort of literary abstract expressionism, the blotches of consciousness.

Apparently, the canon of Western lit wasn't just a collection of voices. It inspired more. Hundreds more. Thousands. Just when I thought I could assemble a life from a set number of great works and turn myself into a walking *Norton Anthology of Literature*, there was more to take in. I'd mistaken a limitless sea of voices for a simple chorus. They were all shouting at once over what might be—I shivered—the fundamental meaninglessness of the printed page. The words of *The Portrait of a Lady* coalesced into sense, not when they touched a reader's mind, but when they inspired more words, more scrawls, more marks. Scholarly papers. Conferences. Living room lit groups. Worlds without end.

Yet the life I'd created from the great works was now far more wordless. My marriage. Our meals. Our vacations. Our fabricated existence with its showy, inevitable happy ending. A romance plot really, in which Miranda and I were the lead characters and lived a perfectly imagined life.

We hadn't had sex in months. Didn't even try. I'd come to this weird place where I couldn't let the voices in my head play around in our bed. It all made sense when I was inside her. It all made sense when I was inside a book. It never made sense when I was inside both, which is the only way I could still be me. I also didn't want to fantasize myself into other plots when we made love. In some weird reversal, some strange backward leap I'd never planned, I wanted one damn thing that books hadn't touched. There had to be a place without illusions. And if not in our marriage, where?

But by demanding something outside of the plots that coursed through my brain, I'd turned my life, our lives, into the Kodachrome negative of a wedding photograph. A reverse-tint show of ghostly figures that didn't inspire words, that was itself a blank. A clean page. And perhaps—I felt a chill in my marrow as I sat at that library desk—the desolate, unfathomable bottom under all hopes. Our marriage was all present tense, all now, an ongoing fresh start. A spot in time without a plot. Nothing but possibility. Nothing but promise. And so nothing at all. When you read yourself into existence, nothing's your fault. And nothing's your own, either.

I shoved James's novel in my bag and sat back. Except when we read, when do we ever willingly surrender our consciousness to another's control? We talk to each other, our thoughts flitting this way and that. We have dinner together, still in our own heads. But we read and let someone else take over our brains. Their thoughts become ours.

Thoreau. James. Brontë. I'd given them free access to my head. If I hadn't, I'd have been left with my own thoughts, which were monochromatic and meaningless. If this was the real truth of my quest, if this was the real reason I read and reread and reread, then I'd been wrong to steer clear of Prescott. The only answer was more. And more. Like the goddamn pages of *The Portrait of a Lady*.

The library lights must have dimmed to indicate closing time, then flicked to their night setting, every third fluorescent lit across the ceiling. I didn't notice, and in those pre-9/11 days no one came to check. I stood up and stretched. Why was it so quiet?

Downstairs, the doors were locked. I rattled the handles, then wandered the reference room, the open stacks. I wasn't panicked. A library was like home, too. Or could be, if the books would just stay pure. I considered lying down among them, spending the night in their musty smell. But I could hear Miranda's voice, too. "Don't be absurd!" she would say.

I found a phone on a librarian's desk and called for help. A security guard arrived, a guy about my age with blond hair and fleshy acne scars. He undid the doors. Outside, the night was just above freezing, almost balmy after years in Wisconsin.

"Hang on a minute," he said as he locked up. "You can't haunt the library."

I smiled and tried to act casual, but I could no longer sling my book bag across my big stomach. I tilted like Humpty Dumpty as I carried the satchel in one hand.

"This is an actionable offense," the guard warned. "I could write you up."

I'd been holding on tight since Chaucer. Maybe since seminary. How good it would feel to loosen my grip and let the voices run free! Let them multiply. Let them be the only point. Instead of answering him, I giggled and quoted *The Portrait of a Lady*: "You must be prepared on many occasions in life to please no one at all."

The answer to my loneliness had to lie in mouthing what I knew. I'd once quoted Blake to my buddies at a bar and seen the poet a few hours later. That had been the one, true, unsullied moment of belonging I'd ever felt in my life. So why not beg for more?

The guard didn't seem to care about my existential dilemma. "What the hell are you talking about?" he asked.

"One can't judge till one's forty," I said, quoting more James, "before that we're too eager, too hard, too cruel."

The guard took a step back. "You better skedaddle. You got anybody to look out for you?"

I shook my head. Miranda was asleep. Rona was with her kids. Prescott was who could guess where. Thad, Melody, Alex, all the other people who'd cared about me? I'd lost them. I was alone. But how could that be? There were still so many voices. Miranda's, first of all.

"I'll be fine," I said, suddenly the voice of reason. "You ever read American lit?"

"Shit, no," he said. "I don't want to see you again. Get outta here."

Half an hour later, I slipped into bed, the sheets warm and soft. Miranda backed her hips into my crotch. "Home?" she asked.

I nuzzled my nose into her hair. "Mmmm," I said.

Our breathing fell into sync. She was becoming a national figure, invited to speak at conferences about the place of women in business. She seemed to use me as her Prescott, a different sort of "x marks the spot," the place where things weren't always a corporate, for-profit struggle.

In the end, I told myself that ours was the only plot that mattered. I could reread it forever. The home I'd always wanted, the place I felt most comfortable. And truly blank. Empty. Real. The page that promised the most was the one without any writing on it. Otherwise, print got scribbled over, and the narrator got lost in the mess. Words were just marks to cover up the truth that now was and forever would be a quantum zilch, melting into the past—and so always into a new story that could inspire more stories, other voices.

Heroic, I fell into a deep sleep.

Miranda and I got up early the next morning.

"Warm up the shower while I take the dogs out," I told her.

We were throwing a dinner party that evening, as we did almost every Saturday. We lined up eight guests at a plated affair. Miranda sent out formal invitations, never to any grad students or profs, mostly to our socio-economic set. Or hers. I ironed the linens and cooked the courses.

I let the shelties run wild in the backyard, a leafy expanse ringed with bare lilacs. Their craggy limbs made a twisted cage. The dogs seemed carefree, everything I could be if I kept this story as blank as it should be.

I found Miranda in the shower's fog. We kissed: lightly, barely. We bathed together every morning. I washed her hair, then she washed mine. I soaped her back, then she soaped mine. We never once had sex in the shower. Like a long time ago in another shower.

In other words, this moment did what a good narrator would have wanted it to do: it held the past as a resonance, an echo. Like *The Portrait of a Lady*, which had become more reverb than plot, more texture than sense. That novel held as many voices as anyone could stuff inside it. It was and wasn't about me. Which meant it mirrored my life. Which surely meant I was home.

Miranda and I toweled off. I weighed over 260 pounds. She never said anything about my weight. Her silence seemed like redemption, another blank page.

She walked out, and I sat down on the edge of the tub, my stomach on my thighs. I was proud of being fat. I was the jolly academic. And married to the woman I loved. This was my best story.

That evening, candlelight gleamed off the oak molding. Soft music filled the dining room. There were grilled hanger steaks, a buttery herb sauce, and savory pumpkin custards, along with a little mâche salad on the side. Who doesn't love mâche?

At dinner parties, Miranda and I now performed our marriage, staged our happy ending. Curtain up! We never once admitted to each other that we knew we were doing this, that we matched our sterling, an estate-sale set, finely polished and engraved with initials other than our own.

One of our guests was a tech wonk who'd cashed out and lived a country-club life. Sometime into the third bottle of wine, he decided to break the chitchat to ask me a heavier question. "What'll you do if you don't get a job after grad school?"

Our cue. As usual, Miranda took the lead. "Oh, Mark's going to be fine," she said. "He's going to buy a few Armani suits. Aren't you, dear?"

"Do they carry Armani suits at the big and tall shop?" I asked, head down.

I heard nervous giggles from our friends. I'd never once seen a knowing look, the clue that our guests knew we'd rehearsed these lines at a string of dinner parties.

More confident, I went on. "I'm going to offer my services to L'Etoile."

It was the five-star restaurant in Madison, a vanguard of the new American dining scene, so innovative that it had already been featured in all the glossy food magazines.

"With a degree like mine," I said, "I can provide scintillating conversation for those dining alone."

Sure enough, broader laughter. Truly, there was nothing as funny as a humanities grad student. Miranda sat on the opera board. I was on a commission to revamp the T.A. program at the university. I was a year late with the first chapter of my dissertation and we could afford bottles of '88 Meursault.

Except that night, I looked across the table and caught Miranda's haunting, green eyes. She was staring at me. I shuddered. Were we off-script?

Silently she mouthed, I know.

I flushed and went numb. I cleared plates and brought out the lemon tart. Had something happened to her, too? Had she reached a limit to the story we were telling? Or did she know I was heroic?

After our guests left, we cleaned up in silence. Sudsy water soaked my sleeves. *I know* tolled in my head. I and silence, some strange race. Wrecked. Solitary. Here.

"I've got work to do," I said when Miranda carried the last plate into the kitchen. "I thought I'd head back to school."

She seemed beat: a busy weekend, then the start of the next work week, one great rush.

"Can I leave you to. . . ?" I asked.

She looked at the mess. Maybe she wanted someone else to clean up what life did when we were otherwise pretending to have a good time. "Of course!" she said.

I pointed to my cheek, expecting a proper peck. "Good night."

Later, I aimlessly drove around Madison, peering at closed convenience stores, looping the shopping mall parking lots. *What* did she know? That I foresaw something worse than a psychotic break when a poet walks out of the dark or Hebrew characters dance on a page? That I couldn't make a real story out of the thousands of voices in my head? That I was slowly becoming the author of a failed story I couldn't stop telling?

Even now, I wonder if Miranda saw the future. Was she the major prophet in my life? Did she know I was about to force her to play the consummate heroine? A James heroine, at that? Did she see that in the face of something that finally proved unsolvable, her only reaction would be to give in, give up, and let me lead her over insanity's lip, the one I knew so well?

That night, I came home and slept on the couch. I wanted to face my fears. Or dismiss them. Either way, for the first time since Alex pulled his bullshit in our dorm room, I yearned to be left on my own. Loneliness was better than *I know*.

Sunday was easier: Bloody Marys, one after another, a bottle of wine that evening. By the time Miranda asked me about sleeping downstairs the night before, I could shrug it off in a tipsy lurch: "I didn't want to disturb you."

On Monday morning, I slept late, heard Miranda leave for work, and got to campus around noon. I sat in my office, reading bits of books I knew, until Rona stopped by. She was trying to put together more graduate funding but was falling in debt. She was still mad at Prescott, but she'd put him on her dissertation committee. "He knows everything," she'd explained.

That day, in the middle of one of her broadsides about the indignities of grad school, she must have noticed I wasn't paying attention. "What's up?" she asked.

"I'm fine."

"Good," she laughed, "because I hate whining from people who have an office with a view."

I didn't have any way to respond. She should have had my appointment on staff. She was a better scholar. A better teacher, too.

Truth is, I wanted to tell her that getting married to Miranda was the best thing I'd ever done, that we fit each other perfectly, and that I knew it because our lives matched all the other plots. Wasn't that the reason I still read? To see myself where I'd already imagined myself? And wasn't that the heart of the marriage argument? To match your own love with what you've read about?

Instead, I said something I didn't mean: "*The Last of the Mohicans*? Cora and Natty? They never get together."

"Shit," Rona said, "you, too, can't let Prescott go."

And with that, as if the mention of his name granted us permission, I leaned in and we kissed. Easy, adult, just like that. Although it, too, wasn't what I meant.

Rona backed up. "What are we doing?"

I shrugged.

"No, seriously," she said. "Explain it to me."

I wanted to. I wanted to tell her that sometimes I couldn't remember what day of the week it was, what month, what season. That I walked around campus in spring thinking, Well, winter's almost here. That I got lost running errands because I was rehearsing novels and poems in my head. That I'd stop at a pay phone and call Miranda and she'd help me find my way back. But that I actually wanted to keep driving farther into the Wisconsin prairie because there must be someone out there who looked like me, who acted like me. Because I passed through the world without ever seeing my face reflected in a single family member's, even a single character's in a single book. But it didn't stop me from looking. And looking. And looking.

Before I could say any of that, Rona kissed me again, longer, better. We shut my office door and fumbled with buttons and collars. She was aggressive, more so than Miranda. She bit and clawed.

When I did the same, Rona lost interest. She straightened up, cocked her head and said, "I always thought you were gay."

"Yeah, right," I replied, all stagy male bravado as I'd once been with Melody. "You're not going to get off that easy."

I reached into my pocket, took out my silver pillbox, and unfolded the paper that Immy had given me.

> *Life is so short, any skill takes so long to learn, any attempt is so hard, any victory is so sharp, any joy slips away so quickly—by all this I mean love.*

"It's a prayer," I said.

"Where'd you get it?"

"It dropped into my life from heaven," I said. I thought I was lying.

Rona shook her head and handed it back as she buttoned up. "Throw it out. You don't need it. We done?"

I nodded, silent.

She left and I tried to organize the files she'd scattered across my desk when she'd pushed me into them. Eventually I sat in my institutional metal chair and nodded off. I've always hated naps, considered them a sign of indolence, a violation of the Puritan who lives along my spine. This time, I woke up mid-afternoon and considered it a good sign. Maybe I was making much ado about nothing. Maybe I was growing up. Or at least growing older, inching closer to the end of my story, a full tale. Which still didn't make sense of Miranda's *I know*.

I heard a rap at my door and opened it to see Nate slouched against the wall. A senior business major, he'd taken my upper-level course as an elective. He was a strange kid, a little like me: all silence, then overflow. He and his girlfriend dropped by our house once in a while for dinner. He loved Wisconsin football. After my class, he loved Cooper, too. I wasn't exactly his Caddie Anderson. More a former prof who'd become something like a friend.

"Want to go for coffee?" he asked.

We walked out of the building and into an icy blast. Since the weekend, the weather had turned back to winter. Gray, menacing clouds scudded across the sky. The wind bit so hard that I pulled a scarf tight against my neck, although I was sweating like a beast, a fat man trying to keep up with a twenty-year-old.

We headed up State Street. In his spare time, Nate had read all the Natty Bumppo novels.

"What else did Cooper write that's important?" he asked.

His seafaring romances? I thought. Who reads that crap? Except me?

"Maybe you should branch out," I said. "How about Harriet Beecher Stowe?"

"From *The King and I*?"

I couldn't make up this Midwestern innocence. "Yes," I said. "Sure."

We chose one of the new coffee houses, long removed from Madison's hippie protest days. The plate-glass window was squeaky clean. I couldn't imagine hurling one of the ergonomic chairs through it.

We got a couple of espressos, found a spot up front, and watched the passing students.

"I've been thinking. . . ," Nate started, then faltered.

I'd taught long enough to know where this discussion was headed. A new English major! Oh, joy.

But he surprised me.

"Thinking of getting married," he said.

"Congratulations!" I nodded, more at ease. Maybe we weren't friends. I tried to be parental. "As long as you wait until you graduate."

"Until I *am* graduated," he said.

He was definitely my student.

"I mean, you and Miranda have it so great," he said. "I want that."

That innocence again. I envied it. "Oh, I don't know," I said. "We're just giving it our best. We don't really know what we'll do if I end up with a job where she can't...."

Nate put his hand over mine on the table.

Madison was a progressive place, but in 1990 the gay bars had darkened windows. Men didn't hold hands in public.

I left mine where it was. The feeling wasn't the same as it had been with Alex, the high Gs at the drop of the parabola. It was more like a quick stab, the sharp blade of irony. I could barely feel it over the roar in my head. Could this day get any weirder? Miranda, Rona, this kid. Fucking polyphony. Was I going to see Blake next?

Nate looked out the window. His hand relaxed, cupping mine. "How does anybody know what's right?" he asked.

I hitched up on one hip but still didn't move my hand. I hated his question. Each of the great books knew the right way to see life. They hollered it. Just read, I wanted to say. Yet this current cliché, the professor and his student, was unbearable.

"I thought you wanted to get married," I said.

Nate kept his eyes on the window. "You once said the frontier was a metaphor for the inner life."

"I did."

"And you said the closing of the frontier marked the inward turn in American thought."

"I did, although someone else said it first." I'd turned my body into a barrier. "Nate, we're not...."

"I know we're not. I might. I don't know."

"You're not making sense."

"Yes, I am. There are so many ways to be married."

I gasped. Immy. Her words in his mouth, an overlay of time, the past creating the present. Why was my life so full of echoes? Was it really that hollow? Or was it finally, truly a plot? One scene a mirror for another. One scene a backdrop for another.

Was Immy's face behind Nate's? I hadn't heard from her in years. We'd tried holiday letters, but I hadn't kept up my end of the deal.

I was breaking other deals, too. Nate's hand felt warm. It felt like when I held a good book. It felt like when Miranda touched me. My carotid fizzed again.

The coffee shop door swung open. In walked Dr. Keller, my Chaucer advisor. My story continued to fold in on itself, the pulpiest of plots. I could barely breathe. I knew there was a small medieval conference in town, but I hadn't written to see if she'd show up. She, too, was supposed to have disappeared into the silence of a finished tale.

Dr. Keller had been to our wedding. She knew Miranda. She saw me. She saw Nate. I don't know what she saw.

"Mark!" she said.

Nate jerked his hand back. Mine stayed where it was.

Dr. Keller cocked her head. Wispy hair fell onto her forehead. "Mind if I join you two?"

Isn't this what I'd always craved? The sheer thrill and utter dread of all the plots at once?

Letting the vertigo go, I imagined more. I saw Prescott walk in. *Onward, lad!* And Rona. I could still taste her on my lips. Immy, too. Thad, Alex, Melody. And Miranda, who was supposed to be the embodiment of *chesed*. Would she work late tonight or be home on time? Would she get something to eat at the office? Should I keep her dinner warm? Or eat both portions?

At the back, didn't I see my buddies from Baylor, Pastor Daniel, Jared and his hick mother from Canton, my own mother and dad? This present moment was like the ending of one of those big Victorian novels in which the author says, "Here's what happened to everybody in the years ahead."

Dr. Keller didn't notice the horde around her. "In all the coffee joints in all the world," she said. Or they said. Maybe the whole crowd said it.

She looked hard at Nate, then headed off to order.

I turned back to him. The crowd seemed to dissipate in his eyes.

"How do you know her?" he asked.

"Old story," I said. "But Natty Bumppo was right. The prairie is where we're all headed."

He seemed let down. "You still haven't told me what the hell the prairie has to do with any of this."

I didn't lie. "There's no gradient change to the horizon."

"Who the hell wants that?" he asked. "And while I'm at it, fuck off."

Dr. Keller came back as he stalked away. "Student?" she asked.

"Former," I said flatly.

Dr. Keller rolled her eyes. "The worst. So how's life? What are you writing on?"

I spread my hands out on the table again. "This."

"Doesn't sound promising. Don't you want to come back to Chaucer?"

I shook my head. I'd broken through the crosshatch of timelines. Which meant I was fully in time. Like everyone else, I was in free fall.

"Anything wrong?" she asked.

"I'm just waiting to see what happens next."

"Aren't we all?"

I looked at her. "No. *You* know what's happening next."

"A chaired professorship, I think." She'd gotten the Minnesota job.

"Told you," I said. "The goddamn world's all before you."

She scratched a mole on her neck. "On second thought, don't come back to Chaucer. American lit needs you."

I took it as a compliment. We chatted some more. She was dating a medievalist at another college. "That's a tragedy in a dead dialect," she grinned.

I got up to leave, said I'd call her, invite her over to dinner with Miranda, though I knew I wouldn't.

I walked back to campus, my coat open to the bitter cold. I wanted to feel something outside my own head. I passed my office and went straight to Prescott's. To my surprise, his door was open. It would be the last time I ever saw him.

No lights were on. The sunset filtered through his blinds. He must have heard my footstep because he called out, "Natty! How's life?"

Refusing to go beyond the door jamb, I launched into the truth, as if he were the right person to hear it, as if he was in any shape to hear it. I could smell the booze.

"I'm not sure what to do," I said. "I don't even know why I'm in grad school anymore."

My wail was vague enough for him to understand. He shambled toward me and steadied himself against his desk. The bottles clinked inside. "You've always known what to do," he said.

I looked down. "No, I've always let books tell me."

He laughed like old times, his breath rank. "Natty doesn't have the luxury of an existential crisis."

I surprised myself with outrage. I didn't know what I'd come for. But I suddenly knew what I wanted to get away from. Him. And his bullshit.

"For God's sake," I said, "Natty's nothing *but* an existential crisis! He never knows which side he's on. The settlers? The Native Americans? The British? He's everywhere. And nowhere. So when the story's over, he ends up dead out on the prairie."

I seemed to have hit a nerve. Prescott shuffled back toward the window and yanked up the blinds. The day had somehow turned brilliantly cloudless, shockingly bright. Sunlight angled off the lake. I saw how filthy his office was: binder clips, corks, hairballs. He was so pale that his skin seemed blue. But he swung his arm out to take in everything beyond the window, a greasy Parson Weems pulling back the curtain on the story that started it all.

"Walk the land, lad," he said. "It's always been your answer."

Fuck off, I wanted to say, echoing Nate, echoing Rona from that first semester in his seminar. I knew this vaunted promise, the nightmare of wandering in the wilderness. "I'm a lecturer in the department," I said instead. "I have commitments."

"I'll handle it for you."

"Sir, you cannot handle it."

He stared me down. "You think just because I drink I can't. . . ."

I gasped to shut him up. I wanted to save him from his words, from his truth, the way I wanted someone to save me from mine.

"You don't get it!" I said. "There's nothing to handle. I'm not going anywhere."

"Light out for the territories!"

"There are no territories! The world is settled. Besides, what would the department say? What would my students say? Not to mention my wife?" I knew I was pushing it further than he intended. "I'm not you. I'm staying put."

He chuckled and looked at the sky. "Natty can do anything."

"And for the last time, I'm not Natty!" But I couldn't move, held there by him, a singularity of despair, a black hole of human loss, the true gravitational well in any of our universes.

Prescott stared into the space between us. "Walk through the forests, the prairies, Mark. Here is where we are healed. Here is where we find ourselves. You must keep walking until you find what you are looking for. The whole time I've known you, you've been a man with nothing behind you. You must find a landscape that makes sense of you."

His eyes went vacant; his breath, shallow. He didn't motion me out. He just stood there, an alcoholic with the decency not to drink in front of me, a man whose love of books had emptied his life until the shell of his body was the only space in which his voice found resonance. He was hardly a god, much less a saint. Prescott was a run-of-the-mill sinner, the sort of person I never wanted to be and the only sort of person who ever really matters.

I walked back to my office and packed up. In my car, I couldn't make the seatbelt fit across my stomach. I tugged and tugged. I screamed with the windows closed. I didn't feel any better for doing it.

I didn't drive out to North Dakota or Montana, as Prescott would have. I needed to get home and make dinner. Miranda and I were having Vietnamese filet medallions and coconut sticky rice.

I roared the car out of the garage and held the horn down for two blocks, a metallic drone, one note, cacophony for the unimaginative. Students stared from the sidewalks. I gave them the finger.

When I pulled into the driveway, I tried not to notice the neat flower beds, the manicured lawn. I got in the house out of breath and let the dogs out. As they barked every squirrel off the property, I went upstairs to my office, sat down, and stared at my books, the shelves stuffed with them, the stacks in the corners.

"Liars!" I called out to them.

No, I was. But I'd told myself so many stories, I could no longer tell the difference.

How to Turn Your Life into More than One Plot

Step 1: Start on a Sunday afternoon, early spring in Madison, snow on the crocuses.

Get ready to settle in with Miranda. You'll have spent the weekend grading papers for a course on the creation of the modern world in literature: ten novellas, four by Henry James. You have two sections, fifty undergrads each.

Miranda will have taken to reading books from your courses. She wants to "get you." She's working her way through Edith Wharton.

Walk in from cleaning up the kitchen. Make this bit nonchalant. Your relationship is fragile. Convince yourself it's because you can't maintain the border between fact and fiction. Convince yourself that you don't have the right story yet. Which will conveniently justify the reason you have to keep looking.

Say: "Listen, what are we going to do about your job? How long can you stay here before you have to transfer somewhere else? I'm not finished with my dissertation and I. . . ."

"About three chapters. What would I do if I up and followed you? If I. . . ."

"I meant, what would I do for work? Cooking dinner doesn't count. So we move away from Madison and I just sit on my ass and play the good wife while you. . . ."

Sorry. I know it's important for you. But I love teaching, love it when my students want me to make them lists of books to read, when we sit in coffee shops and. . . .

"I'm not being the victim. We're supposed to be in this together. We're supposed to figure out how this is going to work, any of this is going to. . . ."

"What's this? You know. Us."

Step 2: Move to a late afternoon on Monday.

You'll have enrolled in yet another seminar. Your tenth, eleventh? It's hard to keep track. Get ready to present your paper in class while daydreaming about a rack of lamb you've got in the fridge. Rosemary and oregano? Lemon and garlic?

Cooking is fun. Like playing house. You've heard one of the literary quants refer to it as "the only unalienated labor in the modern world." You've held onto that one. You've also lost about thirty pounds by the usual methods: low-fat this and low-sugar that.

Miranda hasn't said a word about the diet. Which makes you feel more alone. You want someone to call you out, to tell you what to do. In any event, your clothes hang off you like bags, even if you're still sixty pounds overweight.

You've stretched your Ph.D. program to seven years. You're close to believing your own arguments, although the doubts are fun, a frisson of secrets, even if you've got no one to tell them to.

Prescott died a few months ago. Cirrhosis, the last refuge of scoundrels. You stood with a few others at his grave in the gray chill. Afterwards, you drank a bottle of cheap wine in your car. "This is what 'walk the land' gets you," you said to yourself.

Remind yourself that you'll never get your seminar paper's argument right if you keep rehearsing the past. Plus, you've got to impress the unsympathetic new hire at the head of the table, a guy a few years your junior, now on your dissertation committee. He plots American literature with the history of the stock market.

Say: "My paper is about the way reading novels makes you an atheist. Basically, you can't be a reader and a believer. I'd like to start by talking about the wall between what is and what could be, between this world and the imagined world—and how novels force you back and forth across that wall until it no longer means anything. In so doing, they ruin any chance for faith in anything other than the concrete reality underneath their fiction. In other words, they push us back to bedrock to judge the validity of their imagined worlds.

"Take Henry James. His fiction makes us reconsider the reality of the social order by creating a complex fantasy of that order—thereby making us judge how right he is by pushing us out of *his* world and back onto *our* side of the wall, where we begin to understand the fiction of the structures that model our own manners and morals. We judge our real world by his fiction and come to doubt our faith in our own social codes—and ultimately, our faith in the very notion of faith. We finally realize that hope is just faith without a creed."

Step 3: Follow up with an early evening the next day.
You went out for dinner last night. The wunderkind prof had declared your paper overthought. "Where's the heart?" asked the guy who's developing an algorithm for the genres: comedy, tragedy, romance.

After that letdown, you wanted to meet Miranda at a public restaurant, to put on the display of who you two are, then drive home and fall in bed half drunk. Sometime in the night, you woke up and decided you wanted to be in love without being in a relationship. You decided this is what scholars meant by "post-modernism."

Tonight, you're getting around to that rack of lamb. Sear off the meat and shove it in the oven. Polish off some red wine. Plummy stains in the glasses will remind you of what you can lose.

Miranda will be reading the paper. Hand her a glossy food magazine, the sort that lie all over your house.

Say: "Look at this crap. French bistro is coming back? Have these hacks even been to Paris? Remember that last trip? How many Michelin stars did we rack up? We should throw a dinner party. Who can we invite? This weekend? I'll do some gougères, then I could follow those up with. . . ."

"What? Twenty-five minutes or so before the lamb's done."

"Oh, no, no, I'm a little tired. Worn out. And we're a little old for quickies, aren't we? I mean, later tomorrow night we could plan to, make a date to . . . But thanks. That's really nice. It's nice to know I've still got it. Hahahaha. Or you. You've still got it."

Step 4: Wake up early on Wednesday morning.
You and Miranda no longer shower together. She's usually driving in at this hour. She's got one of the first car phones anybody's seen: a lug of technology that includes a rotary dial and a handset mounted under the dashboard.

This morning, she won't be barking orders at anyone. She'll be sobbing, her head on her folded arms at the table as the sun comes up. She'll be wearing her typical black suit. The jacket will stretch over her shoulders. There's nylon in the wool.

Try to comfort her. Pat her back and think how warm that suit must be in the summer. Think about Henry James's *The Ambassadors*. Lambert Strether survived a Paris summer in wool. It's hard to imagine him breaking down.

Stop it. You can do tragic. But you have no words for what this moment is. It's tricky, because you're losing interest in the great books. They seem fake, although your life seems faker. Which makes no sense.

Say: "Goddammit, we just have to keep trying. You've only been off the pill for three, four months. The doctor said it could take a while. We're not young. Thirty-two, thirty-three, I mean, we're not...."

"But it *is* nice, this quiet in the house. I mean, it wouldn't be the worst thing if...."

"No, no. Of course, I want a kid. I just mean that if it didn't happen...."

"I know, I know: we'll keep trying. I know, I know: we have to."

Step 5: Flash to mid-afternoon that same day, a late lunch.

Camp out with Nate at Madison's first scent-free restaurant. You're surrounded by 1990s hipsters in white T-shirts and sleeveless wool vests, the first of this kind anyone's seen. Feel as if your life has become very up to date.

Nate's finally changed his major. Not to English. To theater. He's also added a year to his undergrad program and dumped his girlfriend for a boyfriend, a redhead in a trade school, who may hit him. You've seen marks on Nate's arms, purple bruises with a sickly yellow edge.

Maybe to salve his own hurt, maybe because Nate sees something in you that you can't see in yourself, he regularly asks you out. You've been back to his apartment a few times. You lie down on his twin bed, unzip, and jerk off together. You tell yourself he doesn't really turn you on. You tell yourself that the best stories connect sex and love. You notice that his bedspread is cheap and scratchy.

Besides, you like it when he winds his foot around your ankle in public. He'll start to reach for your hair. Ward him off and say: "Don't go to grad school where you did your undergrad. Don't shit where you...."

"Stop it. I'm not putting you off. I am older than you. I do know more. Listen, you need distance to look serious. You need. . . ."

"There's no *we*. We've been over this. We can't be a we. Even if you are beautiful. You are. Don't let that jerk tell you otherwise. If anything, he's your real problem."

Step 6: Follow up the next day, Thursday afternoon, with a brown bag lunch for academic job seekers.

The meeting will be about interviewing skills. The tenured set will talk about ways to be casual. In five bullet points, they'll discuss appropriate chitchat with a hiring committee.

Don't feel any pressure. You have a healthy IRA and no debt. You've been on staff so long that you have fifteen interviews at the Modern Language Association conference. Be excited about the one for Kalamazoo. You have a history with that place. You're nothing if not a master at folding time in on itself.

And if all those interviews don't work out? Just this morning, Miranda rushed to the airport for business in Austin. There's a hint of a new job, a bigger position, a C-something. COO? CEO? You've never heard letters in this order before.

But right now, you need to fit in. Try to model the group's concern. It's hard to be a grad student for years on end. The role wears thin. So play it comic, antic. Say: "Who knew it would end up like this? I mean, I wanted to read and here we are trying to get jobs, out in the world. We're not made for the world. Right? Because how will any of us pay off our student loans? I mean, a first job pays what? Twenty-five a year? We all need to find some rich woman and seduce her. Or some rich man. Hahahaha. That's the only answer to grad school."

Step 7: Find yourself that same Thursday afternoon in a hotel room downtown.

You've met Rona like this on and off, sometimes weeks between, sometimes days. You don't have an exact number of times. That's how you know it isn't serious.

You can count the exact number of times you've jerked off with Nate. Five. That's also how you know it isn't serious.

Sneak into a room on the top floor without paying for it. Rona knows the manager because she used to wait tables at the restaurant off the lobby. And anticipate the twenty-first century. Tell yourselves it isn't adultery if you only go down on each other.

Although today doesn't go according to plan. Sit in the red chairs near the window. The city will twinkle in the dusk. Rona will have just gotten her diagnosis: breast cancer, stage four. Prognosis: thirteen, fourteen months.

The fabric in her vintage Chanel suit will stretch across her breasts. Wonder if there's nylon in it. Wonder what happens to dresses when the breasts are gone, when the person is gone. Does a dress hold its form, waiting on the hanger for the woman who will never come back?

Start to cry. Hate yourself for being a narcissist. Try to be strong. Rona's a part of your life. A part that's not in any other plot. Mourn its loss. No, mourn *her*, you asshole. She's sitting right across from you with all her hurt, all her hopes dashed.

See what happens when you forget to let books do the heavy lifting. Things get lost in the ruins of time.

Look up. She'll be crying. Mourning, too, although you know she'll be more concerned for her kids, herself, not for you, a fact that has kept you safe until now. She'll hiccup a question, a call for hope: "When are you and Miranda going to have children?"

Say: "I think being childless is the only way to go—with the wars and the way the economy is. I can't in good conscience bring a kid into this world. I don't know what's going to happen to us in ten, twenty years when everything. . . ."

"Oh, sorry. I can't get my head around your news. I can't. . . ."

"No, no. I don't mean it that way. It's not *news*. It's. . . ."

"Okay, yes, we want to have kids. Sure. And while I'm at it, I'm sorry."

"For what? For this, us, all of it, I don't even know anymore. I've never been any good at living. I'm better at reading. Better at believing. Which is of no help to you, to me, to anyone. Which is why I'm sorry, because I can't even get out of my fucking head long enough to realize this is about you, not me."

Step 8: Realize you have to find a temporary resolution on a Friday afternoon at your house.

Miranda will be flying back to Madison. So far, no job. She sounded upset on the phone. But you're more so. Rona. Your life. The pieces of it.

Call Nate. You want to lay your eyes on another person who knows you, who cares about you. Do they all have to disappear? And the ones who don't of their own accord, do you have to work so hard to make them disappear?

When Nate gets there, open a couple of beers. Put on a CD of Bach's Goldberg Variations. It's now your favorite, a wild ride through all that one song can be.

Sit on the floor in the living room. As the music swirls around you, say something about Bach, something absurdly professorial, something Nate usually eats up. Instead, he'll lean over and kiss you.

It's the first time you've been kissed by a man. It doesn't feel good. Or bad. Is there a word for it? The only one you can think of is "demoralized." Which makes no sense.

Nate will sit back on his haunches. "Well?" he'll say. "Now what?"

Stay silent. Where are the fucking words?

He'll look away and deflect into frets about school, life: simple at first, then angrier, slowly turning this moment into something understandable. He'll finally say, "I can't believe you made me change my major."

Tell him he's free to do whatever he wants. Hope he isn't. Sip your beer in silence.

He'll stand up, call his boyfriend, and leave, slamming the front door.

Finish his beer but pour yours down the drain. Think of little gestures like these as symbolic of something or other. Don't worry about what.

An hour later, drive to a dinner party on the deck of the gorgeous home of that cashed-out tech wonk who comes to your dinner parties. There are several couples: lawyer types, state government types. Usually, Miranda, who fits in. And you, who don't. These people know nothing about grad school, younger men, or dying lovers.

Over the grilled tenderloin, say: "She's supposed to land in an hour or so. Of course, we'll follow her career. We have to, right? I mean, she's got all the opportunities. And I can teach anywhere, right? I mean, this is what it means to be married to the big executive. I just didn't know it would mean I'd have to. . . ."

"Jealous? That's not fair. I'm a modern guy. I'm probably more of a feminist than she is. I believe it all. I think believing it all is the only way to save yourself."

Step 9: And end up on Friday night, sometime after midnight.
Miranda will be upstairs when you get home. "Hey, babe," she'll call out as you quiet the dogs at the front door.

Before you head up, crack open a bottle of red wine. Grab two glasses. In the bedroom, her suitcase will be open, clothes strewn on the bed. She'll be unpacking on the far side.

Take your position across from her. Ask, "How was it?" as you hand her a heavy pour.

She'll smile, her teeth slightly crooked, so beautiful, so human. "Shit, it's a man's world," she'll say.

Something will give way in her. She won't cry like Rona. Or rage like Nate. She'll seem at peace. As if her bones have settled into familiar angles.

"It's nice to be home," she'll say.

Nod. Act like you understand.

Soon, the lights will be out. Tell yourself that talking in the dark is the best intimacy.

Say: "They're asking what we're going to do. Who? Everybody. Our friends. Shit, it can make my head spin. Are you sure we want to rush into getting pregnant when. . . ?"

"Yes, we have to take our chances. I guess I've read too much. I know what can happen. I know how these things end. Plots, you know. They don't always turn out the way we. . . ."

"I know, I know: books don't predict real life. You don't have to tell me!"

Henry James in Venice

That fall, I taught my American novella class to well over fifty seniors in a cinder-block science building. All the desks were filled; a few guys sat on the floor. The smell of formaldehyde wafted in from the hall.

Sometime during our discussion of Henry James's *What Maisie Knew*, we got into a rousing debate about Maisie's fate and restrained options. Abandoned by her mother and father, she's little more than post-divorce weaponry, a barb her parents toss at each other until they walk off to their new relationships and lives.

At one point, Maisie wants to make things easy on her benefactor, her now-former stepfather, Sir Claude. Her mother married him right after the divorce, then left him, too, with Maisie in his care. Sir Claude's a decent man with few funds and little imagination. He just wants to get on with his life. But without him, Maisie will be alone in Victorian England, where children are disposable capital. Innocent as ever, she gives him an out. He can leave her with her penny-poor nanny and they will fend for themselves. His moral obligation will be over.

A student with blond hair in a ponytail grew impatient with this late Victorian morality tale. "These people are idiots," she said. "Can't they just say what they mean?"

"Can anyone?" I asked. "Doing so would fill the silence around us, the same way a book does when you're inside it. But the great works of Western literature prove their redemption is impossible. They end. They disperse back into the silence. And here's the bigger problem: they do it more quickly than we do. Everyone in this room has lived a length of time longer than it takes to get lost in the biggest novel or poem. Ultimately, the great works of Western literature leave us and we go on. How? That's the question. How?"

To finish my point, I reverted to my old ways, or the ways of my mentors, reciting a sentence from the *What Maisie Knew*:

> *She chose the soft method of silence to satisfy him, the silence that after battles of talk was the best balm she could give him.*

That I'd located the moment when the great books failed me in a sentence from one of those great books was an irony I'd been destined to embrace from the get-go.

Frankly, I was worn out, left most days without a thought in my head. I walked the sidewalks to and from class with nothing more than a ringing in my ears. My life had fallen into tawdry affairs, then out of them, until I had no idea who I was. Until I was indeed my greatest hope, a blank page. Until I was the new Prescott.

Yet I craved human touch. Miranda and I no longer put our hands near each other in bed—although we did so in public: kissing lightly, running fingers along each other's spines. We'd been reduced to those finger exercises of affection, the ones I used to cherish, the ones we could busk for the rest of our lives.

Of course, my students didn't know any of that. "What *are* you talking about?" that co-ed asked.

I thought I'd been so honest. Plus, I quoted literature. Why was she so upset?

She went on: "People don't just end. They get married, have kids. And those kids live on. That's how the world works."

I looked around the room and had a vision, a minor one, more like a poetic moment, but the last time the scrim of my world ever tore open. I watched my students dissolve from scruffy twenty-year-olds into swaddled newborns, each one somebody's baby: all silent potential, hope incarnate, the most important piece of the human puzzle.

We did lots of jigsaw puzzles when I was a kid. Stacked on a closet shelf, their boxes tore over time and inevitably a random piece fell to the floor. One of us would pick it up and shove it back in a box—often the right one, sometimes not. A lot of the puzzles had one piece that didn't fit. As a kid, I'd set it over the final gap, gingerly, as if I didn't want to hurt it.

The last time Miranda and I were in Dallas, I got out a puzzle and set up the card table. Sure enough, there was a misplaced piece. I put it akimbo in the last spot.

Miranda pointed to it. "Hey, it's you," she said.

Tears started to my eyes. Was I mad? I had no words.

She saw my reaction and tried to solve it, an old gambit with us. "You're adopted," she said, as if the facts were incontrovertible, nothing to be feared. She chucked me under the chin, probably because my parents were in the room with us. "Or did you forget?"

I didn't want to be reminded that day in class either. I pulled a Caddie Anderson on my baby-students. "Get out," I said. "Just get out." I even fluttered my hand at them.

Some looked startled; most were probably happy to take a breather from the nut who was their prof. As they walked out, waddled out, maybe crawled out in diapers, I asked myself, Who saves *them* from the silence? Their parents? Their friends? Their future spouses?

No one, I thought, proud of that steely truth, still a Puritan at heart. But something about that vision, something inside that co-ed's answer to how life goes on, even James's words themselves—all of those things fit together. Some jumble of words and visions gave me an idea. I finally knew how to save myself, if no one else.

Miranda and I hadn't been able to conceive. We also hadn't slept together for a year. She was more and more upset. I felt steadily guilty, as if I were being punished. But I didn't want a child—mostly because I didn't want to be nailed into the story I was telling. As that co-ed pointed out, a child would have made it complete. So the way out of the plots of my life was to make one that would be grand enough to silence all the others and cram our marriage into it.

A real baby could give Miranda and me the right story and preserve the silence that had always been my natural state. But a fake baby could do more! A narrated baby. A made-up one.

To clarify my guilt, explain myself to whoever would listen, and take my marriage to the ninth circle of hell in my own descent, I decided as I sat in that empty classroom to fuse my marriage with a Henry James plot. I wasn't going to go home, get naked, get in bed, and wait for Miranda. I was going to write the two of us into the greatest performance piece of our generation: the infertile couple.

That day, I finally stopped trying to be a narrator and became an author. Not on the page, that cheap pulp that got written over, that couldn't survive a deluge, that lied as often as it told the truth. I would do what no other author could do: stick Miranda and me in a story that explained us. Our hopes and silences would be understandable. Our motivations, clear. Our troubles, identifiable.

Better still, our lives would become closer to what they were: that reverse-tint Kodachrome negative of my adoption plot. And if I were ever caught in a scent-free restaurant with a troubled boy or a hotel room with a dying colleague, I had an excuse. Well, he and Miranda were having trouble conceiving, so. . . .

Isn't that the best story: a new twist on the obvious? We could play it to our graves. Beyond, since we would be the last of our family lines. People might remember us with a sigh.

I wanted to be in the perfect marriage. I wanted out of our marriage. We had the perfect home. I wanted to find my real home. So many voices, so many conflicting vectors of morality and hope, so many damn narrators in my brain. But with the right story, I wouldn't need to hang on. I could hang the thing around my neck. Better, our necks, the characters in the tale. Isn't that what a great work of literature is all about?

Okay, Miranda was the tricky part. But her hand was no longer in the small of my back. She seemed to rely on me, particularly as her corporate life became more demanding. My hand was in the small of *her* back. Who knew that when we built a relationship on dependency, it would be easy to flip it back and forth?

I started to bring up our childlessness more and more at our dinner parties. It was believable. We were in our mid-thirties. Our biological clock—or so they said on TV—was ticking.

I made sure we were around families on the weekends: biking, hiking, even trips to the Madison farmers' market where everyone looped the state capitol counter-clockwise, never clockwise, a model of Scandinavian efficiency. I still commiserated with Miranda when she got her period but started mumbling things about fertility clinics.

At first, she seemed to resist. Not flare up, the way she would in the business world. Just push back gently, the way she did with me.

"I don't think we need. . . ," she said.

I had to have all the right answers, which involve ambiguity and doubt in the best plots. "It's hard to know what we need," I said.

I made an appointment without telling her, then mentioned it one night over vodka tonics. "We probably need help if we want a baby."

She looked away. "It would explain. . . ."

"A lot." I had to be as sure of myself as I'd ever been. Even if it didn't exist, probably *because* it didn't exist, our baby was the best fiction. We didn't need the real thing. We had something better. Something literary. That is, the imagination. And its child, hope. The ultimate surety, something no one could gainsay or prove false.

"When's the appointment?" Miranda asked. Her doubts seemed deeper in her eyes, somewhere under the green.

"Day after tomorrow," I said. "Plan on taking the morning off."

I asked Miranda to drive us to the two-story, industrial building with narrow windows.

"I'm so nervous!" I said on the way there. "They'll probably want to start with me. My dick, my balls." I laughed as if I'd told a joke. "Then we'll really know what's what."

Miranda's hands gripped the steering wheel, the skin white over the bones. Like my dad's hands when he drove me to school. See, I got plot resonance, too!

To this day, I don't know what Miranda thought. She was so determined and capable in her career. Perhaps she, too, lost herself in this story. Once, she'd offered an "I know" as some sort of answer. By now maybe she, too, had gotten tired of holding on. Or maybe she simply chose the easiest way out, even as I tried to break her sanity to save my own. Maybe she loved me unconditionally and was willing to follow me down any rabbit hole. That's the best motivation for a tragic heroine, right?

The doctor was a middle-aged man with red glasses and a black goatee. He looked vaguely Freudian and radiated concern.

We sat in hard chairs and learned about our future, our treatments. We nodded. We held hands. We didn't cry. We should have. It would have made the whole thing more believable.

We walked out and went to lunch at a place that excelled in late '80s décor: white walls, white tablecloths, bold abstracts. As the man, I decided on main-course salads: "Flank steak for me, salmon for my wife."

We looked at each other in gluey glances. We ate our meals in silence, forking up soggy lettuce.

With the coffee, Miranda tried to make a break for it. "Maybe we're going too fast."

Thankfully, the check came. I pushed it toward her. I could only play the man for so long. "Your turn," I said.

We weren't sleeping together because I couldn't stand the dishonesty, although I still couldn't explain what that meant. I wanted to make love with Miranda, but I also wanted to tell the truth—which made no sense whatsoever. What was that truth? The closer I got to it, the more alone I felt.

There was no one like me. I had to make a me that made sense. And if doing so involved pain for both of us, if it muted the person I loved so I could sound the depths of who I was and hear the essential loneliness that was my life, then she was a reasonable casualty in my lifelong war to conquer whatever life was supposed to mean.

I fed us more lines, and we became officially tragic. Not the contented childless couple who buys theater subscriptions and goes on cruises to Patagonia. The struggling couple, made for daytime talk shows, that new medium that sprang from the likes of us.

I videotaped an Oprah show about this new thing called "surrogacy" to watch with a couple who had three kids and a renovated Victorian. We ate bowls of ice cream and huddled around the TV set, furrowing our brows. After they left, I poured two shots of brandy. Miranda and I read in opposite corners of the living room. The wintry cold popped in the walls.

Maybe this sort of thing happens to lots of couples. Alcoholics, drug addicts, serial abusers: their stories lock their partners into believable but horrible sequences. Less dire, most couples surely fold each other into the plots they write. All of us pay the debt of learning to read, of seeing the world as a pattern of mirrored scenes and escalating climaxes. The best stories, the sort literary pros like me admire, include intricate symbolism and that vaunted irony, often with tragedy waiting in the wings. Like the one I was writing.

Miranda endured rounds of tests, blood draws, and invasive procedures. She took her temperature every day, charting her ovulation cycles. The pages piled up beside the bed. Another month gone. Another month gone. We looked at the stack: Exhibit A of our lives. Neither of us looked up and said, "Let's go make love." We didn't need to. We were lost in a good story.

The morning of my solo visit to the clinic, I washed the breakfast dishes, the hot water thrashing in the sink. I let the dogs out and watched them chase a neighbor kid into her house. I rounded them up, recited that quote about silence from *What Maisie Knew*, and got in my car. I inched through rush-hour traffic toward the clinic. The waiting room was packed.

"You were supposed to be here twenty minutes ago," the receptionist said.

I soon faced a nurse in whites and sensible shoes. She was probably used to guys jizzing in cups.

"You need a magazine?" she asked.

"For what?"

"*Playboy? Penthouse?*"

"Good grief, I'm fine."

She handed me a key tethered to a block of wood. "For the private bathroom," she said. "Or there's a public one down the hall with three stalls. Some guys get off on that. Your choice."

I laughed as if she'd told a joke. "The private one," I said.

"That's what I thought." She looked at her watch. "Hurry up. There's another guy waiting on you. How old are you?"

"Thirty. Give or take a few years."

She looked at my chart. "Second door on the left. Get busy."

I carried the cup to the bathroom and locked the door. I pulled my pants down, sat on the toilet, and put the cup within reach. Then I leaned back and closed my eyes, ready to come in the way I'd been practicing ever since Melody, the way I did with Rona and Nate, the only way I ever came, maybe the only way most people do. Eyes rolled back, I tipped off the edge of this world and wrote myself into my imagination, into a story, an alternate timeline. Now, à la Henry James. Why not go with the best?

Her necklaces were a stockpile of glitter. Not ready for dinner, she showed her intimacy in unkempt hair, which was woven into a knot that fell in ringlets around her face.

I kicked back a footstool and stretched out my legs. I wanted to seem at ease, since I was in love with her.

In the height of the Roman summer, she picked up a tumbler of lemonade from her dresser. She ran the glass down her neck, chilling her blood. Then she came out with it. "You needn't worry. I know what I'm doing. I'm going to him." Her words sang like lies, soft pulses in the air. "Unless you want him."

"God, no. He's too much."

She leaned into the brocade. "That's what I came abroad to find. I want my match. Someone who can see me. Someone who can balance me." Her eyes picked up the glow of the fire in the grate, stoked to mitigate the humidity, although the embers added to the heat. "Someone who would scare you," she said.

I'd taken coffee. I refused to be anything but an American. "You're wrong about that. There is no balance. That's a fantasy of novels."

She looked away, smiling. "So you don't want him?"

"He's destined for you."

"And you don't want me."

I gasped. "You are pert!"

She laughed it out. "No, you want to be *me*."

I ducked the shot and set down my cup. "I have always tried to get away from you."

"By coming to my private chamber?"

"By seeking your advice."

"So you can disobey it?"

"So I can choose."

She laughed again. "Is that what I am to you? All the choices? Am I everything?"

I nodded and let her have it. "Or maybe you're nothing," I said.

"Oh, yes, please, let me be nothing." She was enjoying it at last. "You be everything. You set yourself so high in heaven that you miss the things that matter."

Her eyes were dazzling.

"You'll go to him, even if he's cruel?" I asked.

She thought it through. "I love him."

"What happens when you don't?"

"Today is enough. But you wouldn't know about that. You've never been now. You've always been then. Or next."

I thought I had her. "Now is nothing. It is always passing away."

"Precisely," she said, her smile tender and welcoming. "There are no stories about now. You can only narrate it. You have to live it."

I emerged with the cup in a paper bag.

"Good job," the nurse said.

A week later, we got the results. I was normal. A perfect count. What a relief. *We* weren't infertile. Miranda clearly was.

In the logic of these clinics, the man's problem was solved with a sum: 100 million sperm per milliliter. The woman's was more ambiguous, even melodramatic. I'd saved the juiciest role for my wife. I congratulated myself. I also hated myself. Authors! What can you do?

Of course, Miranda could have stood up and hollered, The fuck are you doing to me? But as long as I kept the story moving, she seemed to slip forward in its stream, as I used to zip along those in condensed novels. We spent thousands of dollars on tests and never once had sex.

That spring, in the March light that was the compensation for the ongoing Wisconsin winter, we bundled up and went for a walk after dinner. Our neighborhood was full of tricycles and swing sets. In the intervening years, twentysomethings had bought up the bungalows. Young parents met us with knowing eyes. We smiled back. We knew who we were: the strolling, childless catastrophe.

We didn't talk much. My mania for plot stalled whenever we were alone. What good is a book if no one reads it?

I looked at the bare patches in the front yards, the would-be gardens still frozen hard. When I started writing us, I didn't know what would happen next. Now I did. The moment I got the plot right, as it finally ticked along almost like magic, I saw its ending. Prescott had been right: I needed a setting, at least for this part.

"Let's go to Italy," I said.

Miranda shook her head. "I can't get the time off. State contracts are coming due."

"You're the boss!" I reminded her.

"And you're teaching."

"Spring break. I'll take an extra week."

"Is that allowed?"

Many of my former peers were on far-flung appointments. Rona was in the middle of her second round of chemo. I was the endless adjunct, the chapters of my dissertation a messy bundle.

"Nobody cares," I said. "It's academia. Besides, we've always wanted to find your family in Tuscany."

All we knew was that Miranda's grandmother had been born in a tiny village north of Lucca. By now, most of the immigrant generation had died off. Her parents had come back into our lives, although they never once came to our house or spent a holiday with us. Still the American success story, they wouldn't want to talk about this past, about poverty close to starvation.

We walked by kids in heavy coats skipping rope. We both looked away.

"I could make it a tax break," I said. "There's always another paper to write, another conference. Look, I'll pull together something on James. We'll go to Tuscany, then on to Venice. I can do research there. I'll say I'm working on . . . his travel essays."

She was still unsure.

"The luxury of living in Italy," I said.

"We're not moving there!"

"His words, not mine."

"Sounds tempting."

A few weeks later, we drove the hills northeast of Pisa in search of something we called "roots." We'd collected a few hints from Miranda's cousins. "A small place just outside the main village." "Near a bend in the road."

We came to a rundown village. We knew no one and didn't speak the language. But one house had the right feel. It was little more than an abandoned building, a cow stall with extra enclosures, crumbled walls, and hay. It tipped against a rock outcropping.

"No one's lived here for years," Miranda said—which sealed it. We took pictures. I positioned her for the right angle.

"Stand here," I said. "No, closer."

She momentarily seemed to want out. "You can't really mean. . . ."

"This is your grandmother's home," I said, confident, definitive, even though the place was nowhere, nothing.

I congratulated myself on how lucky she was, how lucky I'd made her. I gave her what I'd never had. I gave her a family history. The long tale.

She seemed to relax into it. "Nonna did mention cows," she said.

I smiled. "I want to be in the next shot! Over there! By the cliff!"

Afterwards, we drove down the mountain to Lucca for a night at a five-star haunt with tall gates and flowery wallpaper. We checked in and went upstairs. Giddy, we tickled each other in the elevator. "We rounded this bend and there it was!"

In the months ahead, we'd show the photos to everyone. At a restaurant with friends, Miranda would pull them out and pass them around. At dinner parties, I'd retrieve them and let our guests feel that Miranda had discovered her place, somewhere to be from. I'd slip in something about my origins story. Or the lack of it. My backdrop textured her tale, a subplot in the larger melodrama we were living.

That night, we went down to the hotel's dining room around nine, the stars bright outside. Under drippy sconces, we were that typical, childless couple, the sort who don't talk over dinner, who sit alone together, vigilant and formal. We got through three courses, forks in our left hands. We polished off two bottles of Tignanello, an inky red with little fruit. We went back upstairs and tucked in.

After she fell asleep, I opened the pill box on my night stand and pulled out Immy's prayer.

> *Life is so short, any skill takes so long to learn, any attempt is so hard, any victory is so sharp, any joy slips away so quickly—by all this I mean love.*

I'd read enough now. I knew the words weren't Immy's. They were the opening lines of Chaucer's *Parliament of Fowls*. He'd cribbed them from Horace. James cribbed them for one of his stories, too. Everyone was playing a part. There was nothing original. We all work in the dark and do whatever we can. What's left is the madness of art.

I tore Immy's prayer to bits and blew the pieces onto the carpet for the morning vacuum cleaner. Then I plumped my pillow and lay back. Because I was an English prof, a professional reader, people always asked me, "What's your favorite book?" Maybe every committed reader gets that question. But it always unnerved me. Favorite? How could I pick? I loved them all.

Or had loved them. Now that I was an author, had created a plot and written our lives into it, I finally had the answer: James's *The Portrait of a Lady*. And if I had to pick one part of it, its end, when Isabel Archer realizes she's married the wrong man, Gilbert Osmond, the cruel art collector, as cold as a drafty room. She is locked inside.

She flees to her best friend, Ralph Touchett, who's back in England and riddled with TB. On his deathbed, Ralph tries to tell her how it all adds up. I knew the passage by heart. "*You said just now that pain is not the deepest thing,*" Ralph says. "*No – no. But it is very deep.*" He pauses, then goes on. "*It passes, after all. But love remains. I don't know why we should suffer so much. Perhaps I shall find out. There are many things in life. Remember this: that if you have been hated, you have also been loved.*"

Those words had become my mausoleum, my Armstrong-Browning library. They contained me. Soon, they'd let me go.

I woke a little after five. Early light seeped in behind the curtains. I showered quietly, dressed, and headed downstairs. I rousted the concierge and asked for coffee in the garden. I chose a small table near the back wall. A trellis stretched overhead; songbirds flitted in the vines.

Time slipped by. I stared at the gravel. I'd chosen someone who understood me. Who made me happy. Who loved me. I'd almost gotten that story right. But "almost" doesn't cut it. I had to change the tale. At the time, I thought by being like Chaucer and shoving another one into the book of my life without ever finishing the thing.

Miranda joined me later, at a more reasonable hour. We kissed as we always did when people were watching.

"I'd like to head into Lucca for some sightseeing," I said, a plan in mind.

She hesitated. "But Nonna's village. . . ."

"We got shots of her house. We don't really need anything else, do we?"

She looked away. "We have what we need."

I'd checked the guidebook and found the address for an international bookstore. We were set to leave for Venice the next morning.

In town, we walked on the stone ramparts. The grass below was brilliant green in the Tuscan sun. It was a perfect day to start taking a marriage apart.

We found a bench. She had some paperwork in her satchel. State contracts had arrived at the hotel for her. They gave me the perfect chance. "I have a quick errand," I said.

"Eighteen inches," she answered, as if I'd asked a question.

I looked confused.

"The necklace you're going to buy me."

I couldn't have afforded one, not on an adjunct's salary. Lately, we'd fallen into the shitty, competitive games that some couples play when there's great income disparity. At dinner with friends, Miranda would say, "If we relied on his salary, we'd be living in one of those awful holes in Madison's tabbouleh belt."

And I'd reply, "Oh God, literature's not worth that!"

Maybe my humiliation was her compensation. It wasn't enough. But it was something.

I left her on the bench and descended into the city.

The bookstore was small and shabby, the beige curtains stained with whorls. The front door sported a peeling decal of a Union Jack. An older woman behind the counter said "Buongiorno," with a British accent.

I told her I was looking for *The Portrait of a Lady*.

She found it on a back shelf. "Why do you want this?" she asked. "It's so out of fashion."

I smiled. The paperback was yellowed, but there wasn't a mark in it. "It's for my wife," I said.

The woman laughed. "Does she know what she's in for?"

"I doubt it."

I paid and walked back to the wall.

Miranda was sitting quietly on the bench, watching couples with their prams and yappy dogs. I handed her the sack.

"All for me?" She pulled out the novel and held it to the light. "Don't you have a copy?"

"Now you do, too."

She paused, seeming to weigh her choices. "I'll start it tonight," she said.

"Wait for Venice. It'll be right in Venice."

Neither of us had been there in years, so we were unprepared for the fact that it had become Times Square. I'd booked an absurdly expensive hotel a few canals off Piazza San Marco. Our room had way too much wallpaper. In the chinks, I could see one pattern beneath another.

Still, we were in Venice. Who stays in their room? I left Miranda and headed out to see Titian's "Assumption of the Virgin" at i Frari, my first pilgrimage whenever I visited. I found a hard chair in front of the church's altar. I looked at the apostles' lifted arms, their twisted bodies. They're reaching for the Virgin as she ascends into heaven. Idiots, I thought. Don't they know how the story ends?

Later, Miranda and I had dinner in a small café: a fritto misto between us, some roasted cipollini onions, a bottle of Friuli white. I said I was tired and went to bed early. She snuggled in next to me, pulled out *The Portrait of a Lady*, and started to read.

Over the next few days, she barely put the book down. I walked the alleys and crossed the canals by myself. She kept reading. Each night, I pretended to sleep, lying beside her, watching her turn the pages with my eyes at half-mast. I heard her gasp more than once.

No wonder. James writes about secrets, about the ways they shape and deform us. His truth is a twofold paradox. Without a secret, you'll never be human. But with one, you'll never be redeemed. I'm getting ahead of myself, pitching this story into the future, telling something now I didn't know then—but here it is, the final reason the great books fucked me up.

Beyond the existential crisis of adoption and the pain of trying to live in the face of a prophesied apocalypse; beyond the promise of coherence as all those plots deformed time around me; beyond the understanding that the great books are our only way to experience the quantum logjam of existence; beyond the bad faith in which books taught me to see the world as peopled with fleshless and bloodless characters—beyond all that, I had no idea who I was because I'm a gay man who likes to sleep with women. I couldn't find myself in a single thing I read.

Is there anything more gorgeous than a naked woman? Except for a naked man? I'm not bisexual. I don't love both genders equally. I love them differently. It all comes down to where I want to be in the dark. Not when I'm making love. That's easy. Or should be.

Instead, I'm truly myself when I'm asleep. When I'm dreaming. When I'm in the middle of another story in my head in the small hours of the night. At that vulnerable moment, do I want to nestle my nose into his skin or hers?

His. Alex's, when he held me one night. Nate's, if he'd ever let me.

A homosexual who loves to make love with women. I'd been right ever since those first condensed novels. I could fit into every plot. And so, because I was interchangeable, into none of them. All the literary genres in the world won't make sense of who I am. I'd been trying to make them do that for years, desperate to solve the riddle of me. I couldn't write desire right because I didn't know what was out of whack in me.

It was, is, and always will be love. It lies in the silence, not on the edges of my story, or your story, but in the bed with us. Love is the quiet and peace after sex, or before it, even without it, the fragmented and wordless space outside of the stories that we know we'll tell when we get up again and go about our lives. In trying to make love match the great works of Western literature, I almost negated my life. And Miranda's, too.

But I couldn't destroy her, even if I made her life hell. I was cruel and heartless in the way authors can be to their favorite characters. And although I thought I was so original, mine was the nastiest plagiarism, a tale that goes all the way back to Eve: the woman takes the fall.

And I know this, too: plots, even in the great books of Western literature, make love too simple. Despite trumpeting their own ambiguity and symbolism, they turn love into an easy dualism, the twin poles of existence: straight or gay, men and women, the eternal mystery. You're one way or the other. Maybe you're both. I'm not. Yet I am. No wonder no one wrote me. I had to. Not with Miranda, but here, in these words in your hand. In a book, the final irony. The joke's on me.

Again, I didn't know the full truth on those nights Miranda read *The Portrait of a Lady*. I only knew that a piece of me was secreted in those pages. I wanted her to see that she might be Isabel Archer, the tragic heroine; and that I might be Gilbert Osmond, the disastrous husband.

I didn't yet know that I was both of them. But at least I'd finally fused with the narrator. And not just any narrator, but the best one, a Jamesian one: barely there, the obscured presence who knows all the secrets, even if he can't tell them flat out.

Read on, Miranda. I'm hidden in that book. Just a few more pages. It's my last place to hide.

What Literary Genre is "Good-Bye"?

When Miranda finished *The Portrait of a Lady*, I wanted at least a small reaction. A sigh, a moan, an exhale. Maybe she'd reach over, try to wake me, and say something, anything. Preferably, "Oh, *that's* you," and let me off the hook.

She didn't. She set the novel on the nightstand, rolled over, and turned out the light, just as dawn's faint glow outlined the drapes. When I got up sometime around noon, I saw *The Portrait of a Lady* in the wastebasket.

I wanted one of the greatest works of Western literature to do in her what it had done in me: to commandeer her brain and lead her to a final understanding of us, of me. But my plan backfired. Not because she didn't get it. Maybe she did. But watching her read drained the life out of me. I knew I was nothing more than a stock character. A coward. A villain.

More importantly, I'd witnessed the act of reading from the outside and seen it for what it was: a temporary, enjoyable amnesia. It didn't reveal me. Or maybe it did, but not in the way I wanted. Mostly, I saw that I was irrelevant, if only for the moments Miranda was in the novel's plot, the one I thought was all about me.

We met around noon over espressos at the gilded hotel bar and said nothing important, nothing about our marriage, nothing even literary. We complained about the price of things in Venice.

"What do you want to do today?" she asked.

I'd expected to be on firmer ground. Someone—well, not me—would be changing her flight to head home. But we were still where we had been. I felt loose, as if my arms were coming out of their sockets.

"I want to wander the city," I said.

She scrunched up her nose. "I'd rather get a facial, work out. Doesn't this place have a gym? I'll meet you here for a drink after dinner." She kissed me, a proper peck, and walked off.

I left for the alleys and quays. For once in my life, I didn't take a map. The sun was so bright that the blue sky was the idealized reflection of the scummy Adriatic.

I'd finally found my perfect mirror: Miranda reading. Of course, I'd seen her read before. But I'd never *watched* her doing what I did for a living: turn page after page, night after night. The great works of Western literature had driven me to distraction. They'd also kept me alive. But no book or poem ever let me catch a full glimpse of the true me, a reader.

Maybe that's another part of the marriage argument. The best mirror is the imperfect, damaged, and beautiful silvering of the person we love.

In the end, I don't have all the right words. I just know that watching her read a book I loved somehow broke the hold of the great books over me. After those days in Venice, I never again saw a poet on a country road or watched Hebrew letters dance on a page. And I lost the fear that I ever would.

As I walked down the quays and into shaded passages, I knew I'd also seen in Miranda what was in me: sadness. It was the hole inside me that Jesus was supposed to fill, the reason I wasn't at home in my body, the reason I tripped across flat floors. It was why I lost myself in literature. Why I wanted to find a voice. Because, in the end, my essence was silence. Because no mother's milk ever let down at the sound of me.

I was the drop in my own stomach, the hollow feeling at the top of the roller coaster hill. When I'd first read *The Stepford Wives*, I'd mistaken the feelings for something *about* me, maybe *in* me. But it was just *me* all along. The unanswered cry of a newborn. And I was the chatter between my own ribs. It wasn't some warning about what would happen if I read too much. Those twinned sensations were about the thrilling hope that reading could salve the silence and the buzzy, abiding knowledge that it couldn't. Sadness was the ground note of my polyphony. I read the great works of Western literature to drown it out. They lied and said they could.

I wandered over to one of the arching bridges that span the Grand Canal, this one linking the basilica of San Marco with the

Accademia, one of the great museums of the Western world. This bridge also linked the two halves of my life: the churchy me who believed I was so empty that I needed to be saved and the arty me who read the great works of Western civilization to get saved.

I watched the vaporetti carrying tourists this way and that. What do you do, I asked myself, when the story you're telling reaches its climax and you're left standing alone in the middle of a crowd?

Books end, as I'd told my students. And we go on. But how?

Miranda and I went back to Madison. I hadn't gotten a single follow-up from my fifteen interviews. I couldn't give the right answers to questions like "Why has your dissertation taken so long?" and "Why does your CV for American lit list medieval publications?"

I was told I was welcome to my temporary job in the English department at Madison for as long as I liked. In the afternoons when I didn't have class, I drove into the Wisconsin countryside. I walked the sidewalks of failing small towns. I stared into empty storefronts and drank watery coffee at broken-down diners.

I saw less and less of Nate and Rona. He was too needy; she, too honest, although now she was also very sick. And I was still a coward. I fell into a celibate monogamy, another ending for the marriage argument.

I didn't pick up a book except to review what I needed to teach. I stopped going upstairs to my home office. I lived in the kitchen, cooking elaborate meals, picking at a few bites, and cleaning up after a bottle or two of wine. Crawling into bed beside Miranda, I'd wait for sleep, and wait, and wait. For what? Another sign? The vision of her reading in that Venice hotel room haunted me until I wanted to cry out in the darkness, wake her up, and say "I know," the way she had once said it to me. I never did.

That summer, Miranda's Austin opportunity came through, a terrific, high-paying job. We talked about living in separate states. Then the final irony set in: hers was the only story I had. I resigned my lectureship and followed her South. We found a two-bedroom bungalow in a trendy downtown neighborhood. "Look, a formal library," Miranda said, passing through to assess the plumbing and the circuit box.

I stared at the built-in shelves. They were pressboard, cheap, white, and pristine. I could trust them to hold my books when I left them. And when I left her.

I was on the wrong side of Isaiah's wall. I'd once thought that it marked off my silly, showy world from his more cohesive one. But I'd had it backwards. I'd settled in the crazy landscape of the imagination's far country and tried to build a home out there with Miranda. Now she'd gone on with her real life and left me stranded in my pretend one.

We signed the papers for the house. I was about to find out what every writer knows: the end of a story is an unforgiving affair. In my past, I'd treated people like minor characters and walked away, or as if we were at the end of some bender that had gotten out of control, as if pretending that the whole thing hadn't happened was a polite way to handle all the broken glass. But I was going to have to do a writerly thing. I was going to have to say "the end." No amount of preaching about the apocalypse prepared me for it.

With Nate, I was my own cliché. I copped out like a modernist, like Virginia Woolf. When I was temporarily back in Madison to wait for the moving truck, I relaxed into an ending like the ones in *Mrs. Dalloway* or *To the Lighthouse*. You turn the page and think, Wait, that's it?

In class, I'd called the modernists' vanishing act "contempt for the reader in experimental form." But Woolf's major novels had so fractured time that it couldn't be put back together, which was about what Nate had done to my story.

I didn't call him or write this new thing, an email. I never explained myself, never said "I'm sorry." I didn't walk away. I just stopped talking. I have no idea if he even noticed.

I saw him on Twitter recently. He's gorgeous if graying, a wry smile and scruffy hair. Time is a skilled abuser. Its survivors forgive its damage.

With Rona, I was a coward. I thought I'd go hard-boiled, noir, Elmore Leonard. I drove to her house, a small one-story with a weedy yard. I used my key and walked in with a nod, trying to play the tough, even when I had to look at the shambles of cancer care, pills scattered on the coffee table.

Stretched out on the couch, she was stick thin and bald. She had no time for my knock-off Humphrey Bogart. "I knew this would happen from the day we met," she said.

Her eyes were sunken but vibrant, her wire glasses taped at the hinges because her illness had destroyed her finances. No book ever prepared me to see her like this. Or to look at death, the true, awful ending. I'd curried heaven and hell, only to be confronted now with their final truth, a silence beyond whatever I'd imagined.

"How?" I asked her. "How did you know this would happen?"

If I was going to go on, not just now but for years to come, I needed to negotiate a way through the future without directions being fed into my brain by books. How *do* people get through whatever comes next without predicting it, guarding against it, and setting it into a plot?

I was a fool to think Rona would have an answer. Dying, she didn't need my folderol. She waved me off. "Just tell me you're sorry and get out."

I didn't. I'd practiced several lies in the car. But when I looked at the bruises on her arms and the lump of scar tissue from her chemo port, all my freshman-worthy compositions fell apart. I said the only thing I could, the sort of balm the great books hope to whip up, an alchemy of hope from the lead weight of despair: "My life is better because you've been in it."

She didn't think the great books needed to be worshiped. She thought they were flawed but necessary attempts at meaning. She dismissed Prescott out of hand yet cozied up to his brilliance. At times, she seemed to understand me better than Miranda, although I knew such thoughts were a bad, boyish excuse for our affair. Worse yet, they killed off my hope that to be known was the same thing as to be loved.

Still, my sentiment caught her off-guard. "Your life is better? Look around you! What about mine?"

Rona took her cane, struggled to her feet, and walked me to the door.

"Don't come back," she said, then smiled, even laughed. "Goddammit, you'll always be a knock-off saint, trying to make the road to nowhere look like a pilgrimage. But thanks for today. It was nice to watch you squirm. Now get out. I need to die on my own."

Actually, she lived another year, way beyond her prognosis, thanks to Red Devil and other chemos from hell. I got a call from hospice at the end. She'd asked to hear my voice, although she could no longer speak. She listened as I repeated that same line about my life being better, the same words in the same order—but not rehearsed, just hopeless, honest, and desolate, that human amalgam that can add up to the truth.

She died later that afternoon, surrounded by her kids. But she's lived in my head every day since. What I wouldn't give to call her up and have her knock me off balance again!

When I got to Austin, the moving van driver informed me that over half the weight of the truck was my library. "And that includes your car," he said. He'd parked my GM Saturn in the center of the semi, then filled the seats and trunk with books before building a wooden frame around the chassis to carry hundreds more boxes.

"You read all those?" he asked.

"Not yet."

"You going to?"

I thought about it a moment. "No," I said.

"But you wanted to get them down here?"

I shrugged.

He walked away, muttering something about yuppies.

I landed a job at a small, Catholic college and taught what I knew (but never James). Rather than free-associating with texts, I now gave formal lectures, twenty-page essays I read word for word. Otherwise, I played the professorial apparition, appearing on campus for classes and office hours. I ran the Writing Lab but didn't always show up when I needed to man the front desk, book the appointments, and organize the adjuncts. Instead, I drove out into the Texas hill country to stare at those escarpments that had once filled me with hope. Now I saw unstable soil over bleached limestone.

For a while, Miranda and I kept up the charade of being infertile, if only for ourselves. She still stacked the pages of her ovulation charts next to the bed. But we never once made love in Austin. We just carried on until we broke up the only way the long-married can: like pages once glued together, now torn apart. A hole in me matched an overlay in her. Jagged edges in each of us could be pieced together like a puzzle.

We met after work at a small restaurant near downtown, the sort of place that served pancakes to the strung-out at three in the morning. We were earlier, more respectable, at six or so. We ordered burgers because it was reasonable to order dinner when dinner was served.

She was headed out of town on a business trip. She looked across the table, pursed her lips, and nodded once, a hard bob. "We're really doing this?" she asked.

I didn't answer. I had all the words but couldn't put together a sensible sentence. We finished our meal in silence. The pickles were so sour that they buzzed my gums.

I couldn't offer her Rona's benediction about my life being better. It was too smug for this folly we'd called our marriage, although it was truer for Miranda than it had been for Rona.

Instead, I asked, "Will you date again?"

Miranda flattened her palms against the table. "How come you never say the right thing?"

I tried to explain. "I'm trying to save myself."

"You're doing a great job."

She wanted a small triumph, the final word. She loosened her palms and came out with it.

"I knew you," she said.

That simple sentence: subject, verb, like the one from that dinner party in Madison years before, but now in the past tense and with a direct object. *I knew you*—what I'd dreamed about, the twin poles of my identity: to be known and to find the moral of my story. I'd become the character who stays true until the end of his tale. I'd embodied another lie from literature.

"I just want to make it clear," she said when I didn't respond, "that I played by your rules."

My jaw clenched. "I didn't mean to hurt you."

"But you did."

"Did what?" I asked. "Hurt you or mean to hurt you?"

"Just stop," she muttered.

I wanted her to say something about our infertility lie, about those pictures of her grandmother's house in Italy. I wanted her to know that I hated myself because she'd gone along with the story. That I'd probably never understand why she did. And that it would make me feel better if she would say she hated me, too.

She never did. So I said something close to it: "I knew what I was doing."

She looked away. "Too bad that's a lie."

She was partly correct. Hindsight is a sachet stuffed with shit. I tossed out another half-truth, the only kind I seemed capable of. "We were never right."

She pushed her fists into her temples to hold herself. "You're wrong. We were."

"Do you blame me?"

"Yes, no," she shook her head. "Or yes, I do, but I don't care."

I was trying to be honest. "We need to get away from each other."

"Because you like men?"

It stunned me. I could see her in bed: on top of me, sure and sexy.

"Not exactly," I said, still unsure of this part of my story. "Remember, I told you that night when I fell off your bed? The Franklin's Tale? But I like women, too. It doesn't make any sense."

She sat back, eying me coldly. "Don't pin this on me."

"I can't," I said, trying to sound brave. "Mostly, I like books."

"Utter bullshit. But you can have them for the rest of your life."

Maybe I wouldn't, but I still had to tell her. I thought it was the worst thing I could say. It stung my eyeballs. "I've never once felt at home."

She threw me a withering look. She was the wrong person to hear my confession, a sure sign our marriage was over.

"Go to hell," she said. "We made a life together. Maybe it wasn't perfect, but it was what we could do. And that wasn't enough for you."

She plunked down money for half the check and walked out. I emptied my wallet and followed her.

"Don't thank me, but I paid off your credit cards," she said in the parking lot.

"What? Why?"

She looked away. "You still don't get it." The Texas humidity was thick around us. "But here's your chance. The big moment. What you live for. The epilogue!"

I had so many things to say. But at the end of our story, I couldn't find any words. I proved myself the hack I'd always been. I plagiarized from the poet William Butler Yeats:

How many loved your moments of glad grace,

And loved your beauty with love false or true,
But one man loved the pilgrim soul in you,
And loved the sorrows of your changing face.

Miranda surprised me, reached over and hugged me. Then she backed up to laugh a little: slightly snide, mostly sincere, very adult.

"And you're wrong again," she said.

"That I loved you?"

"About one man. You don't know the future. You never have." She turned business-like, finally ruthless with me. "Make sure your stuff's gone when I get back. And take all the books. Every fucking one."

In the years ahead, we stopped speaking, stopped emailing, and got a divorce through lawyers. I didn't even show up for the final decree. Ours was truly the end of a Victorian novel: complications that finished at exactly the place anyone could have predicted from the get-go. Years later, their marriage ended like a car crash.

That night, I stopped at an office supply store for boxes. How many did I need? I had no way to cart away all those volumes in my car. I lost my nerve, making the decision harder. I bought ten boxes. Back at the house, I filled two with clothes, then a third with family matters, folders and files. I filled one with saucepans, dinnerware, and cookbooks. I used one for a haul of CDs. Which meant I had five boxes left for the great works of Western literature.

I walked into the library. Like a guy at the end of a love affair who cradles a pillow to his face, I cracked open an old copy of *Great Expectations* and breathed in its musky sweetness. Then I slipped the book back onto its shelf and looked around. George Eliot? That's how I learned about forgiveness. John Milton? That's how I spent a semester pretending I still believed in God. James Joyce? Wasn't college lit amazing?

The phone rang. I missed it, lost in thought in the days before answering machines. It rang again for a longer time. I finally picked up. "What?"

"Surprise," Immy said—didn't exclaim, just said.

We hadn't spoken in years. "How'd you find me?" I asked.

"Called UW. They said you'd moved. Ever hear of this thing called 911?"

"You mean 411."

"Given you, I'm not sure."

I wasn't in the mood. "Fine. But how did you know to call me right now?"

"Buddy, you're always into some *now*."

She was about to be a human catalyst again. Not a character from one of the great books. Like Prescott: always herself. But better: solidly in the world. I told her the story so far.

"Don't say I didn't warn you," she said. "When we first met? Remember?"

I didn't want to congratulate her. "Just tell me what to do," I said.

"Hurray! The world still needs nuns!"

"You're not a nun."

"And this isn't *Sophie's Choice*. Just pick some books and put them in a box. Are you coming out?"

I thought of Alex, of Thad, of *Godspell*. I hadn't read a book in over a year, but I was still trying to be the guy I knew in every plot.

"Out of what?" I asked her.

"As I suspected. Okay, first step. Find a book that means something to you."

I laughed. "You're asking the impossible."

"Do it!"

I filed along the shelves, running my fingers along the spines. "Eureka!" I said.

"You want to tell me what it is?"

"No."

"Dare you."

"My childhood Bible." I opened the back cover. There were the calculations for how long McGovern would reign as the Antichrist.

"Not exactly what I would have suggested," Immy said. "Let's move on to something better. And do it fast."

She sat on the phone for the next hour and helped turn my loss into something rational. I stayed away from almost all of the hardcovers. I needed to stay light. I looked for books without my scrawls. I filled the boxes with paperbacks like William Faulkner's *Soldier's Pay* and Anthony Trollope's *Kept in The Dark*. The only hardcover I packed: that copy of *The Complete Works Of Samuel Taylor Coleridge* from Baylor. Otherwise, I took stuff no one reads, stuff I'd still hoped to read, stuff I now knew I'd never read.

"I can't do any more," I said, exhausted. "Any skill takes so long to learn."

"No, it doesn't."

"You said it."

"Wrote it, didn't say it."

"And stole it," I added.

"Aw, you really are growing up," she chuckled. "You still have that piece of paper?"

"I lost it in Venice."

She sighed. "You're banality made flesh."

But I wanted to tell her more. "You said that prayer was about sex."

She laughed. "You would remember that part."

"Maybe that's why I prayed it so many times. It really helped me to figure out that. . . ."

"Holy fuck, Mark, shut up! Stop being afraid. Stop filling your life with so many words. Just get out and get on with it."

I did. It would prove to be the hardest chapter: to live my life without telling myself the story of how to live my life. But that lay in the offing.

Immy called me a few years later, after she'd gotten her MS diagnosis. Her wife had unexpectedly died. "Picnic, lightning," she explained, trying to be funny, plagiarizing the important part once again. This time, I knew it was from Nabokov. *Lolita*. Humbert Humbert's curt explanation of his mother's death. I also knew enough to call Immy on it.

"Don't grow up too much," she said. "You'll lose that innocence you patent."

She wasn't losing hers. She'd gone back to her order and taken her vows again. "Can't help myself," she said.

After that, she disappeared into the miasma of Catholic Health Services. I tried to find her recently. I couldn't track down an address or an obituary. She vanished, maybe like Elijah, carried into the clouds in a fiery chariot, as would befit one of my minor prophets.

Before I walked out of our Austin bungalow that night, I spotted my teaching copy of *Jane Eyre*. Immy had told me I was making things too hard. I grabbed the book and put it in my back pocket. It was the only great work with my obsessive, obscuring marginalia that

I kept. I left the rest of them for Miranda to clean up, the last promise I broke.

I don't know what happened to the books. I assume she pulped the lot. I'd like to think she kept one or two to remember me by. I wouldn't have.

I drove away, telling myself that I was starting over, that I'd come to the end of this timeline. But I had five boxes of books. I still couldn't do a proper purge. Not yet. And certainly not with *Jane Eyre* in my pocket.

Charlotte Brontë was one of my kind, an evangelical who thought she could get away from the moors. For a while, she led the high life in London, then retreated back to her father's piss-poor parsonage in Haworth.

We're a tough lot, we true believers. We like to gnash before we swallow.

How to Shove a Monk in a GM Saturn

Step 1. Stay up for the call.

The phone will ring sometime after midnight, maybe as late as two if the weather's fine. The voice on the other end will be all panic from the top of the college's brass. "Would you mind? Hate to bother you. Brother Bart's downtown."

Rush to put your clothes on, a one-legged hop. You know Texas. You speak its language. "Would you mind?" means *aren't you one of them?* "Hate to bother you" means *you like your job, don't you?*

Be thankful that Austin is self-consciously '90s hip. Addicted to boosterism, too. You just read in the paper that the city's the number four grunge scene after Dayton. At least it's not a Texas town that shoots queers.

Problem is, you've never liked bars. Not since that joint in Waco where your friend Clay bonded with the bartender over ABBA. You'd rather put on Bach, pour a bourbon, and. . . .

Shit, don't read a book. Do something easier. Listen to NPR. Listen to the crickets. Enjoy your time by yourself. You've spent years telling yourself you'd be better off alone. Fucking enjoy it.

Except now you have to hurry.

Step 2: Make your rounds in a set order.

There'll be three or four spots, depending on the police raids in Ann Richard's Texas. She's said to be a liberal. It's hard to tell. But it'll help that Brother Bart doesn't drive. He takes cabs—which limits the range.

First, go to that small bar near the governor's mansion. In the front room, you'll see ratty pool tables with rattier transvestites, mostly balding, middle-aged men in drop-waist Laura Ashley numbers.

Head for the back room, where the younger guys fill a small dance floor. These are Brother Bart's type. Buff. Tweezed. Callous. Sometimes, they lob insults at the transvestites. You've seen fistfights break out, lace collars torn off.

Your monk won't be there, or at the other small bars. But you'll have done things in the proper order. Head for the big prize: Oilcan Harry's. AIDS is rampant. Gay sex is still illegal. The place is a warehouse of neon and despair.

Tip the bouncer your last twenty bucks, a bicep-y guy in the black tee. He always lets you double-park your Saturn. You slept with him once. He'd seemed so plainsong. "Wanna?" he'd asked at closing time, a quiet question that mirrored your own hurt.

His apartment was spare: a mattress on the floor and a weight set. He insisted on playing The Carpenters. He danced around the room but didn't put on your underwear. You fell asleep with his arm crooked around you, then he kicked you out in the early afternoon.

Tricking with him will be the reason he'll feel entitled to crack jokes now. "I'd prefer it if you drove sumpthin' good," he'll say. "A Jaguar or shit."

Respond with a thin smile. In tax season, you'll try to claim your tips to him were unreimbursed business expenses. The man at H&R Block will frown and say, "You have a strange sense of how things work."

Inside the bar, a ladder wrapped in chaser lights will be pitched against one wall. A drag queen will be standing halfway up, lip-synching *Ain't No Mountain High Enough*.

Look away. Look for the old man in a cowl—which isn't easy. Texas is a repressive place. Dress-up is common. If you can't be yourself, be someone else. For example, a guy who still hasn't truly come out but hooks up with the bouncer at a gay bar.

Spot your mark. He'll be standing near several younger guys, barely out of college. They'll have blond highlights, wide shoulders, and narrow hips. Your guy is past seventy, a little hunched. He'll be leering at them. He'll also be wearing the hood of his cowl over an Izod shirt and skin-tight jeans. He'll look like a chicken in Catholic drag.

Pause as you always do. Try to get over the pain. His? Yours? Don't ask. You won't want the answer. And these days, there'll be no one to give it. No author. No poet. No prophet.

Stroll up to your monk. Play this part casual, despite the sadness that makes you trip along the bar's floorboards. Make conversation, then steer your monk outside. You've done this countless times. Pride yourself on your determination.

Step 3: Start from the passenger side.
Open the car door, tuck his head down, and shove as much of him inside as you can. He'll be drunk, somehow brittle *and* pliable.

Your mother would now make reference to what will clearly be "the bulk of the matter." His butt will stick out of your car door. Try pushing harder, madder.

He'll end up across the shift console, his cowl and shirt bunched up. See the age spots on his back, seborrheic keratosis, the scabby whorls that are the marks of time in men, a sort of lizard skin, a primordial regression, and everything you fear.

There'll be only one conclusion. The job's impossible from this end.

Step 4. Walk around to the driver's side.
You'll need to *pull* him upright, but people are starting to gather. Even in Austin, they don't expect to see a stocky blond guy shoving a monk into a GM compact.

Focus on the task at hand. Don't think about Brother Bart's tenured position at the college. About how his behavior tonight would probably get you fired. Or about how you've already been called to the Dean's office for committing what she called "religious persecution."

You told your students that the character Jane Eyre wussed out at the end of the novel by getting married to Rochester, the guy who locks his first wife in the attic. You said that Charlotte Brontë wussed out, too. She set out to mock God and ended up with a Christian miracle, a voice across the moors: *Jane, Jane!* You called Brontë's novel *and* her faith "a failure of nerve." Two students who tote around enormous rosaries reported you.

The Dean had on a ruffled, white blouse with a turquoise brooch. "We can't be giving students the wrong ideas," she said. She licked a sharpened pencil and made a note in your file. "I'll be keeping an eye on you."

You started to say something about Brother Bart, about how you've been shoving him in your Saturn. Wonder if he has a file. Suspect files are for the secular faculty.

Stop wasting time! It'll be well past midnight and people will be peering through the windshield of your car.

"Is he all right?" someone will ask.

Step 5. Jolly up the bystanders.

Say: "Never better!"

Do this in a hopeful voice. We've been over how. Pitch it up. Alto-ize it. And speak with exclamation marks. "Nothing to see here!"

"Is he religious or something?" someone will ask.

Say: "Who knows what these guys are into?"

Finally, a bystander will ask, "Are you two together?"

You'll be tempted to smart off and say *My dad!* But then you'd be his son and monks don't have sex. Or aren't supposed to. You wouldn't want to get the logic of the story wrong.

Step 6. Open the driver's door.

See his blue eyes when he looks up at you. See the thinning blond hair. See yourself, an older version of the guy in that dorm room mirror so long ago.

Brother Bart's parents probably told him he was full of promise. Imagine him running around his house, a suburban tract home. He's three, maybe four, naked, just out of a warm bath, giggling, laughing, drops of water on the kitchen tiles, a sprint into the towel in his mother's arms, a red thread clearly marking which end was for his face. Now he's found himself in a gay bar at an awkward moment in his life.

Be careful. If you're distracted, he'll try to kiss you. Calm him down with clichés. "There, there, you're going to be fine. Let's get you home to . . . b-e-d." Spell it out. Doing so will seem funny and lead to a moderate bitterness, a nice liniment for what you've lost.

You didn't move fast enough. Those young boys from the bar will have come outside and taken up positions like a Greek chorus. The bouncer will let them hold onto their drinks. He's done you no favors. Wonder if he thought you were any good in bed.

"I thought it was a fetish thing," one of the boys will say. "These old guys'll do anything to get a piece of my ass."

"Look at his sandals!" another will screech. "Like Jesus!"

Don't think how these boys would never notice you. And you're wearing decent shoes. Slip-on Ballys. You bought them on credit. You'll pay them off for seven months, long after anyone in the administration has stopped thanking you. Long after Brother Bart has spent a sabbatical in Europe at the church's expense. Long after you've started dating a guy in seminary because you can't stay away from what you know.

Step 7. Grab his belt with one hand, take his shoulder with the other, and wedge him upright in the passenger seat.

It'll be hard not to hurt him. You've lost the woman you loved, your life with her. What has Brother Bart sacrificed? A few weeks ago, at a faculty party, you heard him say that celibacy "means only women."

Start the car. Ease into traffic. Celibacy? Plus, a pension.

Once you're on the highway, Brother Bart will lean against you and say, "I've still got it, don't I?"

This will seem funny tomorrow when you tell it at brunch over a Bloody Mary with your straight friends. It will seem funny because you have to be able to lose everything and stay human. It'll be the hardest thing you'll ever do. But at least you already know how. It's what the great books teach, what chemistry teaches, what even religion teaches: everything seeks an equilibrium.

When the Dean confronted you about the way you taught *Jane Eyre*, you told her not to worry. You always remind your students that Charlotte Brontë was accused of being an atheist by her Victorian cohorts but that she eventually got married to her father's curate.

"In the end," you told the Dean, "everybody comes home."

The Vanity of Bonfires

How do you live your life without narrating it? You stumble. You falter. You make it up. And not always that well.

One spring morning in mid-February, I slipped into a pair of khaki shorts and a fleece sweatshirt. My lit survey class wasn't until that afternoon, so I stepped onto the deck of the place I'd rented with a cup of coffee to enjoy the Texas air.

Tucked above a cove off Lake Austin, the house was topsy-turvy, built into a limestone ledge that sloped down to a shady dock. The parking area was above the roof. A winding stone walk led to the front door. And a smaller path bent around the rocks to my level, the true first floor, which had been advertised as the second.

Downtown was a few miles away, but the din from the traffic might as well have been on the far side of the earth. The only sound I heard was the putter of a motor boat, hidden behind a curtain of leaves.

I had my copy of *Jane Eyre* in hand. Despite the Dean's concerns, I taught the novel every semester. Sometimes I even carried it in my glove compartment when I went monk-hunting. Of all of the great works, I had the most trouble leaving it behind, this better version of *Great Expectations*, the story of a plucky orphan who stands up for herself and still gets home.

I was slated to give a lecture that afternoon on the part of the novel in which Jane wakes up and sees the ghostly figure of Bertha Mason, Rochester's first wife, in her bedroom mirror. The madwoman from the attic is the image of Jane's future if she stays with this awful man, the one she'll eventually marry.

Once, I'd bellowed about the virgin/whore choices in Victorian society and probably Prescott-ed something about President Clinton and his sex life. These days, I talked more quietly about the first time you see a true reflection of yourself, the absurdly paradoxical notion that the journey to knowing yourself starts when you see another person in the mirror.

"All too often at night, it happens at night," I told my students. "Even in bed," I added, daring another clash with the Dean.

With time to spare, I dropped the paperback on the deck boards, squatted on my haunches, and cupped the mug to my lips. A squirrel raced along a limb. How odd, I thought—because my landlady upstairs was an inveterate gardener. Scuppernong grapes hung off wires. Waterfalls of rosemary ran down the cliff. To Fiona, any squirrel was a bushy-tailed incarnation of the devil, digging up her Eden. She'd recently gone to an industrial supply and bought some horrid toxin. She'd dusted it on apple wedges and laid them around her property. She'd killed every four-legged creature in a two-mile radius. So a squirrel was a rare. . . .

I heard the cock and lock of a twelve-gauge shotgun on the deck above my head. I ducked for cover, spilling coffee on my legs. The blast shook the house and echoed across the lake. When I looked up, there was no squirrel and no limb, just the powdery fog of gunpowder.

Fiona peered over the railing, her gray hair wound in a bun. "Breakfast?"

"You, you, you can't just. . . ."

"Whose house is this?"

I held up my empty mug. "I could have been burned."

"Were you?"

"No."

"Then stop whining."

"You should warn me," I said. I was in my mid-thirties and so battle-scarred that I just once wanted to be the voice of reason.

"Aren't you from Texas?" Fiona asked. "Didn't you hear the pump action? Don't you know what that means?" Through the slats, I could see her feet, pink as a baby's, although she was almost seventy. "All you have to do is pay attention! That's how you'll get better. And get up here. Breakfast won't wait."

Fiona wasn't a prophet. I never met another one of those. She was my healer, a wild-eyed Emily Brontë to my prim Charlotte. She was impassioned about small things and prone to outbursts that calmed into a weird hybrid of Zen and grumpiness. "There's no decent brioche in this state," she once told me, as if she had no other complaints.

She'd moved to the rocky landscape west of town before it became the mass-market redoubt of the Silicon Valley wannabes who were remaking this cowboy capital into a sprawling strip mall. With a hankering for Georgian columns and eight bedrooms, they scraped the scrub brush off the limestone. Fiona responded with an iron fence around her acres. There was no call box. The imposing gate swung out, not in. She either knew you were coming or you didn't.

The one sally from the larger world was by Ladybird Johnson. Every few months, Fiona's house would be awash in bureaucratic nonsense. Phones rang. Messengers arrived. Agents mumbled into walkie-talkies.

The former First Lady was too old to make it down the path to the main floor of the house, so Fiona dragged a picnic table and mix-and-match chairs up to the parking area. The women took tea near beds of phlox and bee balm.

The first time I witnessed the preparations, a thin man in dark sunglasses motioned my Saturn to a stop as I headed to work.

"You're going to eat lunch out today," he said, passing me a tourist guide to Austin. "There's good barbecue downtown."

Later, Fiona showed me the photos. A frail woman stepped out of a black limo. She wore a floral print dress and an enormous straw hat, too big for her shoulders. In one shot, she roared with laughter, her face kind, comfortable, at home in her skin.

I credited Ladybird's happiness to the sacred halo around Fiona's domain, where I finally found time, that modern luxury, and stitched up the slashes in my dreams. Fiona's gift was to teach me the pleasures of being a recluse.

I was thinner, too, not just in my face or waist, but deep in, near the sadness, which now felt more like existence, less like fear. On the bottom floor of Fiona's house, hidden behind a wall of leaves, I let the space inside me resonate with the hollow pitch of the great, spinning world, a drone that was no longer scary even when it was out of tune with my slipshod life as a failing academic.

At least, I let all that happen when I wasn't ducking for cover from a twelve-gauge. I changed into dry shorts and made my way to the upper floor.

We had a routine. Fiona stood silent inside the front door until I rang the bell, even though she could hear my steps on the path. Sometimes, I waited to see which of us would move first. I always did. Once, I knocked. "You know better," she said from the other side.

That morning, when I rang, she threw open the door. "There you are!"

"You scared me to death."

"Don't you expect people to open the door when you ring?"

"I meant shooting at the squirrels!"

"I can't stand them," she said.

"I'm getting used to it."

"Then why were you scared? You never make any sense. Come in, come in." She went off to the kitchen in a swirl of denim skirt.

I smelled strong coffee. Fiona did pour-over years before it was hip, a darkened Chemex on her stove. She often made me breakfast and routinely told me to "buck the fuck up."

Today she forked slices of crunchy toast through hot bacon grease. "You know your job," she sing-songed.

Fiona was an artist by trade, so her home was more gallery than living space, easels everywhere. She painted wild abstracts based on her gardens: all smears and blotches, flowers tossed into the chaos of thick acrylics along with make-up, eye shadow, and pencil scrawls.

In return for breakfast, I read poetry that I retrieved from her study. At first, I hadn't been able to step in that room. "When you're ready," she'd said. "But like I told you, buck the fuck up."

The walls were lined with narrow, beach-house shelves. There were thousands of books, more than I'd ever had, all stacked in no apparent order. Almost every volume was cracked, bent, torn. Frankly, I was glad to read a poem or two over breakfast these days. I was glad to teach *Jane Eyre* when I had to. It was nice to remember who I'd been.

That morning, I chose Ezra Pound and Marianne Moore, nothing I'd ever cared much about, all too modern and brainy. Not like those vast, nineteenth-century novels, reams of consciousness in print. Or that snarky medieval poetry.

In the kitchen, we sat down to sterling silverware and chipped pottery. Fiona bowed her head to pray. "Thanks for getting us here," she grumbled. "Now get us somewhere better or leave us the hell alone."

Then she turned to me. "Eat up. Or I will."

I couldn't. I *was* her prayer. I'd gotten here. I needed to get somewhere better. But how? How could I do it without a book telling me the way?

Fiona picked up the volumes I'd stacked near my plate. "All that poetry. So bookish. It's all about you, of course."

"No, it's not!" Even in her cloistered home, I still spoke in exclamation marks.

She spooned up a bit of runny yolk. "You think that stuff's safe. That it'll put me off. But whoever heard of a person worth talking to who doesn't love all sorts of books? Who doesn't own as many as she can?"

Something clicked in my brain, the almost audible sound of metal clamps. I was sick of hearing *this is so you* about dead words on a page. I had to start over with a clean slate. I'd been practicing for this moment my whole life. I wouldn't shy away as I had at Baylor. Or even as I had at our bungalow in Austin. I'd been a true believer but never true enough. Fiona lived a spare life. I would, too. But I'd do her one better. Mine would be a life without books—not just in my head, but anywhere.

I pushed the poetry volumes to the floor in what I thought was a grand gesture. "I'm gonna take it to the studs," I said, assuming Fiona would understand me.

She sipped her coffee. "Is this about your being gay?"

"It's about getting a new life!"

She smeared green grape jam over the bacon fat on her toast. "Too full right now to make popcorn," she said. "Start tomorrow when I can watch."

I didn't. After breakfast, I drove to school, careening over the hills on a wide highway. My sunglasses were a three-hundred-dollar pair left over from my life with Miranda. I tossed them out of the window and watched the car behind me grind them into the concrete.

In the Writing Lab, I asked students to read their papers aloud so I wouldn't be distracted by print, so I wouldn't be thrown off track. Yes, I'd started getting rid of my books. Or having Miranda do it. But I had to keep going. I had to see how far I could take it. The only way out was to go right to the center of things, the middle of the pit, zero at the bone. That my Puritan ancestors would smile at my crazy notions of purity didn't bother me. I'd show them.

But first, I had to practice a little more. I couldn't jump to the finish line. That evening, I polished off a couple of shots of bourbon, then hauled flatware and dinner plates to the trash, past honeysuckle and blooming jimson weed. I'd live on paper and plastic. What simplicity!

After my shower, I looked at the narrow apartment stove. "Don't need it," I said to no one in particular. I called upstairs and asked Fiona to have it removed.

"I'm just going to have to put it back when you leave," she said.

"Not my problem!"

"No, but you're mine."

The next day, I bought a portable burner that ran off a little propane can.

The next week, I met a woman at school, a textbook rep, back when they circled campuses. We hit it off, went back to my place, and made missionary love, the Puritan dream. Afterwards, I made her pasta prima vera on that burner. We drank cheap Chardonnay out of paper cups. She never called again. I chalked it up to her shallowness. The only people I needed were the ones who got me.

I pared my possessions down to one rug and two chairs. Did I really need two? To a week's worth of underwear. Couldn't I double up? With each bit gone, I felt myself lighten, felt my feet come off the ground.

Those two boxes of clothes from when I moved out? Did I need all that? I was running every morning, a sweaty pleasure in Austin. I needed shorts, T-shirts, and sneakers. Otherwise, I got it down to three shirts, a couple of pairs of jeans, and those Bally shoes. I stood in my closet, fingering the empty hangers. I knew I was still practicing.

The college didn't offer summer employment because the Dallas Cowboys used the campus as their training camp. I had a divorce lawyer's retainer to pay off, so I'd landed a gig writing some of the original food and travel content for an internet start-up called America Online. I'd gotten in touch with the editor by doing this new thing, a Lycos search. In those days, nobody asked for credentials when it came to writing online, which was considered next to worthless anyway. Print magazines still used X-Acto knives and mechanical layouts.

I tossed out my desktop computer and wrote on one of the first IBM Thinkpads with a five-inch screen, just the right size. I filed restaurant reviews and interviewed travel gurus for their best packing tips. Then I snail-mailed my assignments on a five-inch floppy disk. The minute one was accepted, I erased my copy.

I never met my editors. I never even heard their voices. Everything happened in emails. This new world was fit for me.

I started erasing other files off my computer. I stared at the cryptic titles in the early days of Windows—*C://prop-two*—and wondered what I'd hidden there. But if I hadn't opened it in a year, or six months, maybe three, it was ancient history to me and (here's the rub) worthless. I got rid my master's thesis, then my dissertation chapters with their reams of notes. Somebody had a copy. Somewhere. Surely a clean hard drive was a sign of efficiency.

Over breakfast one morning, I told Fiona the story so far. I was proud of my spine, my resolve. "Night tables? Who needs them? The floor's fine for my alarm clock."

She buttered her toast. "Settle down," she said. "You're always so excitable. You have to do all the steps. And you have to do them in the right order."

Stunned, maybe tired, too, I wanted one last easy answer. "There are steps? What are they?"

Fiona burst out laughing. "You have to make them up. Mine aren't yours. Yours aren't mine. Why don't you know these things?"

I couldn't answer. But with that little bit of idealism trashed, I knew I was ready.

I didn't have any bookshelves at Fiona's. I'd lined the volumes from those five boxes against the floorboards on the cool tiles. In one sweep, I sold them all at a colleague's yard sale. I marked prices on the title pages. What's the right price for those complete works of Coleridge? A buck? And *Rabbit, Run*? Fifteen cents?

A woman who'd driven up in a BMW tried to reason with me. "Are you sure?" she asked, dropping a quarter in my hand for *Daniel Deronda*.

I glared at her through cheap, drugstore sunglasses. She added to my triumph. What I needed for the next semester I could check out of the library. "Very sure," I said.

A tobacco-chewing good ol' boy carted my childhood Bible out to a pick-up truck that belched black smoke as he drove away. By five o'clock, there was only one book left: *Jane Eyre*. A few people had looked at it. "A shame it's ruined with all those notes," the BMW woman had said.

I shoved the novel in my back pocket and walked away. Everybody deserves a relic, I told myself, conveniently forgetting that I'd already had two in my life: a silver pillbox that had held Immy's quote from Chaucer and a metal molar bracket from a long time ago. I'd left them both in a dresser for Miranda to throw out.

To my surprise, life moved faster without books. I no longer experienced that temporal dislocation of *wait, where am I?* I thought I was almost free, but zealots know no bounds. Once I'd started, once I'd gotten through my books, I couldn't stop.

I started losing people. I wrote old friends good-bye letters, which I tore up and didn't mail. One day, I set up a coffee date with a colleague, then purposefully missed it. When she called to check on me, I let the machine pick up as I looked out at the trees.

The next day, she confronted me in the hallway of a poured concrete building on campus. "What gives?" she asked. She had streaked blonde hair and a pronounced Virginia accent.

"Gay," I said, the first time I'd ever used the word to explain myself. It didn't. Mostly because it was out of context. But *gay* was just one syllable, three letters, suitable for a pared-down life. It covered the possibilities.

Back in Dallas one weekend, Mother and I peered into her closets, crammed sky-high with boxes, all labeled with indelible ink. Baby clothes. Matchbox cars. Was she about to complain about the lack of space?

Instead, she said, "Do you remember that tape recorder you had?"

"Not really," I lied.

"I still have it." She sounded triumphant. Didn't she know how to get through this world?

My beat-up satchel sat on an eyelet bedspread. We were trying to negotiate my new life, mostly by not talking about it, our way.

My parents had lost things, too: the hope of their son married to an up-and-comer, the belief that he was straight, their struggle to control him. Their smiles were wan, less stretched.

"I even have all those tapes you made," Mother said. "Do you want them?"

"Definitely not."

"What can it hurt?"

"You'd be surprised."

When I headed out the next morning, I wanted to let her know how serious I was, so I left my change of clothes behind. I walked out with an empty satchel.

She left a message on my machine. "Do you want me to save these jeans?"

I didn't call her back. I reasoned that to start over, I needed to get my life down to just one voice in my head.

With so little left, I could finally rehearse my losses, especially in front of Matt, my first boyfriend. We'd met one night at the bar while I was searching for a monk. Matt was in seminary, so he and I had a lot in common. Isaiah! Lying! I thought he'd understand my purge.

The sun glinted through the leaves as we sat on my deck and I paraded out my missing triumphs: my fifth-grade autograph book, my *Oxford English Dictionary*, my two dogs, my retirement accounts.

Matt was liberal and mortgaged. He had thick hair and an endearing mole under one eye. He also had an unshakable belief that he was somehow right about this broken world. Some days, I hated him so much, I could feel sparkles along my thighs. That's when we had the best sex, a frenzied brawl.

"You sure you won't miss that stuff?" he asked me, watching a heron down by the dock.

"There's only one way to find out!"

I wanted him to acknowledge my heroism. Clearly, he didn't care. He aced his Hebrew classes without studying.

I couldn't let him off that easy. "We live in a time of collectors," I preached. "People want to horde. Attics, basements. We're our own swap meets. People don't lose enough."

"How much is enough?" he asked.

"I'll let you know."

He turned to face me. "Am I next?"

I was stunned at his . . . honesty? Vulnerability? Who cares! "Watch your back," I said.

"I have a better idea," he smiled.

He slipped off his shirt and I kissed his smooth chest. We went to bed and made love in the hot afternoon. *Am I next?* Did he think I was a loveless freak? I knocked his forehead into the bed post and left a bloody scrape. I also whispered "I love you" in his ear. If I had nothing, if I carried around my sadness as my only possession, I could say anything, even to a guy in bed.

Later, when he stepped out of the shower, he asked where I wanted to go to dinner.

"Go home," I said.

He looked bemused. "You really know how to treat a guy."

I smiled. I did. I'd made it down to almost nothing, a shining perfection—although I still wasn't a freak. I was just a guy who was trying to figure out how to get through this world unscathed. Not a monk anymore, barely a mystic, I still liked a nice meal out.

I took myself to a bistro downtown: nouveau, hip, a joint I'd reviewed for AOL, with an open kitchen and empty, antique picture frames on the brick walls. I ordered the veal cheeks in a blackberry/tequila sauce. Without a book in hand, I felt naked, clean, a newborn at last. I tucked into my dinner with great relish, then heard the laugh before I saw her.

Miranda walked in with a big group, probably her direct reports and corporate counsels. She was out of her suit and in a black linen dress. She still wore pearls.

I'd made that same laugh happen time and again: the shake of her head, her hair loose and free. Her life was going on, getting bigger, while mine was diminishing, getting smaller. No matter how hard I tried, I couldn't polish the past clean. What if I finally amounted to nothing more than the skin I carried around?

I put cash on the table and scurried out a side door. It was the last time I ever saw Miranda. I'd finally lost what I'd never wanted to lose, even when I called myself "gay."

Outside the restaurant, the night air was hot, well past ninety degrees. I drove back to Fiona's and settled into bed alone. Life was a mishmash, a mess. What I wanted wasn't what I got. What I got was what I'd wanted until I got it. That's not a story, I told myself. Okay, maybe a farce. But not a way to live.

I needed to lose something else: this overwhelming sense of always trying so hard. *That* was the easiest way to avoid a plot.

The next day, I broke up with Matt on the phone. He seemed relieved. "Have fun!" he said before he hung up.

I was getting close to being able to start over. Or so I reasoned. I told my students that they could accept their grades, that the final was optional, mostly so I wouldn't have to administer it, so I could lose one more thing I should have done.

Out of the blue, I got an invitation for my first press trip, a nice perk from those online writing gigs. For some reason, the government of Lombardy had decided the region needed better coverage. The bureaucrats rounded up ten travel writers and parked us at the Villa d'Este on Lake Como.

"I feel like I'm finally growing up," I told Fiona over breakfast before I left.

I still expected sympathy. But she said, "It's about goddamn time."

I landed in Italy and laughed at my spare life and the lavish hotel. I spent the afternoons in a deck chair by an Olympic-sized pool that floated on pontoons in the lake.

This was the first time I ever encountered professional writers. Some could barely clean up for dinner. They sported askew ties and stained blouses. Just when they managed to get their clothes on right, they took them off to get involved in hackneyed bed tricks.

I heard one couple talking about me through the vent in the small hours. "Do you think he's gay?"

I pounded on the wall. This is my story, I wanted to yell. Stop trying to tell it.

On my way back to Austin, I had a couple of AOL assignments about New York: pieces on the restaurant scene, a short article on piano bars. Frankly, I was so new to being gay that I thought every bar with a piano was a piano bar.

I landed in a cheap motel in Midtown East, over by the Lipstick building, a true wasteland. My room had a cracked basin and a rotary phone. To do some research, I plugged my Thinkpad into the dial-up modem and signed into an AOL chat room before the after-work rush.

Someone told me about Marie's Crisis. "You get to sing through *South Pacific!*"

It sounded like hell. Bach and bourbon for me. Also, fewer and fewer exclamation marks.

One guy was having none of my earnestness. "Why's a guy from Austin in NYC M4M NOW?" he wrote in a private chat box.

I told him about my assignments, but he didn't seem impressed by writers. I brushed him off, although I did check out his profile. *Being kosher means having a separate pan for the bacon.*

When I'd gathered enough suggestions about piano bars, I started signing out. With the last notions of a purge still in my brain, I closed each of the open windows before I closed the program. The last one on my screen was the one he'd used to contact me. For some unknown reason, some chance or grace or fate I still can't understand, I typed, *You still there?*

We messaged back and forth until three that morning. He didn't know a Baptist from a Methodist. He'd never read Henry James. He wondered if Wisconsin was one of those "square states." He loved good food and better wine. He suggested we meet the next day.

I assumed he meant for a hook-up.

"At eleven," he explained. He mentioned a Greenwich Village coffeehouse.

"We're meeting for lunch?" I wrote, a Texan at heart, naïve to the rhythms of New York.

"LOL," he wrote back. "Breakfast."

I showed up early and stood by a parking meter outside the coffee joint on Christopher Street. Guys paraded past in white T-shirts and Calvin Klein jeans. But I knew mine the minute he came around the corner. He was impossibly tall, model-thin, in drapey linen pants and a beige shirt.

I feinted the punch and ducked my eyes. He walked up, pulled up my chin, and kissed me.

"I wanted to do that last night," he said. "Damn online."

"How tall are you?" I asked, stalling, trying to catch up.

"Six-four."

"There are no six-four Jews named Bruce."

"Pleased to meet you."

Later that night in my wretched hotel room, he picked up *Jane Eyre* from my suitcase. I'd taken the book to Italy. It was still my relic. One last thing.

He thumbed the pages, looking at my notes. "How many times have you read this?"

"Don't ask." We were propped against the wall on musty pillows. "Want to borrow it?"

He shook his head. "Novels? They're like God. What's the point? Isn't life enough?"

I leaned against him. "Where have you been?"

He bent down to kiss me. "Maybe waiting for you."

I don't believe in love at first sight, even though it's happened to me three times. Alex. Miranda. Bruce. It's the stuff of books. Bad books at that. It's contrived and trite. Maybe it's my lot. I'm still no good at irony.

Or maybe it's my compensation. Seconds after you were born, you looked at your mother and fell in love. Later, horrible things might have happened. Or not. Maybe your relationship with her stayed true, an abiding connection. In any event, for those first moments you and she experienced the stuff of pulp fiction, the thing everyone dreams about: love at first sight.

I didn't get that moment. I've always been looking for it. Maybe fate was busy evening the score. Or maybe life really is the random confluence of timelines. But twice before, and then on Christopher Street in the summer sunshine: Bruce.

Some people hope for a straightforward story. Like "married, then gay." Or "in the closet, then out." They want a lie followed by the truth. I wanted that, too, because I reasoned I could get an easy moral out of it. Like "honesty is the best policy." Or "always tell the truth." Aesop endings, fit for a children's book. Lies, too.

So this is my final marriage argument: no one's life strings out in a line. We all have to make it up as we go. Not once, but over and over again. Life won't end in a neat moral.

Except this one: Reader, I married him.

We search for signs and wonders. We scrape the cosmos for answers, trying to read our horoscopes in the light of stars that have long since flamed out. We're searching for the pattern, the form, the shape that will make sense of our existence.

It's just a story, just the way we think we see time spooling out behind us. We don't come into this world trailing clouds of glory. We pick up whatever glory we get as we go along. And that's what we should tell: the hurts and helps, the sorrows and laughter, the follies and jollies.

Mostly, we're trying to talk about love, the oldest plot we know, the one we get wrong all the time, and the only one we have any chance of getting right. Our hope is to look up on a crowded street, see a smiling face, and a kiss a stranger who can live at the center of our story without becoming it. From there, the thing practically writes itself.

I'd thought the great works of Western literature lied because they ended. But every time I opened one, it was helping me practice the only way to survive the ruins of time. On the first page, from the first line of poetry, the great works were teaching me how to set a new story in motion. This moment right now holds all the possibility of an in-the-beginning from which we can start spinning our lives into the only story worth telling: the one we're too busy living to narrate. And let's hope it's the one about love—however it comes, in whatever form it takes, a winged chariot from heaven or a stranger on a city street—because that story is the only redemption there is.

The Book of Life

Once upon a time, Bruce had an apartment in a seventeen-story, red-brick rectangle of a building that framed a full Manhattan block at the northern edge of Chelsea. His third-floor one-bedroom faced the interior garden with a small fountain, open to the sky. The hollow space had such perfect resonance that a soprano across the way often stood at her window practicing scales. Hers was a disembodied voice, the fundamentals of music, lost among all those identical square windows stacked up and down, right and left as far as I could see.

Beyond lay New York City, long before the hedge-fund mania or even the dot-com bust. In 1996, there were no art galleries in Chelsea, no club kids in SUVs, no models slumming it at the diners. Across Tenth Avenue, the High Line was a rusted hulk. Bombed-out buildings stretched to the Hudson River.

Without competition from Starbucks or Olive Garden, hundreds of bodegas and small shops lined the avenues, a kingdom of entrepreneurs before VC money paved the streets with gold. Bakeries didn't brand. Cheese wasn't artisanal. And coffee came in blue Styrofoam cups with Greek columns.

New York wasn't a paradise. It was filthy. The cross streets smelled like rancid meat. The avenues were worse. But the city was still scaled to the people who made it home.

Our first week was both blissful and tough, the sort of mishmash I'd always avoided by reading too much. Bruce was an advertising freelancer, so he had time on his hands. I had the summer off but classes to prepare for in the fall. In the afternoons, we wandered around Greenwich Village, strolling into housewares boutiques set next to grimy sex shops, before the internet shuttered both trades. I got childishly petulant when he didn't want to go to a midnight movie or get up at six to see the sunrise from the top of his building.

Sure, I had my doubts. For one thing, he turned up his nose at bourbon and knew a lot about cocktails made in a blender. For another, as we sat on his couch one afternoon, watching a "North By Northwest," he said he preferred musicals to "this sort of stuff."

I took a hot shower and thought about packing. But he licked my shoulders as I tried to towel off. Doubts, shmouts!

We got dressed and trekked down to the World Trade Center to sit in the plaza between the towers, ahead of the afternoon commuter chaos. Otherwise silent—not wordless, just quiet—he nibbled the top of my ear. I cupped his thigh. More and more people hurried by. StarTAC flip-phone antennas stuck up above their heads. No one noticed us. It was a recluse's blue yonder.

"How many people are there in this city?" I asked, expecting him to know the answer.

"Too many."

Before I could stop myself, I asked, "And how many have you slept with?"

"Does it matter?"

I wanted to say, I missed the whole coming-out thing. I lived in the '50s during the '70s, in the '60s during '80s. I've spent my whole life out of sync.

Instead, I said, "I guess the number's important. AIDS, you know."

He nodded. "Okay. First, I'm negative. And B, hundreds. I didn't count. Was I supposed to?"

He told me he'd come out to his friends in 1979, to his family a couple of years later, around the time I was at Baylor, sleeping with Melody and playing house with Alex. He was a charter member of half a dozen gay organizations.

How could I ever live up? "I've slept with six," I said sheepishly, although he hadn't asked.

Wasn't this backwards? Wasn't his big number supposed to feel like the confession?

"This month?" He wasn't looking at me. He was looking at the open sky between the Twin Towers.

"No, in my whole life," I said. "Unless you count a publishing rep who didn't like pasta prima vera. Then seven."

I expected Bruce to push me off, to walk away. Instead, he leaned over and pulled me tight against his chest. "No wonder you listen to what I say. You don't have a ton of people up in your head."

I didn't tell him there were more sorts of voices than the people he'd slept with. But as I leaned against him, I knew my job: knot those strands from my past and hold them tight, a tether leading out of the darkness behind me.

I could have stayed on that bench all night. "Is this how people do it?" I asked him.

"What?"

"Life."

He shrugged. "I guess."

I hadn't meant "life." I still had no way to talk without being a literary jukebox. But I wanted to know if they really lived in this happy/unhappy, relaxed/tensed, peaceful/confused mess that seemed to sum up how I felt. How did they go about their days without worrying about whether or not every moment fell into perfect coherence with all the others? How did they carry on without wondering if the smallest gesture wasn't some grand example of meaning itself?

Well, if there's no answer, I thought, then here goes. I sat up and told him the truth. "I was married to one of the people I slept with."

These were the days before same-sex marriage. He knew exactly what I meant. His eyes got bright, excited. "Do you have kids?" he asked.

He was dreaming of a life I couldn't give him. I shook my head. "It's a horrible story. Do I have to tell it?"

He seemed disappointed. "Yes. When you're ready."

I wasn't. We walked back to his Chelsea apartment as the asphalt breathed its heat to the sky. I again tried to slow things down. I told myself that I was making too much out of Bruce. I just wanted the summer fling I'd missed with Alex.

But Bruce didn't conduct Bach with a Bic pen or telegraph baffling messages across a dorm room. Instead, we spent the rest of the evening in bed, connected along the skin if still alone deeper in, wary yet somehow happy when we were wound around each other. I would eventually come to understand that ours was the kind of sex middle-aged adults get as a reward after everything else: passionate but forgiving, quiet but intense, mostly because there's less to prove.

I flew home to be alone for a week or so. We called each other four, five times a day. Then Bruce flew to Texas in early July. I snuck him down to my apartment, pushing him along the winding path ahead of me, even when he wanted to admire Fiona's gardens.

"It's like a national park," he said when I got him inside.

I thought I'd be smart and ask him which one.

He seemed confused. "Does it matter? Aren't they all the same?"

I wasn't worried about what Fiona would say about a man in my bed. I was worried about what she'd say about *this* man. Once, I'd brought seminary Matt to breakfast and poetry. She'd fried up five eggs, taken two, and passed the plate to him. She'd wanted to see if he'd leave me one or two. He'd taken all three.

But Bruce? After I rang the bell, she flung open the door, took a look at him, and said to me, "You found an El Greco!" She trudged back to making pour-over, humming a mindless tune.

He admired her paintings and listened to the poetry I'd chosen. Emily Dickinson's lyrics: blasted swaths of despair, on the edge of wordlessness.

> *After great pain, a formal feeling comes. . . .*
> *My life had stood a loaded gun. . . .*
> *The soul has bandaged moments. . . .*

All the while, Bruce looked out at the live oaks.

As Fiona made another pour-over pot, I asked him what he thought.

He asked Fiona if he could have her recipe for the *mole rojo* she'd spooned over the eggs.

"Hold onto him," she whispered to me as we left. "New Yorkers know everything."

By late August, I was still making it up, back in Manhattan at Bruce's apartment. For the first time in my life, I could hear my own heartbeat as I fell asleep.

One afternoon, I pulled the covers up to my neck and told Bruce about Miranda. The light outside looked sticky and thick. The windows across the way seemed cast in a haze. The air conditioner blared an icy blast into the bedroom. I had to talk over it, but I'd never told the whole story to another soul.

"Are you disappointed in me?" I asked at the end. My body sagged in ripples, empty skin where I'd been fat.

He shook his head and kissed me. "I'm just glad you're here," he said. "And whose life makes sense?"

"But don't people want theirs to?" I was steadier on my feet, but I still didn't trust them.

He sighed. "Do you want to go out for dinner or call in?"

I thought he was avoiding the hard stuff. I got up and showered, then found him in the living room. He read the paper as I made a pot of coffee. I was on my second cup, lying against him, when he said something that took my breath away: "I've been thinking about what you said."

"About Miranda?"

"Sort of. I think we have to talk about the future."

I righted myself, picked up a sofa cushion, and pressed it to my chest. "I don't believe in the future," I said. "I'm not religious anymore."

"Sure," he nodded. "But let's talk through ours."

How could I? The future was all plot, a timeline told but not lived. I was terrified I'd ruin yet another version of my life, especially if I started spinning it out in front of me.

Then it hit me. Of course! He wants to break up. Summer was winding down. I could begin again. If I had to. Maybe I wanted to. I knew what to do now: the steps, the right order. Sure. Why not?

I disappeared into the kitchen and pretended to clean the coffee maker. I needed time to work on my soliloquy. To mitigate the hurt, I had to be the lead, the one with the big speech. We can't. You won't. I shouldn't.

When I came back in the living room, Bruce was sitting in the same place, in almost exactly the same position, as if I'd gone through a time warp and come back to a conversation in progress.

I still wasn't ready for it. I dragged him out into the city and took us shopping on credit. I made him try on lots of clothes. I was undone by his hips, his smile. I assumed I was seeing them for the last time.

He got tired of dress-up, grabbed a couple of hard ciders at a bodega, and pointed us to the pier that jutted into the Hudson River at the end of Christopher Street. It was once the site of The Village People but far less glamorous in the mid-90s. The sunset light was harsh, a pitched glare from the west. We picked our way across broken slats and bong pipes. Around us, graying men in starched shirts stalked impish boys in midriffs.

We got to a concrete pylon and dangled our legs toward the sludge below. We popped open our bottles and clinked the necks. I had the speech ready. Take a deep breath, I told myself. Look at the sides of his eyes, not into them. Ready. Set. . . .

"I want to live together," I said instead.

For once, I'd said what I meant, not what I should have said, not what I'd written in my head. It wasn't the poised conversation from a novel. It was just my voice telling my desires.

Bruce didn't blink, despite the light. "I think I do, too," he said. "Especially after everything you've told me. We've lived such different lives. Maybe we should try living the same one."

I swallowed hard.

He pressed on. "But I'm going to have to insist on something," he said. "Monogamy."

"Monandry," I corrected. "And it's a Parthian shot, in case you're wondering."

"What are you talking about? I mean, we have to stay faithful."

I looked away and thought of seminary, of Alex and Rona. The past didn't resonate in the present. It just sat back there, still an "is," not a "was."

"I don't have a great track record," I said.

"Me, either," he echoed. "But we'll try. Right?"

I nodded. I could be honest. I wasn't expecting him to be.

Yet he wasn't done. "No matter what, one of us has to move."

"That's easy," I said, a little flip, maybe brave. "Someone gets in his car and drives."

"I don't own a car."

"You know what I mean."

"I don't," he said. "Not with what you have."

I looked across the Hudson at the Colgate clock in Jersey City. It ticked out minutes that didn't matter on a weekend at the end of summer. *Not with what I have?* I'd lost it all: lots of it because of the divorce, the rest because of my mania for purging, for being the last Puritan standing.

"I don't have much," I said.

"Don't lie. You're an academic. That's an identity."

I thought of monks in gay bars. "I told you, I can't play a character anymore."

"You can't help it. You talk like people should listen to you."

"*Ex cathedra*?" I asked. When he looked confused, I added, "Latin. The way the Pope talks."

"Right. Christians. Shit. Anyway, you do. You think you deserve to be heard."

It stung, especially after my confession. "Doesn't everyone?"

"I'm a trained chef who went into advertising. I have to force myself into every conversation."

I blinked in disbelief. He looked like a model, a Jewish Scott Barnhill. People like him used their looks to get their way. On his trip home from Austin, I'd watched him get a first-class upgrade by flirting with the airline desk clerk. I'd always had to lay low, to scheme and manipulate. Except I didn't seem too good at it around him.

When I didn't say anything, he outlined the next step. "I don't have a full-time job right now. This has to be your decision."

Not my forte, I wanted to scream. I threw red velvet squares over dorm room lamps and faked my way through conference papers. I crafted novel-like motivations for myself, sometimes for others, until I made the person I loved walk into a fertility clinic to prove to myself that not being at home in my own skin wasn't my fault. Now, somehow, I had to make a decision in the emptiness of the bookless library that was becoming my brain.

"So we've come to some sort of an agreement?" Bruce asked.

We clinked our bottles again, the best I could do. I watched a tanker heading up the river, chugging toward Albany.

I flew out the next morning and quit my job a week later, two days before the fall semester. An academic? That didn't seem like me anymore. I figured I had a couple of writing gigs to support me, so I left a handwritten note for the Dean. She called me at Fiona's a few times. I unplugged my phone and threw away the answering tape. Somebody else would have to save the monks.

At long last, I was taking Prescott's advice. I lit out for the territories—only to discover his mistake. These days, the wagons' tracks pointed east, not west.

God save the fool who starts a life without books in New York City, the publishing capital of the world. I drove across the George

Washington Bridge as the sun sank low and burnished the buildings. Bruce had told me it was the end of Yom Kippur, the evening after the Jewish high holy day. The chosen were hungry from the fast and waiting for the final prayer when their names would be written down in the book of life.

"Watch out for traffic," he'd warned.

But I was late. The golden light had gone gray. There were few cars around me. Mine held all I owned: no dogs, no couch, no bed, no rugs, no desk, no knickknacks, just some clothes, that IBM laptop, that old copy of *Jane Eyre*, and a few family heirlooms my parents had forced into my hands when I'd passed through Dallas on my way to Manhattan.

I had a couple bags of groceries, too. I'd stopped at a supermarket back where the suburbs began to colonize the Delaware Water Gap. On our first night together, I was determined to make dinner for Bruce, although he was the one who'd been to chef school. I could still impress him. I put my faith in effort, that Calvinist virtue. Some patterns are hard to break.

I pulled into the bridge's right lane and slowed to a crawl. The silver-blue slats slipped by in a halting rhythm, more jazz than sonata. The city lay to my right, a crush of buildings, a New World squeezebox of granite and limestone, beckoning and beautiful.

I was left with snippets of what I'd read, disjointed lines in a counterpoint's slow decrescendo. It may have been Yom Kippur, but I heard the words from the Gospel of Luke, the words Jesus puts into the mouth of every priest and minister who begins the sacrament: "People shall come from the east, and from the west, and from the north, and from the south, and shall sit down in the kingdom of God."

Centuries of people had come to this city with barely the clothes on their backs. There were the nightmares: some, stolen from the Gambia River basin; some, fleeing the Nazi nightmare, only to be turned away. But there were millions more, the dreamers, pouring into the city for its promise: some, to sew garments; many, still in container ships. And I was a small voice among those. I came because I needed to lose myself in something bigger than I'd imagined. In my relationship with Bruce, yes. And in the human mess of New York City.

I pulled up in front of his building. He was sitting on the stoop. We unpacked quickly. We needed to get the car off the street. What did I know about parallel parking?

"Isn't there a place where I could park head in?" I asked. "Or a garage?"

Bruce looked horrified. "New Yorkers don't pay for parking."

"I'm not a New Yorker."

He nodded, peering into the traffic. "I'll take care of it."

We swapped keys. I went upstairs. His door seemed full of locks. Four? Seriously?

Inside, the apartment was quiet, almost hushed. The living room was dim in the evening light. I'd known him three months, almost to the day. How the hell do people pair up? Or why the hell? I felt that pain in my jaw, ear to ear.

In the bedroom, he hadn't left me an empty closet or an empty shelf. He'd cleaned out half of everything. He'd shoved his underwear to the side of one drawer. He'd pushed his shirts to the side of one rod. Fortunately, I didn't need that much space, even in a small one-bedroom, barely 650 square feet.

I heard him come into the foyer. "Everything okay?" I asked, hanging up my clothes.

He walked into the bedroom. He was rimed with sweat, a low-grade panic at the city's hassles. "You didn't lock the door," he said.

"You didn't have your keys!"

"I would've knocked. Always lock the door. It's a rite of passage. Or something."

"That doesn't make sense," I laughed. "Okay, what else should I know?"

"Don't go into Central Park after dark."

"Charles Ives wrote a symphonic poem about it."

"Whoever he was, he was an idiot."

Bruce sat on the bed and watched me unpack. In a matter of weeks, we'd lost our identities: the bookish pedant and the out-of-the-closet-since-Adam rake, shacked up together. We were silent, tossing our best bravado at our fears. He was watching his life change in front of him, an act I should have found old hat, although it felt as strange as ever.

"This is all harder than it needs to be," I said.

He looked away. "Needs. Right."

I tried to explain. "What's hard is to stay brave."

"Brave?" He shook his head. "Are you afraid of me?"

"Should I be?"

He sighed and walked out. I finished up and headed for the kitchen. It stretched the length of the living room behind a plaster wall, twenty-three feet long but a mere four feet wide. I couldn't stand in front of the oven and open it at the same time. If Sylvia Plath had lived there, she'd be alive today.

I was going to make us a hearty Italian stew. Miranda had always favored the meals of her childhood: thick ragùs, soft tortellini. Years before, I'd worked through Marcella Hazan's cookbooks to oblige her.

And because Hazan was my kindred spirit. She never believed her recipes would work in the New World, so she didn't try to coddle her readers. You'll never make this lamb dish properly because you'll never find Roman lamb. She wanted disciples, not viewers. Hers was a challenge, not a hug.

That said, the apartment had no more than three square feet of counter space. I looked up at the pots hanging from industrial hooks in the nine-foot ceiling. The cookware was within Bruce's reach but beyond mine.

He walked in holding a bottle of wine by the neck. "You ready for some?"

He was so gorgeous, he took my breath away. "Not quite," I said, pointing to a braising pot over my head.

He reached it down.

"What about when you're not here?" I asked.

"You'll need to buy a step ladder."

Who'll take care of me? I thought.

Bruce pulled the rabbits out of one of the shopping bags and held up the two packages like meaty semaphore. "It's Yom Kippur."

I shook my head as if in answer. "So?"

"Trayf," he explained.

Was that what New Yorkers called a light stew with fennel, olives, and garlic?

"Rabbit is the pig of the woodlands," he explained.

I was still holding the braising pot. I felt its weight in my shoulder. I was a guy who'd climbed over the literary wall in his obsession with Hebrew but apparently couldn't remember the basics of Jewish dietary law. Trayf. Forbidden. *And the hare, because he cheweth the cud but divideth not the hoof, he is unclean unto you.* Leviticus 11:6.

I'd forgotten all that. At last, I thought. At last!

"Sorry," I said, smiling.

"Also, we usually have smoked salmon and stale bagels we bought the day before," he said. "We're not supposed to cook."

"I thought you said you weren't religious?"

He pulled more ingredients out of the bag: a bottle of olive oil, a can of diced tomatoes. "What does being religious have to do with breaking the fast on Yom Kippur?"

"You don't want the rabbit?"

"I didn't say that. But we usually stick to tradition."

"Who's we?"

"Jews. Now you and me." He rummaged in a drawer. "Have you seen the corkscrew?"

I wanted to yell, I don't even know why I'm here! Instead, I asked, "So the rabbit? You sure?"

"Found it!" He tossed the corkscrew back and forth between his hands. "No, not sure. But yes, rabbit's fine. Next year, we'll have smoked fish."

"There's a next year?"

He pulled the cork out of the bottle. "It's 5757 in the Jewish calendar. There'll always be a next year. At least until 6000. Then something's supposed to happen. Won't. Never does. But yes, next year."

I asked the next question before I thought about it. "In which there'll be an 'us'?"

"Did you forget?" he laughed. "I'm Jewish. There's always an 'us.' Too many of us for one dining table, most of the time."

"There's just two of us tonight. Is that too many?"

He sighed. "Can you just relax?"

Why lie? "No," I said.

"Then let's have a glass of wine."

And there it was: my fear, anger, horror, and hope, all balled into kitchen repartee. He was already home and I still had no idea what that word meant, even though I'd done the thing I thought I could never do. I'd fallen in love without a book in my hand.

Nobody told me what to do. No minister. No book. No poem. No *I'm Okay, You're Okay*. Which made everything even easier to fuck up.

How to Make Rabbit Stew

Serves 6
And yet there are just the two of us in this tiny apartment.

Spring seems the right time for a rabbit dish. Maybe it's the hope of warmth again. Maybe it's the wonderful way life starts slowing down. *But here I am making it on a September night, Yom Kippur, for God's sake, the first night we're living together. Did I blow it with trayf?* Good rabbits can be hard to find in North American markets. Ask your butcher to order two smaller ones, the meat more tender at the bone after braising. *I also didn't remember that skinned rabbits look like dead kittens.* Keep everything else at the table more straightforward since this is a deeply flavored braise. *There's a spray bottle of disinfectant cleaner on the counter. Is that a hint? Should I clean the wall behind the stove? Or is the bottle always out? Stop! I'm just cooking for a guy who's been to chef school. I'm just trying to remember a recipe from a cookbook I've thrown away. If I fuck it up, it's on me.* Pour a light, crisp, Italian white wine for the best pairing. *Yeah, because everything might go better with a glass or two. Hell, I'd even look better with a glass of wine in my hand. Oh, shit, don't start that. Don't start performing it. Just cook the damn trayf.*

    1/4 cup extra virgin, first cold pressed olive oil
    Two 3-pound rabbits, cleaned and each cut into 6 to 8 pieces
    1 1/2 cups fairly light but fruit-forward white wine, such as one from Friuli
    1 medium yellow onion, chopped
    1 medium fennel bulb, trimmed of its fronds and chopped
    One 28-ounce can diced tomatoes
    1 tablespoon tomato paste
    About 10 green olives, preferably not pitted
    2 to 3 medium garlic cloves, minced

2 rosemary sprigs
2 cups chicken broth
Freshly ground black pepper

1. Set a large pot or a Dutch oven over medium heat for a couple of minutes, then swirl in 2 tablespoons of the olive oil. *Meanwhile, the guy I'm living with for reasons I can't remember has disappeared into the living room. Apparently he trusts me enough that he doesn't think I'm going to set his kitchen on fire. Wait, is it <u>my</u> kitchen now?*

2. Add half the rabbit pieces and brown them well, turning once, about 6 minutes. *Are they sticking? Shit, they are! Do I add more oil? I don't want this thing to be greasy, like I don't know what I'm doing. I should've gone with the filets mignon. I had to show off. I had to make fucking rabbit. God, this is taking forever. I'm going to have to dig them off the bottom of the pot with a metal spatula. Where <u>is</u> a metal spatula? This drawer? Do I just open the drawer? Like I own the place? Calm down. Sing. No, wait, hum mindlessly, the way Fiona did. He liked that. He thought she was eccentric. He probably thinks all Southerners do that. He'll think I feel at home.*

3. Transfer the rabbit pieces to a large bowl and brown the second batch just as well. *Shit.*

4. Once all the rabbit is in the bowl, pour the wine into the pot and scrape up any browned bits as the liquid comes to a boil. *Browned bits? What about the blackened bits? Do I get rid of those? Are they going to be bitter? I like bitter things. Mustard greens, collards. Wait, is that a stereotype? A guy from the South who likes collard greens? Should I start my new life as a stereotype? Well, I'm cooking the wrong dinner for him on his holiday, so he's going to have to learn to like bitter things, too. I've seen him drink Campari without a mixer. Now there's a cliché: the Manhattan sophisticate with his Campari. He'll love the blackened bits.*

5. Pour the remaining liquid in the pot into a small bowl and set aside. *God, the way he looked at my clothes. Was he outraged? Disappointed? I could stand outrage. I could face it down. Is he trying to pick a fight? He went to Austin. He knew how I lived.*

6. Add the remaining 2 tablespoons olive oil and wait a moment to warm it up. *Except we're up to about a cup. Maybe he's glad I didn't drag more stuff into his apartment. Maybe he wants to keep things neat. I like that. Spare. Clean. A new start. I wonder what Miranda's doing tonight. I heard she was dating someone. Probably someone with a big kitchen.*

7. Add the onion and fennel; cook, stirring often, until softened, about 4 minutes. *That was nice. He brought me a glass of wine. Kissed me more than once. Was that a signal? Were we supposed to make love first? Move in, then fuck? Is that the preferred order? Yet I'm cooking dinner. And I'm not even naked. Maybe I should have cooked dinner naked. With all these grease splatters? He can go fuck himself if he thinks I'm going to cook dinner naked.*

8. Add the tomatoes, tomato paste, olives, garlic, and rosemary. Stir well, raise the heat to high, and bring to a full simmer. *I'm doing fine. I don't have to figure out what happens next. I don't have to make this more than it is. I'm just cooking dinner for the guy I love.*

9. Nestle the rabbit pieces into the stew; pour any accumulated juices on top. Also pour in the reserved wine reduction. Bring back to a simmer, then cover the pot, reduce the heat to low, and simmer slowly for about 45 minutes, or until the rabbit is fork-tender at the bone. *Holy hell, I didn't think about that. I gotta man this pot for forty-five minutes? If he comes back into the kitchen, what will we talk about? I mean, what do you say when you move in together? Hey, who cleans that wall behind the stove? Or maybe now is when we should go to bed? When you're dating, you just kind of do it. Do I have to get more formal? Ask? What will you have for dinner, honey? What other holiday traditions can I fuck up, dear? Would you like to have sexual congress now? Slow down. Say it. I'm living with the guy I love in New York City. I know all those words but I have no idea what they mean.*

10. Season with ground black pepper before serving. *Who sets the table?*

Hiding in Plain Sight

The most surprising thing about those first years in New York was the noise in my head. Not from plots and poems, memorized paragraphs and lines. Instead, I felt my anxieties, hopes, fears, and dreams, the internal cacophony I'd papered over with the great works. My thoughts were in sync with the city's blare, the cab horns and sirens.

For some, the din might have been a nightmare. For me, it was like hearing my voice in that tape recorder from long ago and *not* having to separate it from the story I was living. From now on, I had no one—and no book—to blame but myself. At first, it seemed like liberation.

I got a job reviewing restaurants for a tony, late-1990s newsletter that went out to a select list. Bruce took a position as the creative director at an advertising firm that specialized in publishing accounts. He also did some moonlighting in a professional test kitchen, developing product recipes for corporate clients.

One morning, he called me from the Madison Avenue agency. "Where are you reviewing this month

I named a place in Midtown.

"How about lunch there today?" he asked, his bass voice pitched up toward my tenor. Clearly, he had something on his mind.

I made a couple of calls and landed a reservation. The freelancer, I arrived in a dark suit and a polka-dot tie. The exec, he came in Ralph Lauren jeans and a Madiba shirt.

The New York dining scene was stuck in the jump-cut between a stuffy, faux-French vibe and the emerging, new American restaurant, which was more art-directed than frou-frou, more roasted than stewed, more grilled than blanched. Brooklyn fine dining amounted to no more than a couple of places on Smith Street. Queens, unheard of.

Once Bruce and I were seated, the waiter rushed at our table.

"Cocktails?" he asked, looking at the notepad in his hand. The place was packed and loud.

"We're ready to order," I said. "We'll have the tuna and the chicken."

He scratched it down. "No starters?"

"Also, the filet mignon and the salmon." These were still the days of writerly expense accounts, even for newsletters.

"Are you. . . ?"

"And the scallops."

The waiter squinted at our two-top. "The food won't fit."

"Space the dishes out. Or get us a four-top. Also, San Pellegrino."

We moved to a quieter table squashed at one end of the bar, a four-top most people didn't want because they couldn't stage their lunch for the room. All the dishes arrived within ten minutes. Everything had been pre-seared and pre-cooked, a jigsaw puzzle of ingredients and sauces that were assembled to order, even though the restaurant was asking top dollar.

Bruce fidgeted as I took a few notes. He bit the corner of his lower lip, a gesture that drove me wild.

"Where do you want to start?" I asked, trying to concentrate on the plated fare.

He looked almost embarrassed. "I got a call this morning," he said. "To write an ice cream book." He named an editor at a big publishing house. She'd met him at his test kitchen gig a while back.

"I can't write it and keep my nine to five," he said. "Unless you're willing to. . . ."

"Stop," I said. "No."

Help him? Hadn't I told him about me and books?

He sat back and crossed his arms. I cut into the chicken breast. It was crunchy with panko breadcrumbs, a newfangled ingredient. The meat was gently pink at the bone.

I had to say something, give him some excuse. "I like what I'm doing."

"You're paid nothing!"

"Does that bother you?"

"Only that you're not appreciated."

I didn't want to discuss it. I chewed the chicken. Tasteless. "I feel appreciated," I said, hooking my foot around his ankle.

"Okay. I guess I could. . . ."

He hesitated while I pulled the skin off the chicken to see if the meat underneath had been seasoned in some way.

Then Bruce came out with it. "The book should be pretty easy. And everybody's looking for a writer in this town."

I pictured him and some guy, surely a guy, bent over a manuscript at night. I saw them lean over the pages and. . . .

I pushed the salmon fillet off its bed of lentils. The underside of the fish looked both dry and gummy. "I'll do it," I said.

"Do what?"

"I'll help you write it."

"We'll write the book together?"

He seemed confused, but the salmon flaked nicely. "You suggested it!" I said.

"You didn't let me finish. I could write this book on my own if *you* were willing to find a better paying job. Get your résumé out there. Everybody needs a writer in this town."

I pulled the plate of scallops toward me. "I don't want it to be my thing."

"Don't want what to be what?" he asked. "I hope you're not talking about food, given all you've ordered. Or is this about Henry James and the shit you went through? Listen, I'm just talking about a cookbook."

"When you prick them, do they not bleed?" I cut into the scallops. They were translucent at the centers. Perfect.

"Cookbooks are about recipes," he said. "The beef should bleed."

He took his fork and knocked down a tower of tuna chunks.

I wasn't sure what I wanted. But wasn't my new life about making it up as I went along?

Bruce wasn't interested in another of my existential crises. "I suppose they'd let us do it together."

"I never said that," I said, still trying to figure out what to do. Books? I thought. No way. But cookbooks? Are those even books? I mean, real ones. Symbolism, ambiguity, metaphor? Nope, little of those in them.

"The tuna's too rare, don't you think?" he asked.

"I still never said that."

"About the tuna?"

I took a deep breath. "About a cookbook."

"Now you *don't* want to do it?" he asked. "Goddamn it, being in a relationship is like the U.N. Nothing happens without translators."

I wasn't going to make light of what he was asking, or what I'd proposed, or what we'd somehow arrived at together. I'd hit on a compromise that kept him away from a sexy writer at night yet gave me more to do than restaurant reviews.

"Yes, we can do it together," I said. "I'll help you write the book, but I don't want my name on it, okay? Try the beef."

He went for it. "Why not your name?"

"As you put it, 'James and shit.'"

"Even though you write for a living?"

"Online articles. Newsletters. I don't want to be associated with a book."

He seemed to understand. "Beef and black pepper marmalade," he said. "It's a great cliché. Someone serves it and you think, 'That's clever.' Then you remember you've had it lots of times before and start to question your whole judgment in the chef."

"Nice. Can I use that?" I asked. We were already working back and forth. What could be more natural?

"Be my guest," Bruce said. "So you'll do it? The book?"

I straightened my tie. "I wasn't putting you on."

He nodded. "It's hard to tell."

A few weeks later, he signed the contract. In a twist of irony no prophet could have predicted, I had found an anonymous way into the publishing world. If I went nuts again, if I started to channel canonical authors or dress up like Fanny Farmer, I had the perfect out. I could walk away, as I had from Dr. Franklin at Baylor. No one would ever know.

Besides, I'd always liked cookbooks. They were close to my heart: DIY manuals like the Bible. Sure, there's an implicit plot in every recipe. Start here. Finish there. But in the end, the ingredients and the technique determine the flow, not the writer.

Over the next few months, I sat at my desk with a stack of Bruce's notes at hand. I wrote a book without fearing the blank page, without wondering what I was doing, without thinking about William Blake or Geoffrey Chaucer. I was the ghost, handed something to write by the chef, who happened to be the guy I lived with. We were working on a creative project, each with distinct roles. What couple wouldn't envy that?

Back then, editors had tables at the Four Seasons. They hosted glittery pub parties. I never saw any of it. I prided myself on staying out of the muck. Mostly, I liked the steadiness of the work: find the right word, bring the messy kitchen technique into order. And no recipe ever came walking down a country road in the middle of the night.

I flipped through Bruce's cookbooks. I needed to find the right balance between authoritative and avuncular for the headnotes that floated above each recipe. I kept coming back to my favorite, Marcella Hazan. So I followed her lead: no fooling around, all business, let the quality of the ingredients assure the success of the dish.

Was I letting another author help me find my voice? Of course! But not a canonical author. Just a cookbook writer. She'd be out of print in twenty, thirty years.

Soon, the manuscript was done. I passed it to Bruce, he turned it in, got it back from his editor, passed it to me, and I made the changes. I gave it back to him, it went into layout and design, he passed those pages to me, and I corrected them—all with me but without me, not mine and gladly so, but a book nonetheless.

After a stint on QVC, Bruce got invited to make ice cream cocktails on one of the first live cooking shows at the dawn of the Food Network. Far from glitzy, the studios were housed in a faceless midtown office building. The lobby had chipped columns and stained ceilings.

Bruce needed a food stylist. The publisher had run out of money for any more publicity. He thought he might have to turn down the opportunity, so I again agreed to help.

We'd been told the network had nothing on site, so we toted shopping bags of blenders and booze up the elevators to find ourselves on an open half-floor with ugly desks in rows, the ruins of a 1960s stenographic pool.

"Where do we set up?" I asked our producer, a blond woman who held a clipboard as if it were a life preserver.

"You better have everything," she said. Her bangs were swept tightly to one side of her head. "Are you the talent?"

"You mean the author?" I hooked a thumb over my shoulder. "He's behind me."

"And you?" She pulled down the clipboard.

"The writer."

She wrinkled her nose. "Wait? What?"

I tried to explain. "He's the chef. I do the other stuff."

She seemed satisfied. She showed us to two desks, our counter space. Bygone phone number prefixes were etched in the laminate. PL3. RE7.

"Make-up's back there," our producer said, pointing Bruce to dingy curtains hanging from hooks.

"Where are my outlets?" I asked her.

"I told you to bring everything."

"Electricity?"

She rounded her shoulders. "Only on set. You'll have one fifty before we come out of commercial."

"One fifty what?"

"Seconds! Do you know what you're doing?"

This was great fun, despite her panic. "Do you have a cart I could use?"

She sighed again. "What other parts of everything didn't you understand?"

"Just the part about the cart."

"I'll see what I can do."

I sliced strawberries on the laminate. I opened bottles and cleaned jiggers. I got ready for the minute and half in which I'd throw the drinks together before the camera started rolling.

Our producer showed up again with a three-tired, metal contraption, like the cart from an old AV room. The wheels were so rusted that she had to drag it, rather than push it. "You can't take it home," she warned.

I soldiered on with doilies and swizzle sticks until Bruce came back from make-up. He was a clown's mask of foundation and rouge.

"Behold, the author!" I said.

This probably wasn't the best moment for the truth, but our guards were down. And I was so far from the great books that I still didn't know how to work out the timing of honesty.

"I've never made a blender drink," I confessed. "Fundamentalist, remember? Then bourbon."

The mascara seemed to darken around his eyes. "Shit," he said. "But you've watched me."

"Yeah, you. I watched you. Not the drink you were making."

There was no time for a lesson. Our producer hauled him toward the cameras. He glanced back while I put everything on the cart.

The set was a shoddy thing at one end of the floor. I plugged in the blenders and started whirring things together. By the time our producer hissed "ninety seconds," I'd made one of three drinks.

Bruce was in position. The cameras pulled into place. I heard the smack of air kisses from the hosts. I put ice cream, vodka, and ice in another canister, whirred it up, and poured the slushy concoction into a tall glass.

"Fifty seconds," our producer said, a flat-line monotone.

One empty glass left.

Bruce asked, "Do you want me to . . ?"

I pushed him off. Look how competent I was!

"Forty seconds," our producer said.

The lights went up. I threw things into the blender, turned it on, forgot to cover it, and splattered half the drink over the table. I also had it in my hair. Bruce lunged for the cart but one of the hosts pulled him back.

I had just enough to pour the remainder of the drink in the last glass. I grabbed napkins and bowls of party nuts to cover the stains on the set.

"Get out of here!" our producer yelled. "Five seconds!"

She pulled me and the cart back to the food prep desks and swept away the comma of her bangs. "If I ever see you around here again," she hissed, "I'm going to. . . ."

I waved her off. She didn't need to worry. I walked to the windows and looked at the skyline, a jumble of bodegas and skyscrapers. I could hear Bruce on camera, saying something about the best way to keep an ice cream drink thick after blending. I knew he was flying by the seat of his pants. Me, too. Isn't this how people went about their lives?

We left the studio with a commitment for a few more episodes. "Get a real food stylist," our producer said.

We told friends. We laughed and laughed. The *The Today Show* called. And *Good Morning, America*. A two-cookbook deal followed. Bruce and I talked it through. We told ourselves the books were a side interest, despite good sales. We could sustain the pace if we did our separate jobs.

But the schedule got grueling. More cookbooks landed on QVC. They were becoming the sum of our lives. Bruce embraced them, but I kept them at arm's length. I called them "his."

He landed a second two-book deal and quit his job. I was still reviewing restaurants, but had no time to pitch other assignments. I began to interact under the table with publicists and marketers. I got a little jealous as I watched Bruce walk out the door to this publicity event or that bookstore talk.

One summer afternoon, I went for a run along the West Side Highway. I was no longer skin and bones, nor an overweight beast. I was a middle-aged guy out for a jog. And I'd been through enough to realize that I only had myself to blame. I'd set up our world this way. Really, the old way. I felt as if I was back in a fertility clinic, crafting a me who was something like me but who I didn't like. I was hiding again. And in books, to boot. Goddamn it.

I circled back to our apartment, my almost-forty shins aching for the last mile. I knew what to do. I could tell Bruce the truth, even if I kept fucking up the timing.

I broached the topic at dinner. We'd gotten into a hip SoHo spot, Blue Ribbon. Bruce and I sat on the same side of a red banquette. We ordered sushi and fried chicken, as one did.

I looked sideways at him. "I don't think I can do the next two books," I said.

He pulled a drumstick out of his mouth. "Why not?"

"I mean, I don't think I can do them without my name on them."

He seemed relieved. "Is that all? Oh, sure. That's easy. I thought you meant you didn't want to. . . . You've come over a change, haven't you?"

I pictured one of those mountain passes from my childhood hiking vacations. "In first gear, slowly. We'll do this as an official twosome?"

"Sure," he said.

He made it seem so easy. I leaned against him. "God, I love you."

"I told you: I'm not God."

I should have listened. A week later, Bruce signed a contract with just his name, not both of ours.

Working without a plot, the two of us had run headlong into an American story about success and fame, hopes and hard work. As a former creative director, he knew that bringing me into the mix could hurt the brand. His editor wouldn't want that. He didn't either.

And to be fair, he didn't lie about it. Nor did he seem to remember our talk at Blue Ribbon. He read the contract in front of me, all smiles and jokes, sitting at our dining room table over bagels and jam. I looked out at the wall of empty windows across the courtyard as he stuck the contract in an envelope and called a messenger service.

Afterwards, we went to bed and made love. Or he did. I lay flat on my back. He was like a teenager, giddy and proud. It couldn't be mad at him. He looked so happy.

Besides, I'd broken my share of promises. So I thought, Payback's a nightmare. And I thought, See, books are deceptive. And I asked myself, How can I feel so lonely in the relationship I've always wanted?

How? Because the last thing I had to lose, years after minor purges and then the big one, the deepest thing, the thing that hurt the most, the last residue from the great books, was my notion that someday, somewhere, someone would be my hero, my champion, the one who saved me. Maybe from the world. Maybe from the world I set up. Or just because I needed saving. I'd kept my old teaching copy of *Jane Eyre* and stashed it in among Bruce's cookbooks because it best expressed what I ultimately wanted: Rochester. And I'd found him. A liar and a great guy, all rolled into one.

A few days later, a writer from *The New York Times* called. He wanted to do a lipsticky lifestyle spread about Bruce, a cookbook author who lived in a small apartment and fed his neighbors the remains of his recipe-testing.

The photo shoot involved our elevator man in his uniform, Bruce in Comme des Garçons, neighbors and friends gathered around our coffee table. Here's the glamorous woman from across the street with her Pomeranian. Here's the hip writer from across the hall, a woman who's been on Oprah because she knows everything about the city's prostitution rings.

The photographer didn't like the way I looked in any of the outfits. I was thinner but no model. I had an Icelandic body, now built for New York's cold.

Pushed off camera, I stood in the kitchen and washed the dishes that came off the set. I folded napkins and kept the crew in espresso. I wrapped the props and put them in their boxes. The designer had used some of our own things. Authenticity! I put these in our cupboards among the other dishes we'd bought together.

We'd been a great couple. We liked the same things in bed, liked long walks and good meals afterwards. Bruce seemed to accept the sadness in me without having to adopt me or it. Yet I'd told him what I wanted, and it hadn't amounted to a hill of beans.

After the lights were taken down and the makeup artists air-kissed, I put on my coat, took our checkbook, and told Bruce it was over. All these years later, I still tucked the speech I didn't give on the Christopher Street pier in my memory. We can't. You won't. I shouldn't. I gave it in full.

I started to walk out, but Bruce blocked the door. "I won't let you leave," he said.

"But you promised!" I was trying to temper the rage, not really at him, more at me. I should have been a master of this stuff. I should have plotted our love. I was an idiot to let us play it by ear.

He started to cry. He tried to hold me and explain, but he didn't say he was sorry. Instead, he told me his fears. His dad had dropped dead when he was still in college. Bruce had always felt on his own, felt he had to grab hard onto what was his to make sure nothing bad happened again.

He told me about the years of dating married men, about feeling so alone for so long, despite tricking up and down Eighth Avenue. About coming back to his apartment and wanting so badly for someone to be waiting for him.

He looked at me and said, "You always know the answers. Just tell me what to do."

It was the silliest thing I'd ever heard. Me? The answers?

But I could see the hurt, the truth, all of it lying along his skin. I could see his body written over with the promises we'd made to each other. He loved me. And just like me, he'd failed at the promises love must make.

We stayed up all night. When he ran out of words, I started. Not on my story. On the fury under it. I screamed so loud that the neighbors banged on the wall. Occasionally, Bruce tried to say something, but I wouldn't let him. I was really the narrator now.

Sometime after dawn, he went in the kitchen and made coffee. He came back, sat down, and put his head on my chest.

"Isn't there something you need to say?" I asked, waiting for *I'm sorry*.

But he was silent. We'd blown through all the words. All that was left was to stick it out.

We did—through friends, therapy, fights, and determination, about the only way couples ever stay together. And maybe because of this, too: we shared a bed the whole time, even when we weren't speaking. I crooked my body against his, put my nose between his shoulders. I breathed in all that was human and loved, fallible and broken, the organic chemistry of us.

In losing the illusion that someone could redeem me, or that I was redeemable, I learned that the only, last, and real way out of seeing the world as a set, imagined, and coherent story was through forgiveness. I had to forgive Bruce, of course. I also had to forgive myself—not just for hiding in cookbooks, but for the long string of the past that led us to this moment.

I came to understand that forgiveness was the strongest bond, way beyond those in organic chemistry radicals. It kept us in each other's arms. Stronger than love, it made love possible.

Months later, we took ourselves out for a late meal at Gramercy Tavern. I sneered at the quilts on the walls—"how Canton First Monday"—but relished the vegetable-focused fare, impossibly earthy but bright, bitter mizuna tamed by smoked paprika aioli.

We ordered a bottle of wine and settled in. I was still angry but exhausted. Who said that love had to be real? It was easier when it stayed in the far country of the imagination.

I looked at Bruce. His eyes were down; his cheeks, flat. He picked at the eggplant terrine.

I still wanted one more thing: an apology. "You know you're eventually going to have to say you're. . . ."

"Help," he said, his eyes down.

I knew that word. I knew its hurt. I knew its hopelessness. I looked at his graying hair, his thin chest, his narrow shoulders. I loved him more than I could say, mostly because I saw his struggle to say what he meant and recognized its sadness as my own. And yet not. As fundamentally his own. He was more than my mirror. He was my mate.

I reached across the table and took his hand. "I don't know how to help," I said. "I can't save you and you can't save me."

He looked up—not at me, more away, toward the front windows. "How do you ask for forgiveness?"

"I think you just did."

"Does that count?"

"I'm not keeping count," I said. "I used to. It never adds up. It just makes me madder."

I felt a comfy warmth inside me. Something beyond words. Beyond hope. I was a middle-aged man with another middle-aged man in a middle-aged melodrama. Holy hell, I thought I'd never get here.

"Let's go home," Bruce said.

I shook my head. I still didn't know how. "Let's stay," I said. "Let's finish our dinner."

We did, mostly silent, like those couples in fancy restaurants who are comfortable, relaxed, settled into the moment.

Later, we walked out into the New York night, holding hands, trying to hold on. In life, I thought, you think you have to be brave, then you have to be braver.

On Monday, Bruce called his editor and told her my name had to appear on not only all future books but even the ones from the deal he'd just signed. She balked. We thought she might. But we persisted. Well, he persisted. One day while he sat on the phone with her, I went downtown to SoHo and treated myself to a long lunch.

I walked back, content, alone, the truth between Bruce and me clearer, brighter. People fail at love because they break *chesed*. Because they shy away from the words that make love possible, all the words that make up the completely human virtue of forgiveness.

Later, Bruce told me about his conversation with his editor in that foreshortened way of his. She'd asked him if he was going to give back his advance. "If I have to," he'd said.

Tense days passed, then she gave in and I became a named author of books that I didn't choose, of cookbooks that had somehow chosen me. I fell into publishing and became an author in no way I'd ever imagined: a life in books beyond the great books. The joke's still on me.

Dante Alighieri in a Nursing Home

In the summer of 2005, Bruce and I were working on our eleventh cookbook, a giant tome, 900 recipes, our own doorstop. The kitchen was a wreck. The apartment, really. Pots, pans, and cooking gadgets colonized the living room. We had to eat dinner on the bed.

Late one morning, we were trying to figure out how many lasagna recipes the book should include and the phone rang. I rummaged for it among packages of pasta. Bruce was ranting about the lack of space, "not a single place to put my thoughts." I picked up the call and went to the living room.

"A lady has your Bible," Mother said, carrying on as if we'd been having one long conversation over the years.

Maybe we had. Maybe I hadn't been listening. I was forty-five, still trying to figure out how to balance on my feet. I looked out at the apartments across the way. Big drops of rain pinged our window-unit air conditioner.

"This lady was rummaging around a junk shop," Mother said, "when she found it. She told me these places can hide a Renoir. You never know."

I could only think of Canton's First Mondays. "Mostly, you do," I said.

Mother and Dad had seen me through the changes in my life. It hadn't been easy. They didn't speak to Bruce for a year, not even a "hello" on the phone. But they'd slowly changed. They'd come to our commitment ceremony, held at an inn on Maine's coast. Now they visited us every year. Mother cried when I put them in the cab to LaGuardia. Dad put his arm around her as they sped off. They, too, had had to lose the image of the son they'd created from their book, the Bible.

None of which mattered now. "How'd this lady get hold of you?" I asked.

"She saw our address and phone number under your name on the first page. She said to tell you she thought McGovern could still be the Antichrist."

"He's an old man," I sighed.

"You can't be too careful. Anyway, she called me up. Well, she called you. She got me." She paused to figure out how to say what she meant. "Do you want it? Tell the truth."

I wanted to say, How'd you get so fast to the two sentences that sum up my life when it took me forty-some-odd years? Instead, I said, "Tell her to keep it."

"She couldn't imagine anyone wanting to part with a Bible like that. I told her you live in New York."

"You had quite a conversation."

"I told her you loved books."

"'Love' is too easy a word," I said. "How about 'forgive'?"

"You forgive books?"

I looked back at our bookshelves, trying to catch a glimpse of *Jane Eyre*. I could only see cookbooks. I never once looked in them for subliminal messages.

"Not all books," I said to Mother. "Just tell her 'thanks.' It's nice to know that Bible's making the rounds."

I hung up and walked back to the kitchen. Bruce was trying to balance a cutting board on the stove's gas burners to open up more work space. He leveled the board with a measuring spoon underneath.

That Bible held its marks, my marks, a physical object with my pilgrim soul etched on its pages. Someone wanted to find it a home. To send it home. But mine was not right for it. What if that's the whole problem? What if books need the right setting, too? Maybe they themselves, the ultimate backdrop to a life, need their own backdrop. Maybe the great ones need to be read at the right time.

"And we need a break," I said to Bruce, carrying on to him from the conversation in my head. He never seemed to mind. I mentioned lunch at Union Square Café.

We cleaned up and got a cab. It had stopped raining. The city was a steam bath, but the restaurant was so chilled, it seemed to hold an autumn crispness. We got two seats at the bar and ordered burgers, blood rare. We whiled away an hour or more as the place settled into its slow, mid-afternoon pace. We were in no rush to head back into the sauna. But I could hear the rumbles of thunder. The lightning was soon brighter than the halogen spots.

"Maybe we should get out of here," I said.

It was raining again, sideways drops, drenching our cuffs. Every cab was taken. Bruce stepped closer to the street for a better look.

I saw it happen in slow motion. A car came around the corner, too close to the curb, and drenched him in a Niagara of melted newspapers and dog shit. It splattered up my legs, into my waistband. He got it on his shirt, across his face, even in his hair.

"Only city that makes its own gravy when it rains," Bruce snarled.

It was a rehearsed line. He'd used it at cooking schools and on *The Today Show*. It always got a laugh. For the first time, it made me wince.

"It'll stop soon," I said.

Bruce wasn't having any of it. "Let's walk."

I looked down at my black wingtips, splotched brown. "Okay."

We bought an umbrella from a street vendor and huddled underneath. Bruce was tense, irritated. He hoisted the umbrella so far above my head, I got soaked.

Back at our apartment, I took a shower and retreated to the kitchen to make a pot of tea. He'd cooked everything we'd published on that tiny laminate counter.

After a bit, Bruce rounded the corner, toweling off his hair. He'd gotten a little paunch. I loved the changes in him. I loved that I got to watch them. I loved our hermetically sealed life in our rent-controlled apartment.

"I'm done," he said.

I knew what he meant. Not with us. Or with cookbooks. But with New York. His proclamation had been coming for a few years. He'd grown tired of the filth, the noise.

But those of us who choose New York hold it more tightly than the natives. I'd carefully stitched *why would anyone live here?* into *I can't live anywhere else.*

I saw the strain in his eyes. I knew how scary it was when I'd seen it in my own. I also saw the future, not in a prophecy, not in a book, just through the details of our relationship. We were already leaving New York.

That evening, once the rain stopped, I went out to explore the city. I walked the chaotic streets. I loved them for all they'd given me: a life in my own head. I took the subway uptown so I could stroll back to Chelsea.

I passed a big-box bookstore. I had a professional obligation to rescue our cookbooks from oblivion. I found our titles all over the place. Our book about cooking for two was with those about cakes and pies. I replaced a Food Network star's book on a display table with one of ours, then squirreled the glitzier one away among the literary fiction.

Before I headed out, back to my walk, a volume caught my eye: Dante's *Divine Comedy*. Not a cheap paperback. A hardcover, embossed book. *Illustrated*, it claimed. I imagined the old Florentine poet would have been appalled at the showiness.

I'd first read the *Comedy* back with Dr. Olivia Keller. I'd just gotten word that she'd passed away, undone by those moles that threatened her neck and face, a vicious melanoma that took her down in mere months. We'd exchanged a flurry of emails at the last. "Remember me and I'll remember you," she'd said, an odd blessing from the dying to the living.

I picked up the *Comedy* and held it in my hand, savoring the weight, that feeling from long ago. Here were all three parts, *Inferno*, *Purgatorio*, and *Paradiso*, together as Dante never saw them. Maybe as a memorial to Dr. Keller, maybe as a replacement for that Bible that was making the rounds in Texas, I bought the volume and put it in my satchel.

It was heavy. I blew off my walk and felt the book's dead weight in my shoulder bag as I rode the subway downtown.

Bruce had gone out. In our sanctuary apartment, I felt guilty about the *Comedy*, like an alcoholic with a flask. I stashed the book in the hall closet. I'll look at it another day, I thought.

I didn't. We descended into the chaos of realtors and house-hunting trips to Litchfield County, Connecticut, a bastion of WASPs and mayonnaise.

Real forgiveness meant *I want what's best for you*. Even after cookbook contracts without my name and fights at midnight, after mornings in bed and evenings alone, silent, unsure where to fling the anger, at me or him or some combination of us, some place where we joined, I knew we were two sheets of paper still glued together despite the odds. I left New York because I couldn't imagine sleeping with anyone else. Because I honestly wanted to see what would happen next. And because in my bones I, too, was tired of the city's push and shove.

We found secluded acres about two miles from the Massachusetts border in an ungentrified town. An enormous black bear sometimes slept in our driveway. Moose wandered up from the wetlands. The house had no road frontage. It looked out on trees and a steep valley wall. I felt like I'd moved back to Fiona's, although I no longer needed to be a recluse.

We were unpacking in mid-November, the New England chill already leaking through the walls, when Bruce pulled *The Divine Comedy* out of one of the boxes.

"When'd we get this?" he asked.

"We?"

"Okay, why'd you buy it?"

"Isn't it beautiful?" I said.

He turned it over. "Seventy bucks. You weren't kidding around."

I tried to seem very adult. "Shouldn't we have a copy of *The Divine Comedy*?"

"You're asking me?"

"Not really. But illustrated," I laughed. "Tarted up. What would Dante say?"

Bruce ran his finger along the spine. "He'd want to know where his royalties are?"

That night, as darkness enveloped our yard and the hill beyond, I poured a finger of bourbon, opened the *Comedy,* and read the first canto. I didn't get any further. The poem felt forced, silly, bellicose. Dark woods! Wild beasts! Virgil! I tossed the book into one of the bags full of packing tape and Styrofoam peanuts, bound for the trash. No way, I told myself.

Early the next morning, I found the volume on the counter. Bruce, I reasoned. I wasn't mad, just confused. *He* thought we should have a copy of Dante? I still had that teaching copy of *Jane Eyre*. It was somewhere in the basement among the cookbooks. I was never any good at a real purge, although I congratulated myself on the ones I tried. I once saw myself as the sort of guy who could lop off the past. It was another lie I had to stop telling.

I picked up *The Divine Comedy* and thumbed the pages, a tingle in my fingers. I poured a cup of coffee, took the book to the living room, and read the first canto again. Then the second. And the third.

When Bruce got up, I still had *The Divine Comedy* in hand, although I'd stopped reading. There were no car horns, no sirens, no cacophony. I was looking at the light on the hill behind our house. I hefted the volume toward him and asked, "Why?"

He scratched his stomach to think it out. "Did you read it?"

I nodded. "For about an hour."

"Did you like it?"

"I don't know. Coffee's on."

He started for the kitchen. I couldn't let it go. "You should at least tell me to be careful."

"No."

"Don't you think I should be?"

"Yes."

"But you're not going to tell me?"

"Doesn't seem like I need to."

"I'll show you," I said.

"I have no doubt."

I became a reader again. Partly because of Dante, yes. And partly because of Bruce—not just his ability to rummage in the trash and pull out what I needed, certainly not because his hand was in the small of my back, but because our relationship had gotten broken and got put back together by us, not an author. And mostly because I didn't need *The Divine Comedy* or any other book. I'd survived the crash and realized the greatest lie the great books tell. Words alone don't solve much of anything. Living solves life. With words, yes. But with love, too. Sex. Nice dinners. Friends. Family, if we're lucky. As well as trees, hills, and fresh air. Walk the land, lad. Yes, that and so much more.

One cold day with a cloudless expanse of winter blue out the windows, I sat at my desk drafting our twentieth cookbook. The leafless trees were giant sticks, as if some ogre had jammed them in the ground on his way to Vermont. My cell rang somewhere in the house. I heard Bruce answer it, then bring it to me. I muttered something about being busy, but he shoved it against my ear.

It was an administrator from an adult education center. "We'd love you to put together a course for us," she said.

I'd met her at a dinner party a while back. I'd gotten a little drunk and mentioned my former life as an academic. Now I stammered into the phone something about teaching, about how I'd loved it when I did it, but how I didn't have time to. . . .

"Pick something you've always wanted to do," she said.

Bruce and I talked it out. Fiona had taught me how to live in silence. New York had taught me how to live in the noise but focus on one voice at a time. Bruce had taught me how to forgive without forgetting. Maybe I was ready to talk about the great books again. I could try it out and see what happened.

I chose *The Divine Comedy*, a work I could never have taught as an academic, since it was so remote from my scholarly fields.

"It'll be me and two old ladies," I told Bruce. "One of them asleep."

Over a hundred people signed up. The class stretched the infrastructure of our rural area. The administrators had to move my lectures to a nursing home auditorium. I was going to teach a poem about the end of time while surrounded by oxygen tanks.

On the first day, I walked through the lobby, by two gray-haired ladies in large chairs.

"That's the young man who's pretending to be Dante upstairs," one of them said.

The room was large but strangely close, warm and loud. No one from the nursing home came. Instead, it was a collection of locals, mostly retired, although some were my age. There were even a couple of twentysomethings on the back row.

I stepped up to the podium. The room fell silent. My arms seemed loose in their sockets. What had I done?

I looked out. There was no Olivia Keller, no Immy, no Prescott. How could I be fifty years old and already have so many of the dead around me?

I blinked. The audience seemed to blink back in unison. Then I recited my own ad hoc translation of the poem's first lines: "One time, I came to myself in a dark wood. The straight way was lost. And I was in a middle-life crisis. Not mine, but ours."

I, too, found myself again, but my woods weren't dark. They were full of maple and oak, sturdy trees that barely bent in the wind. I lived surrounded by trunks, limbs, and branches, the beginnings of what I'd once cared about most: paper, books.

Within a couple of years, I ran the book groups at five libraries. I taught eight-week literary seminars at three others. All while writing cookbooks.

How had it happened that a guy who couldn't have his own thoughts without their first appearing in a book, who had psychotic breaks and let the great works of Western literature control not only how far he could take his life but how much he could ruin it—how had this guy found his way to being once again passionate about the great works of Western civilization?

Well, Thad had been right, back on that road south of Waco. It's about accepting the damage as fair trade and going on.

In the iron dark of New England, I discovered that there was no full answer to any of the questions worth asking. I didn't choose this timeline I lived. I came into it crying, slapped on the butt and dropped into a family that wasn't mine yet was, all at once. My life couldn't be told. It had to be lived. But I also had to *be* it as I lived it, not before I lived it. That's the only way I could survive it and still be talking, still be saying "once upon a time" even as the trees blazed red and gold around our house and the light started to fade into the evening of my life.

If I, if we, if all of us can go out of this life laughing and crying over the stories we tell, we can be in on the big joke that time itself can't silence. Life can be a comedy, sometimes of errors, but mostly of us.

This Now Connected to Enough of the Others

On a sunny June day, I printed a draft of this book and handed it to Bruce before I headed out to do some gardening. We'd just finished our thirtieth cookbook, a Bible for the Instant Pot, American's newest craze.

He took the draft of my book upstairs to his office and said nothing all day. That night, I woke up and saw him reading it next to me in bed. I fell back asleep. I didn't need to watch him, but I saw pages scattered across the floor the next morning.

He got about halfway through the manuscript, then quit. He didn't say anything for a day or two. I finally pushed it one afternoon when I found him in the kitchen, working on the courses for a dinner party that night, mincing herbs on a cutting board.

I dared it. "I have to ask: where are you in the thing?"

"Thing?"

Over the years, I'd come to think of us as the same height. I was always shocked when I saw photos of this six-four guy next to me.

"You know what I mean," I said.

"Yes, I do." He teeter-tottered a chef's knife through the tiny leaves. "I'm at James in Venice."

"And?"

"I can't."

"We're married," I said. "You agreed to these things."

"I don't remember the specifics."

He put the knife down, stepped back, and took a deep breath.

I braced for a critique, a line-by-line edit.

"These were *our* secrets," he said.

I didn't understand. "No, they're pretty much mine."

He shook his head. "You told me these things in private." He looked down. He was even grayer now. Not just his hair. His attitude, too. "Now these secrets aren't ours. You wrote them, so they're yours again. If you can share them with anyone, everyone, what's special about us?"

How could I tell him what seemed so clear to me? "Have you read the parts about you?"

"Not yet." He went back to prepping the herbs. "Maybe this afternoon."

I thought the story of us would make it all better. I heard him finish up in the kitchen and head upstairs to his office. I heard lots of commotion. He wasn't reading. He was straightening up.

I tried to reason it out: maybe he didn't want to be a character in a story he didn't ask to be in. But by late afternoon, I was furious. He came downstairs as I was setting the table, laying out the plates and silverware.

"I finally got around to that filing cabinet in the closet," he said.

I held my jaw tight. I was about to say, How can you be so insensitive when I. . . ?

"Here," he said, handing me a manila folder. It was smudged and battered, creased at one corner. The tab was in Miranda's hand: *Scarbrough family*.

I opened it up to find my original birth certificate, the one with a gold seal and my infant footprints. I'd used a certified copy for years. This one was post-adoption but the only original there'd ever be.

"Where'd you get this?" I asked.

He shrugged. "Where'd *you*? You must have given it to me."

I sat down at the table and pulled things out of the file. A Valentine's Day card to Miranda. "I'll never love anyone as much as you," I'd written.

I looked up at Bruce. "Have you looked through this?"

He shook his head but didn't leave.

There were a few letters, most of them handwritten, including one from my grandfather to my grandmother in the 1920s when he was working the oil fields in Wyoming. "Had a ham sandwich today," he wrote. "It tasted good." He was as formal as I remembered.

At the back, I found a sheet of legal paper. I saw an old man's crabbed handwriting and looked at the signature. It was an account of my adoption from the lawyer who'd handled it.

He named my birth mother. He said where she was from. He noted the year she was born. And he described her: short blonde hair, quick-witted, in grad school in 1960 and trying to make a bad choice better.

It took me a while to look at Bruce. I could hear the silence between the words—not just the ones in my head, but all of them, in all the books I'd ever read, ever memorized, ever ventriloquized.

Bruce took the letter, read it, and pulled me to his chest. The paper crinkled between us.

I was shocked to discover that I didn't need help holding my bones in place. I just needed to be near him as the strands of the past wove around me, a close fit but warm, comforting, the best thing to take the chill off of life itself.

Here was the way home. Not just my birth mother's information. But Bruce holding me along with my past, then letting me go, so I could finish the table, so our friends could come over, and so I could go about looking for a few more answers to the only question that has ever mattered: what in the Sam Hill is going on down here?

How did Bruce get this folder? Did I take it with me from Austin? I'd thrown away things like this in the great purge. Why did Miranda have it? I've checked around. No one knows. What's more, the lawyer is long dead. And the letter isn't addressed to anyone. It doesn't have a salutation. It just begins "hello," like a note in a bottle set out to sea.

That night, I looked around the table at our friends in the candle glow. I wondered what my birth mother would think. Would she be proud of me? Would she throw back her head and laugh, the way we were doing? Or would she be quiet, imagining all she'd missed, wanting to hear the whole story from the start?

I hoped so. That night, in our dining room, surrounded by people I loved, full of food and wine, the stuff that makes life a celebration, I knew I'd written this book for her. She may never read it. But she's here, the presence, not the silence, between all the words. We don't lose what's important. We bury it between the lines, in the book of life we're writing every day.

The next morning, I got up to let the collies out. They bolted in a rush toward the creek at the back of the yard. The sun throbbed in the sky, but the grass was cool under my feet, a New England gift.

Bruce came out a few minutes later. He had the rest of the manuscript in his hand. "I stayed up and finished it," he said.

I looked at the sunlight, not at him. "And?"

"I see what you're going for here. If you're a reader, you can't be normal."

"Well, I wouldn't. . . ."

"Or a Republican. Family values and all."

I knew what he meant. "Anything else?" I asked.

"Don't talk so much about this Fenimore Cooper guy."

I tucked the manuscript under my arm and whistled for the dogs. I could hear their barks among the trees.

Bruce put his arm on my shoulder. "You're warm," he said. "What's on tap today?"

I'd long put off what needed to be done. "Trying to figure out where we're going to put all those books!" I swept my arm behind me to include the house. "We're running out of space. Do you know what it would take to clean this place out?"

The great works of Western literature again filled our bookcases. Bestsellers were stuck under chairs; literary fiction, stacked in corners. Volumes of poetry? Maybe in the attic. In a box in the basement was a full set of *Norton Anthologies*. I've never been one for a tablet reader. I need a book in my hand. I don't want electrons. I want paper. Ink. Glue. The material stuff of meaning.

The collies charged toward us. They could have used a herd of sheep each. Instead, they were stuck with two middle-aged men who published cookbooks. The dogs, too, were adopted, placed into a story they didn't fit. They never seemed to mind.

Bruce kissed the top of my head, then turned back to the house.

"Where are you going?" I asked.

"To get the phone number of a guy who can build some shelves," he said.

The dogs bounded in with him. I stayed behind, looking out at the hill beyond the creek.

In some torque of evolution, we humans got chipped off nature. We can alter our DNA and bio-engineer our limbs. We plan on building islands as suburbs; we dream of colonizing Mars. Yet we've become aliens on *terra firma,* and sometimes in our own skin. We have to find ways to connect with our world because we're lost in the one place we should call home. So we stitch ourselves back into the fabric of all that is and all we know with the books we read, the stories we tell.

Prescott told me to find a landscape that made sense of me. I had. New England, a Puritan domain, rich in color and history. "Walk the land," he'd said.

Half right, I thought. And collect the books. They're so heavy, they'll anchor our existence on this chunk of rock that's spinning through the void.

I waited another minute in the morning air: alone, quiet. I even risked a prayer, the first in a long time.

"More light, please. As much as you can spare."

Then I turned back to a world of cookbooks and book groups, to a writer's life in a writer's skin. I knew something about where I'd come from, the beginning of the plot. And I could sense its end: two guys facing whatever comes next. More than that wasn't worth the telling.

I also knew the truth about the great works of Western literature, maybe about all the books ever printed. They weren't the way home. But once I got there, they were the best way to make it ours.

Acknowledgments

BOOKMARKED is a memoir with a plot—which means it's 100% true and 90% real. While the timeline hasn't been altered, most of the names have been changed, since no one asked to be included, especially Pastor Daniel, Mrs. Marsh, Caddie Anderson, Dr. Franklin, Dr. Keller, Dr. Prescott, and Rona, all now dead. A couple of the lesser characters are fusions of more than one person in the interest of streamlining my life into something that could be read. Miranda deserves whatever privacy I can give her; Bruce didn't get the same pass. Characters sometimes voice what I thought they were trying to say, or what I believe they wanted to say, or (less often) what I think were my own judgments about me at the time, judgments I suspect they would have agreed with, had they been asked.

Immeasurable thanks to those who had a hand in seeing these words into print: my agent at Writers House, Susan Ginsburg, who never seemed to give up; her assistants, Stacy Testa and Catherine Bradshaw; Genevieve Gange-Hawes, who helped me tame this sometimes sleepy, sometimes savage beast; Susannah Smith, Stephanie Bridges-Bledsoe, Harvey Havel, and all those at Propertius Press; Dan Smith, Kellie Rendina, and all those at Smith Publicity; Virginia Watkins, for long-term love *and* our monthly writing group ("just another forty pages!"); Carrie Bachman, for generously sharing her contacts; Rainey Day and John Erwin, for love and hope beyond comfort; and for Bruce Weinstein, who holds my hand and won't let go on this path called life, even in the dark woods.

If I've otherwise erred, it's on me. Everything else is as it should be.

About the Author

A former academic who now writes cookbooks with his partner Bruce Weinstein, Mark Scarbrough continues to teach literary seminars on the likes of Dante and Henry James, and he also leads a raucous weekly book group at the Norfolk Library in Connecticut. He hosts *Lyric Life*, a podcast devoted to lyric poetry and is about to launch a second podcast devoted to Dante Alighieri, *Walking With Dante*.

For memorable fiction, nonfiction, poetry, and prose
Please visit Propertius Press on the web
www.propertiuspress.com